1997

Global
Economic
Prospects

AND THE

Developing
Countries

The World Bank
Washington, D.C.

© 1997 The International Bank for Reconstruction and Development / The World Bank
1818 H Street, N.W., Washington, D.C. 20433 U.S.A.

First printing September 1997

This report has been prepared by the staff of the World Bank. The judgments expressed do not necessarily reflect the views of the Board of Executive Directors or the governments they represent.

ISBN 0-8213-3794-7
ISSN 1014-8906

Library of Congress catalog card number: 91-644001 (serial)

Editing, layout, and production by American Writing Corporation

This report is the result of work by staff drawn from throughout the Development Prospects Group of the World Bank. The task manager and principal author of the report was Milan Brahmbhatt, working under the guidance of Uri Dadush. Also on the core team were Dipak Dasgupta, E. Mick Riordan, T. G. Srinivasan, and David Tarr. General direction was provided by Masood Ahmed. Comments by many reviewers inside and outside the World Bank are gratefully acknowledged.

Contents

Abbreviations and data notes

APEC	Asia-Pacific Economic Cooperation	HIPC	Highly indebted poor countries
ASEAN	Association of Southeast Asian Nations	IBRD	International Bank for Reconstruction and Development
BIG 5	China, India, Indonesia, Brazil, and Russia	ICAO	International Civil Aviation Organization
CFA	Communauté financière africaine	IEA	International Energy Agency
CIS	Commonwealth of Independent States	IMF	International Monetary Fund
CPI	Consumer price index	ITU	International Telecommunication Union
ECU	European currency unit	LMICS	Low- and middle-income countries
EMU	European Monetary Union	LIBOR	London interbank offered rate
ERM	Exchange rate mechanism	MERCOSUR	Latin America Southern Cone trade bloc (Argentina, Brazil, Paraguay, and Uruguay)
EU	European Union (formerly the EC)		
EU-12	Belgium, Denmark, France, Germany, Greece, Ireland, Italy, Luxembourg, the Netherlands, Portugal, Spain, and the United Kingdom	MFA	Multifibre Arrangement
		MUV	Manufactures unit value (index)
		NAFTA	North American Free Trade Agreement
FAO	Food and Agriculture Organization of the United Nations	NIES	Newly industrialized economies
		ODA	Official development assistance
FDI	Foreign direct investment	OECD	Organization for Economic Cooperation and Development
G-3	Germany, Japan, and the United States		
G-5	France, Germany, Japan, the United Kingdom, and the United States	OPEC	Organization of Petroleum Exporting Countries
		PPP	Purchasing power parity
G-7	Canada, France, Germany, Italy, Japan, the United Kingdom, and the United States	SITC	Standard International Trade Classification
		UNCTAD	United Nations Conference on Trade and Development
GATS	General Agreement on Trade in Services		
GATT	General Agreement on Tariffs and Trade	VAT	Value added tax
GDP	Gross domestic product	WTO	World Trade Organization
GTAP	Global Trade Analysis Project		

Data notes

The "classification of economies" tables at the end of this volume classify economies by income, region, export category, and indebtedness. Unless otherwise indicated, the term "developing countries" as used in this volume covers all low- and middle-income countries, including the transition economies.

The following norms are used throughout:
- Billion is 1,000 million.
- All dollar figures are U.S. dollars.
- In general, data for periods through 1995 are actual, data for 1996 are estimated, and data for 1997 onward are projected.

Foreword

Global Economic Prospects and the Developing Countries is an annual report prepared by the staff of the World Bank's Development Prospects Group. The series provides an annual assessment of global economic prospects as they affect developing countries and analyzes the links between developing countries and the world economy, particularly in the areas of trade, foreign direct investment, and other capital flows.

This 1997 report projects an increase in the growth rate of global output. The improvement is likely to be especially notable for Sub-Saharan Africa, which grew at around 4 percent in 1995 and 1996, and for the developing countries of Europe and Central Asia, which are just now starting to emerge from a painful transition process. Although the East Asian countries will have difficulty maintaining the extremely rapid pace of growth that they have enjoyed in the past decade, they are likely to continue to grow strongly, in part because of the liberalization of world markets.

This report places special emphasis on the role of the "Big 5" developing and transition economies—China, India, Indonesia, Brazil, and Russia—in the future of the global economy. Today, these countries account for half of the world's labor force but for less than a tenth of global output or trade. Currently their share of global trade is only one-third the size of the European Union's share; by 2020, according to the conservative assumptions made by the report, it could be 50 percent larger than the EU share. These changes in the international pattern of specialization will have an important impact on both industrial and developing countries. The report finds that the benefits of this expansion—both in terms of the growth of an important export market for the rest of the world and as a source of imports—will be very large. Although these benefits are likely to be associated with some transition costs, there is little evidence to support two of the most common fears: downward pressure on unskilled wages in industrial and other developing countries and upward pressure on energy and food prices.

In addition to assessing the current state of the world economy, each *Global Economic Prospects* addresses a few important topics. This report discusses the expansion of global production and the costs of making the transition to a more open economy. Since 1990, when the first *Global Economic Prospects* was published, we have seen foreign direct investment flows to developing countries more than quadruple, so that now they are the single most important source of external finance for developing countries. This massive expansion of global production networks by multinational enterprises has brought us to the point where about one-fifth of world GDP today is produced by the parents and overseas affiliates of multinational firms. Foreign direct investment is not just an important source of new plant and equipment; it also represents a crucial link in the global transmission of knowledge. This report highlights the increasingly important role that multinational enterprises play in the transfer of intangible assets, like management skills and technical know-how. It also stresses the importance of maintaining a high degree of competition in host country markets as a prime condition for maximizing the knowledge transfer and other benefits of global production.

The growth in capital flows has been mirrored by the acceleration of international trade. If the pace of change is intensifying, then the ability to adapt is becoming even more critical. The report reiterates previous findings showing little evidence that trade liberalization has hurt aggregate employment—probably the single most important concern—but also underlines that the costs of adjusting to trade liberalization can be larger or smaller depending on the presence of certain conditions. Critical among these is investor confidence, which in turn depends on macroeconomic conditions and on the belief that liberalization will not be reversed. Also important is the flexibility of labor markets and a proper regulatory environment that allows producers to respond to changed conditions. Sometimes the lack of flexibility associated with large and inefficient state-owned enterprise sectors can increase the costs of adjustment.

Global Economic Prospects is part of an ongoing attempt to understand the dynamics of globalization, including its promises and its potential pitfalls. It clearly does not exhaust this extremely important topic. The questions raised by the report are vital, and we intend to come back to them as more evidence and research accumulate.

Joseph E. Stiglitz
Senior Vice President, Development Economics
and Chief Economist
The World Bank

Summary

Developing country growth in 1996 was the highest so far this decade, an estimated 4.5 percent including transition economies. Excluding these economies, growth was 5.6 percent, the most rapid rate in twenty years. Just as important, more low-income countries are sharing in faster growth: in Sub-Saharan Africa growth has run at about 4 percent for two years, over 2 percentage points higher than the trend in the preceding decade, while in India it has topped 6 percent for three years running. The integration of developing countries in the world economy, the theme of the last two *Global Economic Prospects* reports also gained ground: foreign direct investment in developing countries topped $100 billion for the first time in 1996, approaching 2 percent of their GDP. Developing countries' international trade volumes expanded at a robust pace of close to 7 percent, despite a downturn in overall world trade growth.

The external environment for developing countries is expected to remain broadly favorable over the coming decade. World output growth in 1997–2006 is expected to average 3.4 percent a year, more than a half percentage point higher than during the past decade, combined with modest inflation of about 2.5 percent in the Group of 7 (G-7) countries and real short-term interest rates of slightly more than 3 percent. In this setting developing country growth is expected to average near 5.5 percent, double its pace in the preceding decade, accompanied by mounting capital inflows and solid increases in trade of 7–8 percent a year.

This year's *Global Economic Prospects* reviews the implications for developing countries of three important changes in the world economy that globalization is bringing about. First, five large developing and transition economies—China, India, Indonesia, Brazil, and Russia—are likely to emerge as key players in the world economy over the next quarter century. This will create broad new opportunities for trade and investment but will also require significant adjustments in international patterns of specialization for both industrial and developing countries. The sec-

ond change is the expansion of global production networks by multinational enterprises, a trend that has been especially pronounced in developing countries in the 1990s and that opens new avenues for acquiring international know-how and participating in the gains from international trade. Finally, globalization is not only creating remarkable opportunities for countries to enhance their development, it is also posing broad and more complex policy challenges for governments, notable among them the proper handling of the costs of adjustment associated with trade liberalization.

The rapid growth and integration of the Big 5 developing and transition economies over the next quarter century will generate important net benefits for the world economy, but also significant economic adjustments, including those driven by greater competitive pressures in labor-intensive manufactures markets.

Increased integration and faster growth in China, India, Indonesia, Brazil, and Russia—five countries that today account for half the world's labor force but only 8–9 percent of its GDP or international trade—will likely redraw the economic map of the world over the next quarter century. For example, although these countries' share of world trade is barely one-quarter that of the European Union today, it could, under reasonably conservative assumptions, be 50 percent larger by 2020. The share in world output of both the Big 5 and developing countries in general will nearly double, with developing countries absorbing half the growth in industrial country exports over the next quarter century. Model simulations for the world economy in 2020 suggest that the emergence of the Big 5 will generate significant welfare gains for both the industrial countries and most other developing countries, resulting from broader opportunities for specialization along lines of comparative advantage and from improved terms of trade. Importantly, the emergence of the Big 5 is expected to have a beneficial effect

1

on real wages for both skilled and unskilled workers in most countries and regions.

Among developing regions the Middle East and North Africa, Sub-Saharan Africa, and Latin America and the Caribbean derive the largest welfare gains from the emergence of the Big 5. Trade liberalization and increased participation by countries with abundant unskilled labor, such as China and India, are expected to lower relative prices for some labor-intensive products, generating some pressure on unskilled wages in a few countries with closely similar endowment structures. These countries will, however, have the incentive and the ability to offset such pressures by accelerating their own trade liberalization, a policy tending to benefit the most abundant factor of production (unskilled labor), and by undertaking other reforms to improve the efficiency of resource allocation and use. The analysis also suggests that fears that fast growth in the Big 5 will generate significant increases in world food and energy prices do not appear to be well founded.

Participation in the global production networks established by multinational enterprises provides developing countries with new means to enhance their economic performance by accessing global know-how and expanding their integration into world markets.

Several trends in the world today are contributing to the expansion of cross-border production by multinational enterprises and their networks of closely associated firms. These include the liberalization of economic policies in most countries, continuing reductions in the costs of transport and communications, and the growing importance of knowledge and other intangible assets in modern production and distribution. These forces are heightening the competitive pressures on firms in both industrial and developing countries, while also facilitating their efforts to improve efficiency and gain access to new markets by reorganizing production processes on a global basis. A fifth of world manufacturing output today is produced by affiliates of multinational enterprises. A third of world trade is now intrafirm. And in the 1990s developing countries have become the fastest growing location for cross-border production by multinational enterprises.

Perhaps the defining characteristic of multinational enterprises is their ownership of specialized intangible assets, such as knowledge about how to produce cheaper or better-quality products, superior ability to innovate, and special skills in design, styling, promotion, marketing, or sales—assets that create the basis for indirect or spillover benefits in host countries. Such benefits include diffusion of improved management and labor skills, better information about world markets, introduction of new ideas or technologies, and, generally, faster catch-up with best practices in the world economy. The challenge for policymakers in developing countries is to establish conditions that help attract more global production and realize more of its benefits. These include political and macroeconomic stability, open trade and investment regimes, better transport and communication infrastructure, adequate protection for property rights, and a predictable institutional environment without excessive red tape. Ensuring that foreign and domestic firms face a high degree of competition in host country markets is likely to be important in maximizing the spillover benefits of global production.

Concerns about job losses and other adjustment costs still deter many developing countries from undertaking or extending trade liberalization, though the evidence suggests that such costs tend to be more limited than is sometimes feared. Nevertheless, there is much that governments can do to minimize adjustment costs, as well as to carefully manage the political economy and equity issues that trade liberalization may raise.

There is growing evidence that increased openness and faster economic growth go together, suggesting that the longer-term effects of trade liberalization on employment, wages, and income are likely to be strongly positive. To be effective, however, trade liberalization requires resources to be redeployed between sectors. In the process, workers in import-competing industries may become unemployed for a time. The output losses suffered by the economy as a result—the social costs of adjustment—are expected to be temporary, and empirical estimates suggest that they tend to be small, especially relative to benefits.

The size of adjustment costs will nevertheless be affected by the policy environment, and there is indeed much that governments can do to minimize them. Adjustment costs will be lower if macroeconomic stability and other complementary policies strengthen the credibility of reforms and support a quick and substantial increase in new private investment. Adjustment will be delayed and its costs will be higher if labor and other factor markets are distorted and inflexible. Extensive government regulation of formal labor markets can be an important source of such inflexibilities, as can the employment practices of state-owned enterprises in some countries, for example, overstaffing, unrealistically high wages, or excessive job security regulations.

Trade reforms are undertaken because they yield large net social gains. By contributing to improved growth in the longer term, liberalization is likely to make a substantial contribution to the reduction of poverty. And where unskilled labor is the relatively abundant factor of production, it is likely to raise returns to this factor. Nevertheless, the private costs of trade liberalization for specific groups, such as capitalists and workers in the previously protected sectors of the economy, can sometimes be large. Given that these losses are usually more concentrated among a few groups than are the larger but more widely diffused gains from trade, the opposition to liberalization will often be more focused and better organized politically than is support for it. Thus understanding and managing the political economy dimensions of the reform process may well be essential to its sustainability in the long run. In addition, it may also be desirable, for equity reasons, to implement carefully designed social safety net measures to assist the most vulnerable groups that may be adversely affected by reforms.

The outlook for the external environment for developing countries is perhaps even more favorable in the next ten years than in the last ten, contributing to the expectation that aggregate developing country growth will increase markedly in the coming period. Nevertheless, some developing regions remain better positioned than others to adapt to a rapidly changing external environment, suggesting that wide disparities in economic performance will persist.

The international economic environment for developing countries remains favorable, though it is likely to be one characterized not only by burgeoning opportunities but also by increasing challenges that place a premium on adaptability to change. The main features of this external environment include broadly stable world macroeconomic conditions, expanding flows of private capital to countries maintaining sound policies, and world trade growth at a solid 6–7 percent a year, underpinned by consolidation of the multilateral trading system and continued policy liberalization.

Current projections look to an improvement in developing country growth to 5.4 percent in 1997–2006, up from 2.6 percent in the past decade. (Excluding transition economies, growth rises from 4.4 to 5.5 percent.) Growth is expected to increase in every region except East Asia, where it should still remain high. Sub-Saharan Africa and the Middle East and North Africa, two regions where incomes fell in the last ten years, are expected to achieve positive per capita income growth. But the projected pace of about 1 percent would remain below that in high-income countries. In some of these countries basic political and macroeconomic conditions for investor confidence are still lacking, and many enterprises remain relatively cut off from foreign markets and competition because of policy weaknesses, institutional impediments, and inadequacies in transport and communication services. The same is true of some economies in Europe and Central Asia, although most of the countries in the region are expected to recover much of the ground lost during the difficult transition to a market economy. Developing countries in South Asia will continue to show faster growth in output and investment and will further increase their share of world trade. Though there is still some way to go before firms in India are fully exposed to international markets, recent reforms there have proved resilient and growth in the South Asia region is expected to improve on historical trends. Countries in Latin America, which have become considerably more integrated into the world economy over the past decade, should also experience a substantial acceleration in growth in the next decade, though in some large countries in the region the risk of macroeconomic instability persists.

Prospects for the global economy are among the most promising for growth and poverty reduction in developing countries in many decades. However, such encouraging projections must be qualified by significant areas of risk for individual countries, including macroeconomic imbalances or financial sector weaknesses that increase exposure and vulnerability to external shocks. Strengthening the framework of institutions and improving access to information to allow markets to work more effectively will be an important consideration for development strategy in many countries.[1] Growing competitive pressures and rapid transformation of the world economy along many dimensions will give unprecedented weight to the ability to handle change. Careful management of the transitional strains associated with global integration will be an important task for all countries in the coming decades. This is a lesson underlined by the experience of the late nineteenth and early twentieth centuries, a period that saw first a great expansion, then an erosion, and ultimately a reversal of integration. As to the risks to the natural environment from faster growth in the long run, greater reliance on market forces is likely to be reflected in many countries in more efficient use of natural resources such as energy. Demand for a cleaner environment rises with income, and so growth in developing countries will also be associated with greater incentives for policymakers to implement strong environmental policies over time. Nevertheless, given the complexity and scope of this issue, it is clear that analysis of the environmental implications of global integration is an important task for further research.

Note

1. Joseph E. Stiglitz, "Agenda for Development in the Twenty-First Century," in Boris Pleskovic and Joseph E. Stiglitz, eds., *Annual World Bank Conference on Development Economics 1997*, Washington, D.C.: World Bank, forthcoming.

Prospects for developing countries in a fast-changing international environment

Developing countries as a group experienced both higher growth and lower inflation in 1996. Trends in low-income countries and regions were especially encouraging. In Sub-Saharan Africa real per capita income increased for a second consecutive year. In India growth was over 6 percent for the third year running. Private capital flows to developing countries rose by a third to a new record, and foreign direct investment (FDI) exceeded $100 billion for the first time. International trade volumes continued to rise relative to output in most countries. Developing countries increased their participation in multilateral and regional trade liberalization agreements: some forty signed the World Trade Organization's 1997 Agreement on Basic Telecommunications Services to liberalize the $600 billion global telecommunications services market, and Turkey established a customs union with the European Union in 1996.

Greater international integration over the past decade has contributed to higher growth in many developing countries, a point discussed in *Global Economic Prospects 1996*. Yet it is obvious that not everything is well. Many developing countries that lag in policy reforms risk becoming marginalized in a more integrated world economy. Recovery among industrial countries has also been uneven. Growth in Japan and continental Europe was weak or erratic, averaging only 1.7 percent and 1.5 percent in 1991–96, respectively. In many European countries unemployment rates now hover around postwar highs. Even in the United States concerns about falling wages for low-skilled workers cast a shadow over an otherwise exceptional combination of sustained growth, falling unemployment, and low inflation. These difficulties have contributed to growing debate over the potential consequences of globalization and increased focus on structural reforms as a way to improve long-run economic performance.

What are the long-term prospects for the developing countries in the light of fast-changing global conditions and the likely progress of international economic integration? An important question that policymakers face

as they look toward the new millennium is the implication for both developing and industrial countries of the integration of China, India, Indonesia, Brazil, and Russia into the world economy—the "Big 5" developing and transition economies, which account for half the world's labor force. The answer depends critically on the progress of reforms in these countries, but also on continued efforts by countries everywhere to achieve a more liberal international trade and investment climate. To assess the risks to the process of globalization, it is possible to draw some lessons from the experiences of the late nineteenth and early twentieth centuries, a period that saw first a great expansion and then a gradual erosion of global integration, culminating in widespread protectionism in the interwar period.

This chapter reaches several conclusions:
- The global environment for developing countries remains broadly favorable. Industrial countries are seeing modest growth, low inflation, and moderate real interest rates. Progress on a wide range of trade and investment liberalization initiatives should allow the faster growth in world trade and international capital flows of the past decade to continue. In this environment, and given likely trends in policy reforms, aggregate annual growth in developing countries is expected to rise to 5.4 percent in 1997–2006 from only 2.6 percent in the previous decade, improving in every region other than East Asia, where it is nonetheless expected to remain high. Wide disparities will persist, however. Despite encouraging recent evidence, it is too early to say that the two regions that have lagged others in growth and investment in the past ten years—Sub-Saharan Africa and the Middle East and North Africa—are on a firm recovery path.
- Despite the favorable long-run outlook, it would be imprudent for developing countries to assume that recent exceptional conditions will continue in all respects. Stronger growth in industrial

countries in 1997–98 is likely to support a rise in interest rates from recent low levels. Growth in private capital flows to developing countries—especially interest-sensitive portfolio bond flows—may therefore slow. Countries where flows are financing high current account deficits and where domestic banking systems are burdened with bad debt problems may then be vulnerable. In general, globalization is demanding higher-quality macro- and microeconomic policymaking from governments over a broader and more complex field, including not only macroeconomic stabilization and trade liberalization but also enhanced competition and improved regulation and supervision in financial, telecommunications, and other service sectors.

- Rapid growth and global integration of the Big 5 low- and middle-income countries over the next quarter century will imply a dramatic increase in their role in the world economy, producing significant changes in global patterns of resource allocation, production, trade, and relative prices. The analysis suggests the likelihood of considerable benefits for industrial and most developing countries from improved terms of trade and better allocation of resources along lines of comparative advantage, as well as benefits for both unskilled and skilled workers. Significant competitive pressures in world markets for labor-intensive manufactured products will, however, increase

incentives for countries to maintain open, investor-friendly policies that help them secure profitable niche markets in the world economy.

- More countries are looking to global integration as an important vehicle for improving their economic performance. The experience of the late nineteenth and early twentieth centuries—with first an expansion and then a reversal of integration—cautions against complacency, however. Although today's globalization is better grounded in several ways, history suggests eventualities in which it could be undermined; for instance, growing great-power rivalry, failure to maintain a sufficiently broad social consensus in favor of integration, and international macroeconomic instability.

Global environment for developing countries

Since the mild recession of the early 1990s, developments in the world economy have contributed to the consolidation of a notably stable international macroeconomic environment. High-income OECD countries, which account for about 60 percent of developing countries' exports, have registered modest growth in gross domestic product (GDP) of 2.5 percent a year since 1994. Though world trade growth slowed in 1996 from a cyclical upswing in 1994–95, it was not much below the 6.3 percent averaged since the beginning of the decade (table 1-1). Inflation

A broadly favorable external economic environment is forecast for developing countries

Table 1-1 Global conditions affecting growth in developing countries, 1974–2006

(*Average annual percentage change, except for LIBOR*)

Indicator	1974–80	1981–90	1991–95	1995	Estimate 1996	Forecast 1997–2006	GEP 1996 forecast 1996–2005
Real GDP in G-7 countries	2.5	2.9	1.8	1.9	2.3	2.6	2.8
Inflation in G-7 countries[a]	10.1	4.6	2.8	2.0	2.1	2.5	2.6
World trade[b]	4.8	4.2	6.3	9.1	5.4	6.4	6.3
Nominal LIBOR (six months; US$)	9.5	10.0	4.9	6.0	5.7	6.2	6.1
Real six-month LIBOR[c]	0.2	5.0	1.7	3.2	2.5	3.1	3.3
Price indexes (US$)							
G-5 export unit value of manufactures[d]	11.6	3.3	3.6	8.1	–4.2	2.2	2.5
Petroleum price[e]	29.4	–7.7	–8.8	0.0	24.1	–3.8	–1.4
Nonfuel commodity price[e]	–2.2	–5.4	0.5	1.2	–1.7	–1.5	–1.6

GEP is *Global Economic Prospects.*
a. Consumer price index in local currency, aggregated using 1988–90 GDP weights.
b. Average of merchandise export and import volumes.
c. Deflated by U.S. consumer price index.
d. Data for G-5 countries (France, Germany, Japan, the United Kingdom, and the United States) weighted by exports of manufactures to developing countries.
e. Based on World Bank indexes and deflated by the export price of manufactures.
Source: World Bank data and staff estimates.

remained low, averaging below 2.5 percent through 1996 and into 1997. These conditions, and efforts to cut budget deficits in many countries, contributed to continued moderation in real international interest rates, a significant factor encouraging private capital flows to developing countries. In this relatively favorable environment, aggregate developing country growth in 1996 edged up for the seventh year in a row to an estimated 4.5 percent, with improvements registered in Latin America, the Middle East and North Africa, and South Asia. Sub-Saharan African countries grew by almost 4 percent—an exceptional pace for the region—for the second year in succession.

Economic growth in industrial countries, perhaps still the single most important element in the external environment for developing countries, slowed sharply in 1995. However, it revived in late 1996, and is likely to gather pace in 1997–98 (figure 1-1). Import growth in industrial countries, which had slipped to around 5 percent in 1996, should also pick up. Faster growth will, however, tend to pull interest rates higher. One risk is that unexpectedly strong cyclical growth and a surge in interest rates may dampen private capital flows to developing countries, as happened in 1994. Countries that rely heavily on interest-sensitive or short-term flows for external financing and that have significant domestic banking system problems may be especially vulnerable to a downturn in flows.

Among the major industrial countries, growth remains most firmly based in the United States, averaging an estimated 3 percent in 1992–97 and contributing to a remarkable reduction in unemployment. Strong growth in early 1997 prompted modest monetary tightening by the Federal Reserve, a move that will help prevent a significant acceleration of inflation from current low levels, while permitting output growth near its potential path of 2–2.5 percent. In Japan growth averaged less than 1 percent in 1992–95 but jumped to 3.6 percent in 1996 as a result of hefty public investment and the effect of low interest rates on housing and business investment. Growth will likely slow this year as the large fiscal deficit built up during the recession is reduced. But private activity should be supported by the effects of a weak yen and low interest rates, the latter also recommended by the need to improve profitability in a banking sector still heavily burdened by bad debts. Growth is expected to rebound to about 3 percent by 1998.

In many continental European countries a promising recovery in 1994 faded in 1995, and growth in the European Union (EU) slid to only 1.6 percent in 1996, sapped by weak fixed investment spending, low consumer confidence, and de-stocking by firms. Unemployment in the EU remained near 11 percent in 1996, some 8–9 percentage points of which are estimated to be structural in character (figure 1-2). Factors contributing to structural unemployment include

A mild pick-up in aggregate G-7 growth occurred in 1997

Figure 1-1 G-3 and G-7 real GDP growth, 1989–97

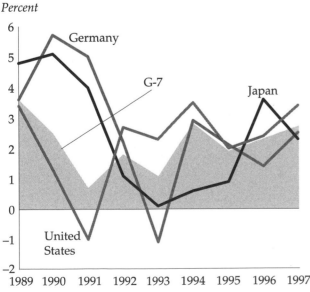

Source: OECD data.

EU unemployment is still high

Figure 1-2 Unemployment rates in industrial countries, 1989–96

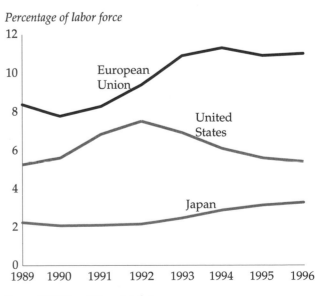

Source: OECD and Eurostat data.

overly generous unemployment benefits, constraints on firms' ability to hire and lay off workers, and high and rising employment taxes (OECD 1994). Signs of a mild recovery emerged in late 1996 and early 1997, stimulated by exceptionally low short-term interest rates and depreciation of exchange rate mechanism (ERM) currencies against the dollar. These factors weighed against the near-term negative effects of fiscal tightening undertaken to meet the Maastricht criteria for the European Monetary Union (EMU). Projected EU growth of 2.5 percent or so in 1997–98 would not, however, allow a rapid reduction in unemployment.

High-income OECD country growth is projected to average 2.7 percent in 1997–2006 (table 1-2). Growth in continental Europe and Japan should slightly exceed consensus estimates of potential rates as existing output gaps (estimated at around 2 and 4 percent of potential GDP, respectively) are eroded. More fundamentally, longer-term growth will also depend on the extent of structural reforms to improve supply performance by enhancing competition, especially in the service sectors, which now account for two-thirds of output in industrial countries.[1] The potential payoff to such reforms is suggested by the persistence of substantial productivity gaps across countries that are only partly explained by differences in physical and human capital per worker (table 1-3).

Case studies of retail distribution, telecommunications, electricity generation, and airline and road transportation provide convincing evidence of overregulation and lack of competition as important reasons for poor productivity.[2] The OECD calculates that regulatory reform in just five sectors—electricity, airlines, road transport, telecommunications, distribution—could add 1.5–2.5 percent to incomes in continental European countries and Japan (OECD 1996). The benefits for developing countries from such reforms include broader export markets deriving from higher incomes in advanced countries, the ability to import cheaper and better-quality tradable services, and efficiency improvements in their own service industries deriving from more intense foreign competition. These gains will be enhanced by ongoing multilateral trade liberalization in services. Other benefits of structural reforms in industrial countries may include a lessening of harmful protectionist policies and—because reform of inefficient service industries has a high priority in many developing countries—a richer store of experience and lessons.

Developing country growth is expected to average over 5 percent in 1997–2006

Table 1-2 World growth summary, 1966–2006
(Annual percentage change in real GDP)

| | | | | | | Forecast | |
| | | | | | Estimate | | GEP 1996 |
Region	1966–73	1974–80	1981–90	1991–95	1996	1997–2006	1996–2005
World	5.2	3.3	3.1	2.0	2.9	3.4	3.5
High-income countries	4.9	2.9	3.1	2.0	2.5	2.8	2.9
OECD countries	4.8	2.8	3.0	1.8	2.3	2.7	2.8
Non-OECD countries	9.2	7.7	6.5	7.0	5.8	5.6	5.5
Developing countries	6.7	4.7	3.0	2.3	4.5	5.4	5.3
East Asia	7.5	6.4	7.7	10.5	8.6	7.6	7.9
South Asia	3.7	4.0	5.7	4.6	6.5	5.9	5.4
Sub-Saharan Africa	4.7	2.8	1.9	1.5	3.8	4.1	3.8
Latin America and the Caribbean	6.9	4.9	1.6	3.2	3.4	4.2	3.8
Europe and Central Asia	6.6	4.8	2.5	−6.4	−0.3	4.5	4.3
Middle East and North Africa	8.7	4.9	0.8	2.6	4.1	3.6	2.9
Memorandum items							
Eastern Europe and the former Soviet Union	6.7	4.9	2.3	−7.6	−1.8	4.6	4.4
Developing countries excluding Eastern Europe and the former Soviet Union	6.3	4.7	3.2	5.0	5.6	5.5	5.4

Note: GDP is measured at market prices and expressed in 1987 prices and exchange rates. Growth rates over historic intervals are computed using the least squares method.
Source: World Bank data and baseline projections, June 1997.

Table 1-3 Productivity measures for selected industries
(United States = 100)

Country	Manufacturing[a]			Distribution[b]	Electricity[c]	Telecoms[d]	Airlines[e]
	1960	1985	1995	1990	1993	1992	1993
United States	100	100	100	100	100	100	100
Japan	19	69	73	71	77	81	54
Germany[f]	56	86	81	101	27	63	64
France	46	86	85	95	46	68	51
United Kingdom	45	60	70	78	27	69	101

a. Value added per hour.
b. Sales per employee.
c. Gigawatt-hour per person engaged.
d. Revenue per employee.
e. Ton-kilometer per unit of operating expense.
f. Federal Republic of Germany for 1960 and 1985.
Source: Pilat 1996.

Global inflation and interest rates

Global inflationary pressures remain subdued. Median consumer price index (CPI) inflation in developing countries (excluding transition economies) slipped to 7 percent in 1996 from 10 percent in 1995. Consumer prices in industrial countries increased by less than 2.5 percent for the fourth year in a row. Excluding increases in volatile food and energy prices, core inflation fell below 2 percent. Elements contributing to today's subdued inflation include the firm anti-inflation stance of major central banks in the 1980s and 1990s and its adoption by ever more countries. In Europe the Maastricht criteria provide many smaller countries with a focus to undertake tight monetary policies to bring inflation down. The persistence of large output gaps in Japan and many European countries further militates against any significant revival in inflation over the next one to two years, even as growth revives.

More remarkable still is the low and stable inflation experienced in the United States in the context of a mature recovery, high capacity utilization, and tight labor markets. Recent analyses suggest that structural changes in the U.S. economy may have reduced the nonaccelerating inflation rate of unemployment below earlier consensus estimates of around 6 percent, perhaps by as much as 1.5 percentage points from its peak in the early 1980s (Stiglitz 1997). About a third of this fall is attributed to an increase in the labor force of groups with low unemployment characteristics, such as mature baby-boomers. A gradual adaptation of workers' wage aspirations to the slowdown in productivity growth after 1973 is thought to explain perhaps another third. The remaining third of the fall can be plausibly attributed to increased competition in product and labor markets due to factors such as regulatory reform, trade opening agreements, and decreasing unionization. CPI inflation in the Group of Seven (G-7) countries in 1997–2006 is projected to average only 2.5 percent a year.

Long-term government bond yields remain moderate

Figure 1-3 Real ten-year government bond yields in G-3 countries, 1987–97

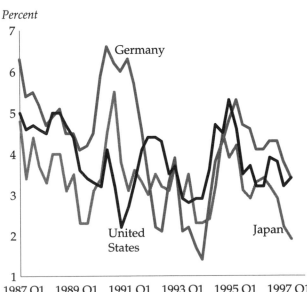

Source: IMF and World Bank staff estimates.

Long-term real interest rates (ten-year government bond yields, less annual CPI inflation) remained within a moderate range in 1996 and the first part of 1997 (figure 1-3). In the United States long-term real interest rates were 3–4 percent in 1995 and 1996, moving to the upper end in early 1997 as activity strengthened and monetary policy was tightened. But in much of continental Europe low inflation and subdued activity will likely keep short-term interest rates low through 1997. With the approach of the EMU, long-term rates in many European countries fell several hundred basis points in 1996 to converge with German long-term rates, which themselves fell below 4 percent in real terms. In Japan zero inflation, concerns about growth, poor profitability and weak balance sheets in the banking sector, and sharp fiscal consolidation in 1997 suggest little pressure for higher short-term interest rates until 1998, while real long-term rates, at about 2 percent in early 1997, were the lowest in a decade.

Interest rates in Europe and Japan are expected to trend higher in 1998 with reviving growth. As higher investment demand in Japan and Europe makes a greater call on world savings, the role of fiscal consolidation in sustaining moderate real long-term interest rates will increase. Structural deficits remain significant in all major industrial countries, though they have fallen in many and prospects for further progress are good (table 1-4). In the United States there is broad political consensus on the goal of achieving a balanced budget by 2002. In Japan the 1997 budget aims to reduce the fiscal deficit by 2–3 percent of GDP. And in Europe the Stability Pact concluded at the end of 1996 to strengthen the basis for the EMU provides for fiscal deficits not to exceed 3 percent of GDP and to

balance over the course of the business cycle. With continued progress on fiscal consolidation, real long-term rates in the G-3 countries are projected to average around 3.5 percent in 1997–2006.

World merchandise trade: an intriguing slowdown

Growth in the volume of world merchandise trade fell to an estimated 5.4 percent in 1996 from the 9 percent averaged in 1994–95, years of upswing from the recession of the early 1990s. Growth in import volumes fell sharply in all major regions, with the exception of Latin America and the Middle East and North Africa. The downturn in world trade is unlikely to be fully understood until more detailed data become available, but some points can be made. First, as in previous cycles, some deceleration from the world trade boom of 1994–95 was expected (figure 1-4). Second, domestic demand growth in continental Europe, a key world trader, fell unexpectedly in late 1995 and 1996 (figure 1-5). Third, manufactured components and parts in sectors such as machinery and transport equipment occupy an increasingly important part in world merchandise trade. This trade was depressed by a sharp cyclical downturn in international inventory demand in electronics and semiconductors. Direct effects of the overall downturn included sharply lower export growth in Eastern Europe and

Structural deficits remain significant

Table 1-4 General government structural balances in the OECD
(Percentage of potential GDP)

Economy	1992	Estimate and projection	
		1996	1997
United States	–4.0	–1.7	–1.8
Japan	0.5	–2.9	–0.9
European Union	–5.2	–3.6	–2.5
Total OECD	–3.8	–2.6	–1.7
Memorandum items			
OECD fiscal balance[a]	–3.9	–3.2	–2.5
LMIC fiscal balance[b]	–2.1	–2.4	–2.0

a. Actual general government fiscal balance as a percentage of GDP.
b. Actual consolidated central government balance as a percentage of GDP. LMIC is low- and middle-income countries.
Source: OECD 1996; World Bank data and projections.

World trade growth slowed in 1996

Figure 1-4 Growth of world GDP and exports, 1981–96

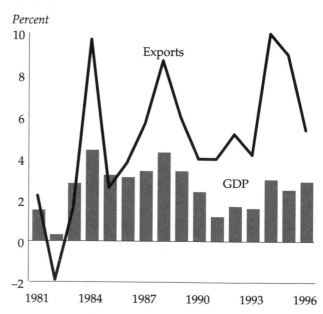

Source: World Bank data and staff estimates.

East Asia (box 1-1). Growth in Eastern European exports (in European currency unit terms) slowed from 25–30 percent in 1995 to 5 percent in 1996.

Looking forward, world trade growth is expected to pick up in tandem with industrial country growth in 1997–98, reaching a longer-term trend of around 6.4 percent (table 1-5). In the near term the 1996 import slowdown was sharpest in Europe and Japan; the upturn should particularly benefit exporters with orientation to these markets—Sub-Saharan Africa, the Middle East and North Africa, and transition economy exporters in the case of Europe, and East Asian exporters in the case of Japan. In the longer run trade growth will be supported by policy changes embodied in the Uruguay Round, new multilateral initiatives, continuing unilateral liberalization on the part of many developing countries, declining transport and communications costs, and growth in multinational production networks.

Trade in services and new multilateral liberalization initiatives

Commercial services such as travel, transport, communications, and financial and professional services are of growing importance in world trade. Commercial services exports touched $1.2 trillion and accounted for about 20 percent of world trade in 1996, having grown

at a 12.5 percent (nominal dollar) yearly rate in 1985–96, outstripping the 9.5 percent growth in the export of goods. Commercial services export growth in developing and newly industrialized regions averaged 12 percent a year in 1991–95, twice the rate in industrial economies (figure 1-6). Increases ranged from 20–30 percent in China, Thailand, and the Philippines to 10 percent in Egypt, India, and Russia.

The internationalization of services is expected to accelerate, thanks to improvements in communication and other information technologies, increasing competition in the delivery of services, and—partly in response to these forces—multilateral trade liberalization under the General Agreement on Trade in Services (GATS) of the World Trade Organization (WTO). The GATS negotiated under the Uruguay Round set out the main multilateral principles that should govern services trade, such as most favored nation status, national treatment, and market access. It secured specific commitments to liberalize in many sectors, with governments agreeing to continue work on sectors such as basic telecommunications and financial services. The milestone February

---

Industrial country import growth fell sharply

Figure 1-5 Import volume growth in industrial countries, 1994–96

Percent (year-on-year)

Note: Three-month moving average.
Source: IMF data; national sources.

Box 1-1 What caused the 1996 slowdown in East Asia's exports?

East Asian export growth slumped to less than 5 percent in volume terms in 1996, from an average of some 15 percent in 1991–95, affecting virtually all countries in the region. The fall was even sharper in nominal dollar terms given the linkage of many Asian currencies to the rising U.S. dollar. Signs of recovery emerged in the second half of 1996, especially strong in China while weaker in other economies, such as Thailand. The 1996 slowdown appears to have been largely cyclical, reflecting:

- Weakness in industrial country import demand.
- The adverse competitive effect of the appreciating U.S. dollar, to which several Asian currencies are tied.
- A cyclical slump in international demand for electronics and semiconductors, especially serious for East Asian countries, which are among the world's top offshore electronics assemblers.
- Supply constraints, overheating, and real exchange rate appreciation in several countries, resulting from years of continuous rapid economic growth.
- Special factors, such as tax changes in China and weather-related supply constraints in Thailand.

Not all of the slowdown may have been purely cyclical, however. A part of the rapid growth in East Asian intraregional trade in the early 1990s may have been a one-off surge, reflecting relocation of production of labor-intensive goods from Japan and the newly industrialized economies to China. Completion of this relocation may now be slowing intraregional trade growth.

Developing country trade growth is expected to average over 7 percent

Table 1-5 World merchandise trade, 1981–2006

Indicator and region	1981–90	1991–95	1996	1997–2006
World trade growth[a]	4.1	6.3	5.4	6.4
World output growth	2.9	2.0	2.9	3.4
Import growth by region				
High-income countries	5.1	5.8	4.8	6.2
OECD countries	4.8	4.7	4.9	5.8
Non-OECD countries	7.9	13.2	4.4	8.1
Developing countries	0.4	7.9	7.6	7.2
East Asia	6.4	15.5	7.2	10.0
South Asia	4.2	9.8	3.7	9.1
Sub-Saharan Africa	−3.4	3.2	5.8	5.3
Latin America and the Caribbean	−0.9	14.7	10.9	6.6
Europe and Central Asia	0.6	3.1	7.5	5.8
Middle East and North Africa	−1.3	−1.0	4.9	5.2
Export growth by region				
High-income countries	4.9	6.0	5.3	6.3
OECD countries	4.5	5.2	5.0	6.0
Non-OECD countries	8.6	11.6	7.3	8.1
Developing countries	1.7	8.5	5.8	7.2
East Asia	8.2	17.1	6.1	9.4
South Asia	6.0	12.0	6.7	10.7
Sub-Saharan Africa	−0.2	0.7	2.3	5.5
Latin America and the Caribbean	4.2	10.2	9.5	6.7
Europe and Central Asia	−0.1	3.8	3.7	5.0
Middle East and North Africa	−2.2	3.6	4.4	4.4

a. Growth rate of the sum of merchandise export and import volumes. Growth over historic intervals is computed as compound annual rates.
Source: World Bank data and baseline projections, June 1997.

1997 Agreement on Basic Telecommunication Services among sixty-nine members of the WTO, including forty developing countries, is the first of these continuing negotiations to be completed.[3]

International trade in telecom services is estimated at around $50 billion in 1995, less than 10 percent of world telecom service output but rising fast. Telecom services trade includes cross-border provision, for example, international phone calls, which increased from 4 billion to 60 billion minutes in the two decades to 1995. Foreign investment to establish a commercial presence also rose sharply in the past decade, as major telecom firms participated in privatizations of public telephone operators worldwide and established foreign subsidiaries, joint ventures, and strategic alliances with other multinational providers. The fact that foreign firms can often contest service markets only through direct investment means that trade liberalization has to go beyond border barriers, such as setting tariffs, to address complex "behind-the-border" issues dealing with foreign investment, barriers to entry, competition policy, and industry regulation. The meat of

the Agreement on Basic Telecommunication Services is in fifty-five detailed market access schedules setting out full or partial commitments to achieving competitive conditions in basic telecom services.[4]

Why the urgency attached to concluding the agreement? Telecommunications services are an increasingly important sector of the world economy, growing at 4.6 percent in the first half of the 1990s—twice the rate of world GDP growth—and valued at $600 billion in 1995.[5] Although developing countries account for only about 20 percent of the world market at present, they are its most dynamic segment. Growth in main telephone lines in developing countries averaged 14 percent a year in 1990–95, compared with only 3.5 percent in industrial countries. Telecom services are also a critical productive input for economic activity: worldwide, firms now spend more on telecom services than on oil (WTO 1997). The size and quality of telecom service infrastructure is significantly associated with economic growth.[6] The infrastructure is also an important factor for participation in the global production and trade networks established by multinational firms. And it is the medium over which developing countries can boost service exports in areas such as processing insurance claims or airline tickets, data entry, or programming. Improving access to low-cost, high-quality telecom services is therefore a major objective for policymakers today.

Technical progress in the past two decades has made possible dramatic quality improvements and service cost reductions. New products and services (cellular mobile, fax, satellite, wireless telephony, e-mail, the internet, private data networks) have proliferated.[7] The extent to which these improvements reach the customer, however, depends greatly on the degree of competition in the telecom services market. This usually entails a shift from the traditional model of the slow-moving, high-cost, monopoly public telephone operator to a competitive supply model based on opening markets to new entrants, liberalizing services trade, and establishing a procompetitive regulatory environment. In the Philippines main line installation by the incumbent public telephone company jumped from about 20,000 a year in 1985–92 to more than 220,000 in 1993–94, the year after competition was announced.[8] International traffic has grown much more rapidly in countries with competitive rather than monopoly markets (figure 1-7). Indeed, governments often have little choice about moving to a competitive model as tech-

nological change erodes the viability of traditional public telephone operators. International call-back services, for example, allow callers to bypass high-cost local phone companies and route calls through low-cost foreign operators. In Argentina these call-back services captured 30 percent of the long-distance market from the traditional operator.

Under the Agreement on Basic Telecommunication Services industrial countries such as the United States, EU members, and Japan undertake the most extensive opening of markets by the start of 1998. An intermediate group of developing or newly industrialized countries, such as Mexico and the Republic of Korea, made more limited but still significant market access commitments (for example, by raising foreign equity participation limits to 49 percent). Many other developing countries agreed to limited market opening over fewer market segments and at a more gradual pace over the next seven to ten years. For many developing countries, which because of their poor telecom infrastructure have the most to gain from liberalization, the agreement marks an auspicious beginning but leaves much to do. Only five countries in Sub-Saharan Africa and two in the Middle East and North Africa signed the agreement.

Even where significant commitments were made, these are only the beginning because there are many

---

Services exports rise in importance

Figure 1-6 Growth of merchandise and services exports, 1991–95

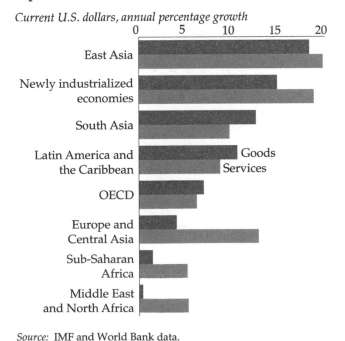

Current U.S. dollars, annual percentage growth

Source: IMF and World Bank data.

International telephone traffic grows rapidly in competitive markets

Figure 1-7 Growth in international telephone traffic per subscriber, 1990–95

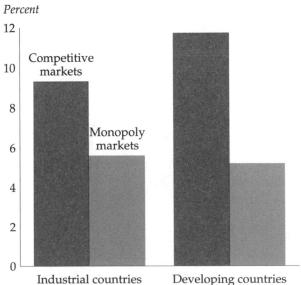

Source: ITU 1997.

13

ways for an incumbent operator to frustrate or delay entry by competitors. Real competitive supply will require broad improvements in the entire regulatory environment, including development of independent, transparent, well-resourced, and competent regulatory agencies, all of which pose big institutional challenges in many developing countries. Many countries therefore included in their commitments a reference paper setting out principles to be used in deciding regulatory disciplines, an innovation highlighting the overlap between international services trade and domestic regulation issues that will likely characterize future liberalization initiatives—for example, the Financial Services Agreement of the GATS, currently under negotiation.[9]

Capital flows and financial integration

Private capital flows to developing countries soared by a third to a record $245 billion in 1996, or 4.5 percent of developing country GDP—up from only 1 percent in 1990 (figure 1-8). Official development finance fell again (to only $41 billion), a worrying trend because access to private flows remains limited—140 of 166 developing countries account for only 5 percent of private flows to developing countries.[10]

Portfolio bond and equity flows accounted for half of the $60 billion increase in private flows. Swift

adjustment measures taken by some Latin American countries after the Mexico crisis succeeded in restoring market confidence. Recognizing more widespread improvements in economic management, credit ratings for countries in East Asia, Europe, and Sub-Saharan Africa also rose (figure 1-9). In the past two years more than thirty countries gained new access to international bond and equity markets. Low industrial country interest rates in 1996 stimulated a voracious appetite for high-yielding emerging market debt, resulting in a dramatic narrowing of spreads over the year. J.P. Morgan's Emerging Market Bond Index rose by about 40 percent over the year. Finally, a broader range of investors continues to be attracted to developing country markets for portfolio diversification. In 1993 there were 560 equity funds dedicated to investing in emerging markets, with a combined net asset value of about $75 billion; by June 1996 there were 1,360 funds, with net assets of $132 billion.

The benefits of financial integration can be substantial and include access to global savings to finance domestic investment, risk diversification in terms of consumption smoothing, as well as indirect benefits in knowledge spillovers, improved efficiency, and strengthening of domestic financial markets. The banking system in developing countries plays a leading role in financial integration and is one of the main channels through which benefits materialize. But financial integration can also mag-

---

Private capital flows to developing countries hit new highs

Figure 1-8 Net long-term private flows to developing countries, 1990–96

Percentage of GDP

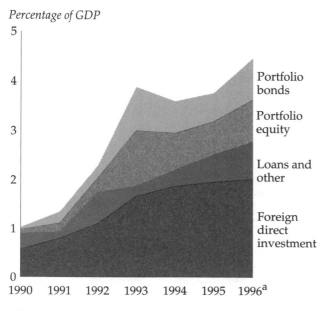

a. Estimated.
Source: World Bank data.

Credit ratings improve in most regions

Figure 1-9 Country credit ratings, 1990–96

Average across developing countries by region

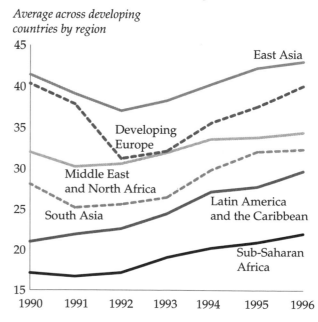

Source: Institutional Investor, various issues.

14

nify the effects of underlying distortions and institutional weaknesses and thus the costs of policy mistakes. The agenda of domestic reforms required for low- and middle-income countries to fully benefit from financial integration will be a challenging one (see box 1-2).

Foreign direct investment rose 15 percent to reach $110 billion in 1996, flowing especially to Latin America, East Asia, and Europe and Central Asia. Flows to South Asia reached a record $2.6 billion in the year, reflecting opening measures in India. Foreign direct investment is now the largest single source of external financing for developing countries, accounting for 40 percent of net long-term flows.

The declining trend in official development assistance adds to the urgency of improving the limited access of most developing countries to private capital flows. An important step in this direction was the agreement on a framework for resolving the debt problems of the highly indebted poor countries (HIPC). The HIPC Trust Fund, established in November 1996, is expected to be the principal vehicle for the World Bank and other multilateral creditors to provide relief on debt owed to them. The Board of Governors of the World Bank transferred $500 million from the net income of the International Bank for Reconstruction and Development (IBRD) to the HIPC Trust Fund as an initial World Bank contribution. Bilateral donor contributions also will be important to facilitate the full participation of other multilateral creditors such as the African Development Bank. The International Monetary Fund will participate in the initiative through special Enhanced Structural Adjustment Facility operations. Paris Club creditors will provide debt reduction of up to 80 percent on a case-by-case basis. In April 1997 Uganda became the first country to benefit under the HIPC Debt Initiative, with a debt relief package that will reduce its debt by $338 million in net present value terms at its completion in 1998.

Looking ahead, although there is a near-term risk to private capital flows associated with the expected rise in interest rates in industrial countries over the next twelve to eighteen months, the outlook for continued growth in private flows in the medium and longer term remains favorable on both the supply and the demand side. Supporting factors include investment in emerging markets as a means of portfolio

---

Box 1-2 Financial integration, capital inflows, and banking sector fragility

Banks usually dominate financial intermediation in developing countries, often accounting for 80–90 percent of the total. Thus, they are often the primary intermediaries for a large part of private capital inflows. The economy as a whole can derive substantial benefits from financial integration, and so can banks in the medium to longer term. For banks, benefits include adoption of more advanced financial technologies, greater portfolio diversification, access to a larger supply of funds, and efficiency gains from economies of scale. Transition toward greater financial integration can, however, involve significant risks for the banking sector and the economy when it is conducted in an environment with large macroeconomic imbalances and where banks are in poor financial shape and inadequately supervised. (Issues raised by the integration of developing countries in world financial markets are examined in World Bank 1997b.)

In the early stages of financial integration emerging economies usually receive significant capital inflows, which, unless fully sterilized by the monetary authorities, allow the banking sector to expand credit rapidly. The result can be a boom in domestic consumption, contributing to an appreciation of the real exchange rate and widening current account deficits. When banks are poorly managed and inadequately supervised, increased lending often occurs without adequate regard for risk, for example, for financial and real estate speculation. Large increases in asset prices result not only from looser credit but also from the general improvement in economic prospects accompanying liberalization (see figure). Rising asset prices and an appreciating real exchange rate boost wealth and so further stimulate spending, growth, and expectations for the future. Rising asset prices also inflate collateral and so encourage further bank lending. These three factors (surging bank credit, rising asset prices, and higher expectations) tend to reinforce each other. Meanwhile, the appreciated exchange rate, large external deficits, high asset prices, and increased indebtedness of individuals and firms make the economy more vulnerable to adverse shocks.

A sudden reversal of private capital flows can sharply reduce liquidity and credit, force banks to sell assets at a discount, and impose high costs on the economy, leading in the extreme to costly systemic banking problems associated with lower (usually negative) economic growth, as occurred recently in Mexico and Venezuela. The consequences of allocating losses among bank stockholders, creditors, depositors, and taxpayers are onerous. The average cost of restructuring banking systems after crises in developing countries is about 13 percent of GDP and 41 percent of total loans, while in industrial countries the cost is 4.8 percent of GDP and 6.1 percent of total loans (Rojas-Suarez and Weisbrod 1996).

Box continues on next page.

An important challenge for policymakers—in addition to maintaining sound macroeconomic policies—is to strengthen the banking sector by aggressively pursuing reform of prudential supervision and regulation. This means building financial institutions, for example, establishing proper legal and accounting procedures and an appropriate incentive structure and upgrading the supervisory and regulatory framework. Because this is a difficult and lengthy process, developing countries may also need to use other policy instruments to manage financial integration in the short term. In particular, policymakers can strengthen banking systems during "boom" periods by encouraging banks to use additional profits to increase their capitalization and increase provisions against future losses. These measures reduce the risk of banks failing as a result of defaults by borrowers and so provide cushions that make the system more resilient to shocks. For example, in Chile commercial banks were able to reduce their stock of nonperforming loans by more than half, while also increasing their liquidity by about 40 percent between 1990 and 1995. In Malaysia banks almost doubled their rate of capitalization in 1989–95 despite the lack of a significant increase in profitability. Loan loss provisions in Venezuela, however, fell before the onset of its banking crisis in 1994, despite deteriorating asset quality.

In addition to building cushions in the banking system, countries can try to curb the credit boom more directly. This may be an important remedy in countries where the banking sector is weak and where private sector spending is biased toward consumption rather than investment. Policies aimed at reducing bank lending include sterilized intervention, increasing bank reserve (or liquidity) requirements, and imposing capital controls. These policies may be effective in reducing aggregate liquidity and limiting bank lend-

ing, but may be costly and highly inefficient in the medium term. They may harm the banking sector by promoting the rise of nonbank financial intermediaries and the creation of complicated schemes to bypass regulations and by exacerbating economic inefficiencies. Although distortionary policies may be advisable in some extreme cases, they do not substitute for structural reforms in the infrastructure and regulatory framework of banking.

*Rising asset prices fuel
the economic boom during inflow periods*

Stock prices during inflow periods

Stock real price index

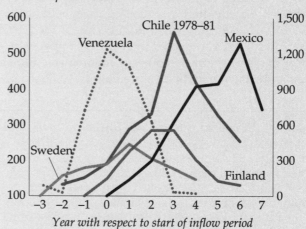

Year with respect to start of inflow period

Source: World Bank 1997b.

---

diversification in industrial countries and continued improvements in export performance, domestic conditions, and creditworthiness across a broader set of developing countries (box 1-3 discusses an alternative boom-bust scenario in which the near-term rise in interest rates turns out much larger than expected). Prospects for official development assistance flows are not encouraging, however, given the movement toward fiscal consolidation in major OECD countries. Better coordination among donors is called for, with aid targeted to the poorest countries.

Primary commodities: after the boom

Unlike the mini commodity boom of 1994–95, when prices for most major primary commodities rose, market developments in 1996 and the first part of 1997 showed few common trends (table 1-6). The beverages price index, which led the boom in 1994–95, has been

driven by erratic movements in coffee prices, slumping in 1996 as a result of bumper coffee production increases in countries such as Indonesia, Uganda, and Vietnam and then surging in 1997 with weather-driven production shortfalls in Brazil. African and other coffee exporters will enjoy buoyant prices for a year more, though a significant price correction looks likely in the next two to three years. Metals and minerals prices, led by aluminum and copper, fell substantially in 1996 in response to weak industrial demand and rising stocks, but prices stabilized in 1997 as world economic activity picked up (figure 1-10).

Cereal prices were up steeply in 1996 for the third consecutive year, the result of a weather-related downturn in U.S. grain production in 1995, as well as longer-term policy changes by major exporting countries that have tended to reduce grain acreage over time. Prices started to drop at the end of 1996, however, in response to a record world grain harvest in the

Box 1-3 Risks in the external environment: a modest boom-bust scenario

The main scenario for the next ten years is of a generally favorable environment for developing countries. But it would be imprudent to count on recent exceptional conditions continuing in all respects. Given robust conditions in the second half of 1996 and the first half of 1997, concerns increased that a near-term consumer-led "boom" and an overlenient monetary policy in the United States could lead to a higher than expected rise in U.S. inflation. A sharp corrective tightening in 1998 and early 1999 could then precipitate a recession (see table).

Analysis of this scenario in a global context leads to some interesting results. Economic conditions in Europe and Japan remain relatively weak, so that the risk of a coordinated boom-bust episode in the industrial countries is low. Policymakers in these countries, faced with weak growth and few inflationary pressures, are unlikely to tighten their own monetary policies. Long-term interest rates in Japan and Europe rise somewhat in response to higher U.S. rates, while growth in these countries slows by 0.2–0.3 percentage point relative to the baseline. But by and large, outcomes in Japan and Europe fail to amplify the U.S.

cycle. This then tends to muffle the effects on developing countries.

Lower U.S. demand for developing country exports and the dampening effects of higher U.S. interest rates on private capital flows would then be the biggest risks in this scenario. Lower import demand in North America has the greatest impact on NAFTA partner Mexico, other countries in Latin America, and some key Asian suppliers. The much milder downturn in Western Europe could have a slight impact on exports from emerging European economies, including Poland, Hungary, and the Czech Republic.

At their highest, U.S. short-term interest rates rise about 175 basis points above the baseline, while bond yields rise about 50 basis points in Europe and 30 in Japan in response to a 100 point rise in U.S. yields. But because the rise in long-term rates in this scenario is roughly half the rise that occurred in early 1994, the risk of this triggering a Mexican-style crisis is relatively small. Nonetheless, adverse interest rate effects could be significant for countries that have received large volumes of portfolio investment and that are financing high current account deficits.

Industrial countries in the boom-bust scenario
(*Average percentage growth for baseline, percentage difference from baseline in alternative scenario*)

Country or group	Boom 1997–98		Bust 1999–2000	
	Baseline	Alternative	Baseline	Alternative
Output				
G-7 countries	2.6	0.2	2.7	–1.1
United States	2.7	0.5	2.3	–2.1
Japan	2.6	0	3.4	–0.2
Europe-4	2.4	0.1	2.5	–0.3
Inflation				
United States	3.0	0.8	3.0	0.5
Japan	0.7	0.1	1.8	–0.1
Germany	1.8	0.1	2.0	0.2
Imports				
G-7 countries	5.9	0.2	5.5	–1.6
United States	7.1	0.2	5.2	–2.5
Japan	6.5	–0.2	5.9	0.7
Europe-4	4.8	0.1	5.6	–0.4
Short-term interest rates				
United States	5.85	50 basis points	6.25	100 basis points
Japan	1.00	0	2.85	0
Germany	3.40	0	4.25	0
Long-term interest rates				
United States	6.50	30 basis points	6.80	90 basis points
Japan	2.95	30	5.35	33
Germany	6.30	15	6.00	25

Source: World Bank baseline and DRI/McGraw-Hill boom-bust scenario, May–June 1997.

Table 1-6 Annual percentage change in oil and nonoil commodity prices
(World Bank commodity price indexes, nominal dollars)

Commodity group	Trends 1981–96				Forecasts 1997–2006		
	1981–90	*1991–95*	*1995*	*1996*	*1997*	*1998*	*1997–2006*
All nonoil commodities	−2.3	4.1	9.5	−5.8	2.1	−3.8	1.1
Agriculture	−3.2	5.6	6.5	−4.4	2.2	−4.4	1.2
Food	−3.3	3.2	9.5	5.7	−4.5	−4.8	0.3
Grains	−2.9	3.8	17.9	16.8	−15.8	−0.9	−0.6
Beverages	−5.8	8.6	1.6	−16.3	16.9	−13.9	0.8
Raw materials	−0.5	6.2	7.5	−6.0	−0.4	4.4	2.4
Metals and minerals	0.5	0.3	20.1	−12.3	2.2	−1.4	1.2
Fertilizers	−2.5	0.7	11.0	15.6	−0.8	−5.7	−0.3
Petroleum	−4.7	−5.6	8.1	18.9	−9.4	0.0	−0.5
Memorandum item							
G-5 manufactures unit value	3.3	3.6	8.1	−4.2	−4.0	4.6	2.2

Source: World Bank, Commodity Policy and Analysis Unit, May 1997.

1996–97 crop year and are expected to be down heavily for the year as a whole. Lower prices will be a boon for many low-income, food-deficit, importing countries, notably in Africa. Higher grain prices over the past few years raised the cost of developing countries' cereal imports by $4 billion, according to UN Food and Agriculture Organization (FAO) estimates.

The other major commodity seeing higher prices in 1996 was oil. Reasons for the unexpected 20 percent price hike included low stocks, shortfalls in non-OPEC production, and the delay of Iraq's return to the market. OPEC producers also displayed more price discipline than in the past. Prices are expected to fall off in 1997, however, and are projected to fall by more than 3 percent a year in real terms in 1997–2006, as a result of improvements in exploration and production technologies, increased supply from non-OPEC sources, and increasing efficiency in consumption. Overall, nonfuel commodity prices are forecast to gradually decline in real terms, at perhaps 1–2 percent a year over the coming decade. In comparison to the large declines experienced in the 1980s and early 1990s, however, this projection is really one of relative stability.[11]

Prospects for developing regions

The prospective external environment is one of both burgeoning opportunities and increasing challenges that will place a premium on adaptability to change. World trade growth of 6–7 percent implies both broadly expanding opportunities for mutually beneficial specialization and exchange, and increasing international competition made feasible by falling trade and transport cost barriers. Private capital flows to coun-

tries maintaining a sound policy environment are likely to be copious, but niggardly otherwise. Declining trends in commodity prices will reduce the potential for large windfall gains accruing to mere natural resource ownership, while rewarding the most efficient producers. (See appendix 1 for more detailed discussion of projections for developing regions.)

Commodity price trends differ after the boom

Figure 1-10 Real commodity prices, 1990–2006

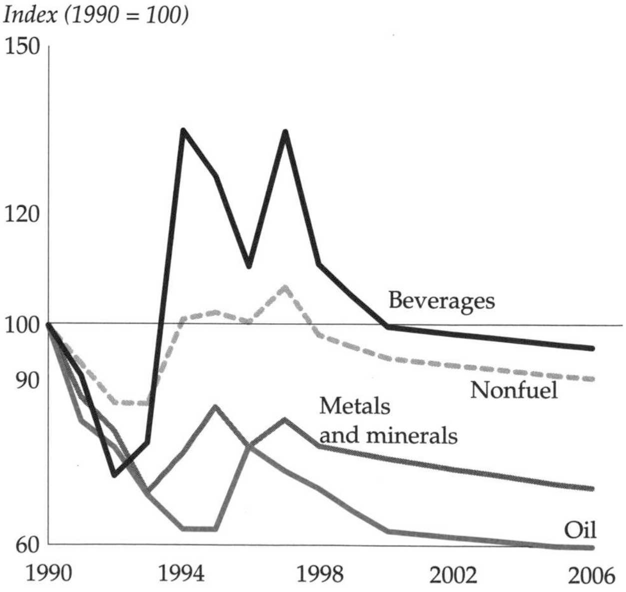

Index (1990 = 100)

Note: Deflated by the manufactures unit value index.
Source: World Bank data and projections.

In this environment the current projections are for an improvement in developing country growth to 5.4 percent in 1997–2006, up from 2.6 percent in the preceding decade (excluding the transition economies, from 4.4 percent to 5.5 percent), with growth expected to rise in all regions except East Asia (where it is still expected to remain high). Three regions where per capita incomes fell in the past ten years—Sub-Saharan Africa, the Middle East and North Africa, and Europe and Central Asia—are expected to see a reversal of the trend. Poverty in South Asia, the region with the largest number of the world's poor, is expected to decline significantly as a result of more rapid economic growth. On balance, the favorable external environment assumed in the projections implies that the growth performance of individual countries will be largely determined by domestic factors, especially policy developments.

South Asia

Long-run growth projections for South Asia have been upgraded by 0.5 percentage point from those published in *Global Economic Prospects 1996* to 5.9 percent. The momentum of economic reforms in the region is being maintained despite political flux and is evoking a robust supply response (figure 1-11). The Indian economy averaged 6–7 percent growth in 1994–96. Stabilization and reform measures introduced in 1991 have removed entry barriers, increased domestic competition, and significantly liberalized the trade and foreign investment regimes. Exports have boomed and, despite slowing, continued to outpace world trade growth in 1996. Key medium-term issues include large fiscal deficits, which hamper investment rates from being raised to the 30 percent-plus level prevalent in East Asia, and the need for major improvements in infrastructure and service sector productivity, both of which seriously constrain potential growth performance. In Sri Lanka and, to a lesser extent, Bangladesh political instability and persistent institutional weaknesses remain primary problems. The external environment is likely to prove favorable, with declining oil prices contributing to improved terms of trade. The benefits of fast growth in world trade should be complemented in the longer term by improved market access for the region's apparel industries as restrictions under the Agreement on Textile Trade are phased out.

Middle East and North Africa

Growth projections for the Middle East and North Africa have also been upgraded by around 0.5 percentage point, on the basis of greater confidence that reforms are being consolidated and will continue in many countries, though at a pace slower than necessary to achieve the desirable major improvements in growth. Growth is projected to average 3.6 percent in 1997–2006, up from slightly above 2 percent in the preceding decade. Egypt and Jordan continue to make progress on macroeconomic stabilization and structural reforms, with growth in recent years of around 4 and 7 percent, respectively. In the Maghreb the signing of free trade agreements by Tunisia and Morocco in 1996 under the EU's Mediterranean Initiative provides a valuable opportunity to commit to far-reaching economic reforms, as it does in Jordan, which signed a comparable agreement this year. Though small, private foreign direct investment and portfolio flows into reforming countries picked up. In Iran recent strength in oil prices has provided a near-term cushion, but there are few signs of enhanced reforms. For all oil exporters current projections of eroding real prices mean this cushion is likely to be temporary. Pressures to accelerate reform, deriving from domestic conditions such as high population growth and unemployment, will also increase. Brisk, sustained efforts to unleash the growth and jobs potential of the private sector by reducing burdensome regulation; significant privatization of the over-large, state-owned enterprise sector; and further trade and foreign investment liberalization are the order of the day.

Growth should rise in most regions in the next decade

Figure 1-11 Average annual GDP growth in developing regions, 1987–96 and 1997–2006

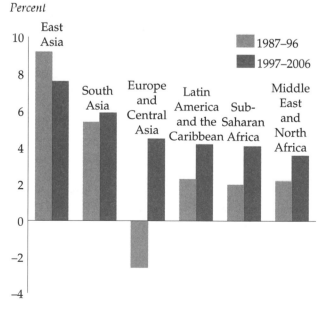

Percent

Source: World Bank data and projections.

Latin America and the Caribbean

Aggregate growth in Latin America and the Caribbean is determined largely by three countries—Brazil, Mexico, and Argentina—which account for roughly three-quarters of regional output. In Mexico and Argentina, which plunged into recession in 1995 in the aftermath of the Mexican peso crisis, prompt adjustment fostered strong export- and investment-led recoveries in 1996, pulling up regional growth to near 3.5 percent from less than 1 percent the year before. Large private capital flows to the region resumed. Though many countries in the region had made much progress with macroeconomic stabilization and trade and investment liberalization in the previous decade, the events of 1995–96 called attention to the need for countries to take on a range of more complex reforms.

These include microeconomic reforms to enhance domestic and especially private sector savings, banking and financial sector reform, and reforms to boost the somewhat sluggish historical export growth, in part by increasing competition and efficiency in sectors providing infrastructure and business services. Progress on reform and adjustment among countries of the region is differentiated, with Chile having made the most progress and Brazil, the giant of the region, still at a relatively early stage. Brazil has reduced inflation dramatically, but slow progress on fiscal consolidation in combination with tight monetary policy has contributed to real exchange rate appreciation and larger external deficits. Nevertheless, with most countries moving ahead with reforms, growth in the region is projected to improve to a little over 4 percent. This rate would represent per capita growth of more than 2.5 percent in 1997–2006, well above the 0.5 percent of the previous decade.

Sub-Saharan Africa

Growth of almost 4 percent in 1995 and 1996 in Sub-Saharan Africa far outpaced the dismal 1.6 percent average in 1981–94. The improvement was broad based, with positive per capita GDP growth in thirty-three countries of the region. Export growth also picked up, and private capital flows to the region, which were virtually nil in the early 1990s, reached about $12 billion in 1996, although much of this went to only a few countries, such as South Africa, Ghana, and oil exporters Nigeria and Angola. Higher primary commodity prices generated increases of around 2 percent in the region's terms of trade, in sharp contrast to the 3 percent annual average declines in the preceding fifteen years. Regional growth is projected to continue to average a little more than 4 percent in 1997–2006, the outcome of several cross-cutting trends. The region's

terms of trade are expected to move down in line with real commodity prices, though much more slowly than in the 1980s and early 1990s. However, recovery in Europe, the region's major overseas market, should encourage exports, while the multilateral HIPC Initiative will help severely indebted low-income countries that are sound reformers reduce their debts.

More important, projections of a return to positive per capita growth of around 1 percent a year from declines of about the same size over the past decade assume that many countries will continue to make headway on fundamental macroeconomic and structural reforms. Although it is too early to say that the corner to self-sustaining growth has been turned, much has been achieved over the past few years. First, conditions for peace are better given the ending of large-scale conflict in southern Africa. The ending of apartheid and the relatively peaceful political transition in South Africa make the forecast of an increase in growth to a modest 3–4 percent (from around 1.5 percent in 1987–96) plausible. This would be a boon to the whole region, although the country continues to face significant hurdles on labor reform and fiscal consolidation. More generally, many countries (as diverse as Benin, Ethiopia, Ghana, Mali, and Uganda) are engaged in a transition toward political pluralism and economic liberalism.

Second, the commitment to reform by a wider range of countries across the continent appears to be firmer; twenty-eight countries are undertaking some form of adjustment, including significant trade reforms. Quantitative restrictions have generally been converted to tariff equivalents with lower average tariff rates and narrower dispersion. Most countries have market-based exchange rates, and parallel market premia have declined from 200–300 percent to less than 10 percent in the past decade. There has been less widespread but still significant progress in macroeconomic management, fiscal administration, and reduction of inflation. Similarly, there has been some limited advance in many countries on privatization, improving incentives for private producers, and raising private savings rates. The forecast could, however, be thrown askew by a number of things. An important one is the potential for policy slippage in the face of declining terms of trade and shrinking government revenues. The fragility of economic recovery in the two large countries of the region—South Africa and Nigeria—also poses downside risks. Finally, the political and economic direction taken by the Democratic Republic of Congo (formerly Zaire) will have continentwide ramifications.

East Asia

East Asia's growth in 1996 slowed to around 8.5 percent from an average of more than 10 percent a year in the first half of the 1990s, as China and some Southeast Asian countries curbed demand to restrain mounting inflationary pressures and, in some cases, growing current account deficits. The sharp slowdown in regional export growth in 1996 further contributed to the downturn (see box 1-1). In some Southeast Asian countries that experienced a huge property boom in the first half of the 1990s, tighter credit and weakening equity and real estate prices put borrowers under pressure, contributing to the emergence of bad debts in the banking and financial sectors. Larger current account deficits and reliance on short-term capital inflows also increased vulnerability to external shocks. Attacks on currencies forced a devaluation in Thailand and smaller adjustments in several other countries. While near-term growth will likely slow, a full-blown Mexican-style crisis appears unlikely because of better economic fundamentals in several respects than in Mexico in 1994. In most countries domestic savings are much higher, for example, and overall external debt and debt service to export ratios are lower.

Given a broadly favorable external environment and the demonstrated ability of regional policymakers to adapt to changing circumstances, the long-term projections for growth in 1997–2006 are around 7.6 percent, only modestly lower than last year, though the risks surrounding the forecast have widened. Policy challenges in some Southeast Asian countries include macroeconomic adjustment to reduce current account deficits to more prudent levels, managing a continued transition to higher value added and more skill-intensive production, improving banking supervision, and implementing other financial sector reforms. In China further development of the institutional framework, reform of the state-owned enterprise sector, financial sector reforms, and infrastructure development remain high on the agenda.

Europe and Central Asia

Expectations for a return to growth in 1996 in the transition economies of Europe and Central Asia were not realized: aggregate output for the group is estimated to have fallen 1.8 percent. This outcome was influenced by slower export growth among Central and Eastern European countries—especially in exports to the critical Western European market—a sharp macroeconomic and financial crisis in Bulgaria, continued decline in Russian and Ukrainian output, and the initial contractionary effects of austerity measures in some countries. Nonetheless, eighteen of twenty-five monitored countries registered GDP gains in 1996 and fundamentals for growth are increasingly favorable for 1997–98.

Accession to the EU—most likely early in the next century—is now an important driver for policy among advanced reformers in Central Europe. The medium-term outlook for Russia and most countries of the former Soviet Union continues to be conditional on extensive and credible domestic reform efforts. Given improvements in the business environment, the response of international investors (and in particular of foreign direct investment) can play an important role in halting the continuing decline of overall investment, supporting economic recovery, and contributing to the technological upgrading and modernization of economies in the former Soviet republics. For all countries in Europe and Central Asia, the next ten years are likely to see stronger economic relations with Western Europe, a revitalization of regional trade, and growing absorption in global networks of production, trade, and finance. Longer-term growth projections of around 4.5 percent are little changed from last year.

Implications of rapid growth and integration of the Big 5 countries

Just five large developing and transition economies—China, India, Indonesia, Brazil, and Russia (the Big 5)—account for half the world's labor force of 3.5 billion and a third of its cultivable land area. Yet these countries' share in world GDP in 1995 was only 8 percent at market exchange rates (or 22 percent in purchasing power parity terms), while their share in world exports was also only 8 percent. If, however, as seems probable, the market- and outward-oriented reforms these countries have initiated over the past ten to fifteen years are sustained and deepened, their role in the world economy is likely to increase dramatically over the next quarter century, producing significant changes in world patterns of resource allocation, production, trade, relative prices, and returns to factors of production. While it is broadly recognized that the world will derive large welfare gains from the emergence of the Big 5, the effects on different industrial sectors, countries, and factors of production will vary, with some bearing a heavier adjustment burden and others seeing especially large opportunities.

Among industrial countries, the prospect of rapid growth in skill- and technology-intensive exports to the Big 5 countries is welcomed. But this appreciation is often tempered by apprehension about the potential harm that manufactured imports from labor-abundant countries, such as China, India, and Indonesia, may do to the jobs and earnings of low-skilled workers in industrial countries. Policymakers in some developing countries too may harbor concerns that competition from the Big 5 may crowd them out of (or prevent them from entering) world markets for unskilled labor-intensive manufactures for a long time. And concerns sometimes arise that rapid growth in the Big 5 may increase pressure on world supplies of food and energy, leading to large price hikes for these commodities.

To evaluate some of these questions, a study was undertaken using the Global Trade Analysis Project (GTAP) database and computable general equilibrium model. The model provides a systematic way of evaluating the impact of changes in trade policies and differential patterns of technical progress and factor accumulation on patterns of demand, production, resource allocation, trade, and prices across industrial sectors and countries. Of course, as with any model, these simulations represent a considerable simplification of the complex forces at work and should be taken as illustrative scenarios rather than formal forecasts.[12] The study prepared a baseline scenario for the year 2020, as well as a low-case scenario assuming a failure to sustain reforms, trade frictions, maintenance of high trade barriers between each of the Big 5 and other countries, and as a result, a slower pace of productivity growth in the Big 5. The difference between the two scenarios gives a partial measure of how the world economy is affected by the growth and integration of the big developing countries.[13]

The world in 2020: a baseline scenario

The world in 2020 in the baseline scenario is one in which the forces propelling global integration in the 1980s and early 1990s have had free play for another thirty-odd years. There is assumed to be considerable trade liberalization over and above the Uruguay Round. Developing countries cut tariffs on manufactures to industrial country levels by 2020, while tariffs on agricultural products are assumed to be cut by a half worldwide. The Agreement on Textiles and Clothing, which phased out the Multifibre Arrangement, is implemented on schedule in 2005. China joins the WTO at some point in the scenario. Continued substantial declines in the price of transport and communications are reflected in a 2 percent annual decline in transport costs.

Within this increasingly open world trading and investment environment, most developing countries and regions are assumed to achieve sustained progress across a broad range of structural and macroeconomic reforms, resulting in aggregate growth for developing countries in the period to 2020 running at 2–3 percentage points higher than in the past twenty-five years (table 1-7). The scenario assumes that the Big 5 achieve solid GDP growth of 5.5–7.0 percent between 1992 (the year to which the model is calibrated) and 2020, underpinned by growth in the capital stock of 5–10 percent and total factor productivity growth clustered in a 1.5–2.0 percent range.[14] Relative to economic performance in the 1980s and early 1990s, the scenario sees a moderation in China's growth rate from the enormous

10–12 percent witnessed since 1982 and a mild improvement in (or continuation of) the robust 5.5–7.0 percent growth trends in India and Indonesia. The scenario also sees a substantial improvement in growth in Brazil, as it moves beyond the adverse shocks of the debt crisis, and in the economies in transition as they move beyond the breakdown of the planned economy.

For China more moderate growth in the scenario reflects in part an easing of measured total factor productivity growth to 2–3 percent from 4–5 percent in 1984–94. The high early rates of total factor productivity growth probably reflected the gains from undertaking reforms with the quickest and largest payoffs, such as liberalizing of agriculture and opening up the favorably located coastal regions, as well as one-off shifts in the labor force from agriculture to manufacturing and services. Major reform challenges for the future, such as reform of the state-owned enterprise and financial sectors and the upgrading of legal systems and other institutions, are more complex and may take longer to implement and bear fruit.[15] India also faces a challenging array of reform issues, including fiscal consolidation, further trade liberalization, and reform of inflexible formal sector labor markets, state-owned enterprises, and the financial and other state-owned or heavily regulated service sectors. Many of the same challenges face Brazil and, although it is difficult to generalize about such a disparate group of countries, the economies in transition, which also face major challenges in developing adequate institutional frameworks. (See appendix 1 for further discussion of long-run reform issues.) The relatively cautious growth assumptions of the scenario presume broadly sustained, if not necessarily spectacular, efforts at reform across a broad and complex range of issues.

The prospect of solid growth is not restricted to the Big 5: the rest of Latin America, Sub-Saharan Africa, and the Middle East and North Africa are expected to see a doubling in growth from the 2 percent or so averaged in the past fifteen years, while other Asian countries continue to grow at 5–7 percent. Such growth, over a quarter century, would contribute to a major decline in world poverty. In addition, the shares in world GDP of both the Big 5 and developing countries as a group double by 2020 (see table 1-7). This increase would be historic, broadly reversing trends of the past 200 years. Developing country growth is estimated to have averaged only around 1 percent a year between 1820 and 1950, about half the rate in high-income OECD countries. In China and India growth averaged only around 0.5 percent a year over those 130 years, or a negligible 0.1 percent in per capita terms. The shares of developing countries and the Big 5 in world output thus fell substantially in 1820–1950, followed by a period (1950–92) when developing and industrial country output shares remained roughly flat.[16]

International trade, patterns of specialization, and relative prices

The scenario's growth, trade liberalization, and transport cost assumptions yield a projection of world trade volume growth averaging near 5.5 percent a year in 1992–2020, not much below the 6 percent rate averaged since the mid-1980s. The high-income OECD countries' share of world exports and imports falls in constant dollar terms from 65–70 percent in 1992 to 40–45 percent in 2020, while that of developing countries roughly doubles to 45–50 percent (table 1-8). Among the Big 5, India achieves the highest growth in exports and imports (11–12 percent a year), reflecting the removal of anti-export bias as protection is reduced from high levels and as international barriers to apparel trade are removed. China is expected to continue its vigorous export growth of 10 percent a year.

The focus of industrial country trade shifts substantially toward the developing countries in the baseline scenario. The proportion of industrial country exports shipped to other industrial countries is expected to fall in value terms from 65 percent in 1992 to 45 percent in 2020, while that to developing countries rises from 25 to 40 percent, the Big 5 accounting for about 10 percentage points of the increase. About 50 cents in every dollar's worth of OECD export growth in the period to 2020 would be exports to developing countries. And developing countries will be the fastest growing markets across all twelve of the broad industrial sectors analyzed, ranging from primary agriculture through various kinds of manufactures to services.

Big reductions in trade barriers and transport costs and the sharp rise in developing countries' share in world income envisaged by the scenario generate significant changes in international specialization. Indexes of revealed comparative advantage provide one measure of international specialization (table 1-9).[17] For high-income OECD countries the most dramatic feature of the scenario is a sharp increase in their specialization in services exports ("other services"), including key categories such as telecommunications

---

Developing countries' share of world GDP will nearly double by 2020

Table 1-7 World growth, 1974–2020, and shares in world GDP, 1992 and 2020
(Percent)

Country or group	Real GDP[a]				Capital stock 1992–2020	Total factor productivity 1992–2020	Share of world real GDP[a]	
	1974–82	1982–92	1992–95	1992–2020			1992	2020
World	2.6	3.0	2.4	2.9	3.6	0.5	100.0	100.0
High income economies	2.3	3.1	2.2	2.5	3.3	0.3	84.2	70.9
OECD	2.2	2.9	2.0	2.4	3.1	0.3	81.5	66.7
Newly industrialized economies[b]	8.0	8.7	7.4	4.9	6.0	1.3	2.3	3.8
Hong Kong (China)	7.7	9.3	7.8	4.0	4.0	1.1	0.3	0.4
Developing countries	3.7	2.6	3.1	5.4	6.0	1.3	15.7	29.1
Big 5	4.4	2.7	3.3	5.8	7.2	1.7	7.8	16.1
China	6.5	10.3	12.5	7.0	9.5	2.2	1.4	3.9
India	4.4	5.4	5.5	5.8	6.7	1.9	1.0	2.1
Brazil	4.3	1.8	4.8	4.6	4.6	1.1	1.7	2.5
Indonesia	6.8	7.1	7.6	6.9	6.9	1.9	0.6	1.5
Economies in transition[c]	3.8	−0.7	−5.4	5.5	7.0	1.7	3.2	6.0
ASEAN 3[d]	6.3	5.6	7.7	7.1	6.7	2.0	0.8	2.4
Rest of South Asia	5.3	5.2	4.0	5.2	5.7	1.4	0.3	0.6
Rest of Latin America and the Caribbean	3.0	2.0	2.2	4.2	4.0	0.9	2.1	2.9
Sub-Saharan Africa	2.2	2.0	2.1	4.2	3.4	0.8	1.2	1.7
Middle East and North Africa	2.2	2.0	2.1	4.2	4.1	0.3	2.3	3.1
Rest of world	3.3	2.4	2.6	5.6	5.8	1.4	1.2	2.3

a. Constant 1992 U.S. dollars using market exchange rates.
b. Republic of Korea, Singapore, and Taiwan (China).
c. Because of data limitations economies in transition are modeled as a group.
d. Malaysia, Philippines, and Thailand.
Source: Global Trade Analysis Project; World Bank data and staff estimates.

Table 1-8 Trade growth and market shares, 1992–2020
(Percent)

	Exports			Imports		
	Growth	Share of world		Growth	Share of world	
Country or group	1992–2020	1992	2020	1992–2020	1992	2020
World	5.5	100.0	100.0	5.3	100.0	100.0
High-income economies	4.0	76.5	51.6	4.3	74.3	56.6
OECD	3.5	67.8	40.4	4.0	65.3	45.3
Newly industrialized countries	6.5	7.4	9.7	6.3	7.2	9.4
Hong Kong (China)	6.0	1.3	1.5	5.7	1.8	1.9
Developing countries	8.1	23.5	48.4	7.3	25.7	43.4
Big 5	8.9	9.0	22.0	8.5	8.7	20.1
China	10.0	3.0	9.8	10.2	2.8	9.9
India	12.0	0.7	3.9	11.0	0.8	3.2
Brazil	7.2	1.2	1.9	6.8	0.9	1.3
Indonesia	8.8	1.1	2.7	7.8	0.9	1.8
Economies in transition	6.2	3.0	3.6	5.9	3.4	3.9
ASEAN 3[a]	9.6	2.8	8.4	8.6	3.0	7.0
Rest of South Asia	8.0	0.5	0.9	6.8	0.6	0.8
Rest of Latin America and the Caribbean	6.7	2.8	3.9	5.4	3.5	3.5
Sub-Saharan Africa	6.7	1.7	2.4	5.3	2.1	2.1
Middle East and North Africa	6.4	5.2	6.6	5.4	5.9	6.0
Rest of world	9.4	1.5	4.2	8.1	1.9	3.9

Note: Exports and imports in constant 1992 dollars.
a. Malaysia, Philippines, and Thailand.
Source: Global Trade Analysis Project; World Bank data and staff estimates.

and financial services. These countries broadly maintain their specialization in capital- and skill-intensive sectors such as heavy manufactures (not shown in table 1-9) and machinery and transport equipment, while sharply reducing their presence in labor-intensive sectors such as apparel. In primary agriculture the freer agricultural trade environment results in a mixed picture, with North America and "other OECD" regions (including countries such as Australia) increasing their specialization, while the EU shifts resources out of this export sector.

Improving education and fast capital accumulation allow the Big 5 countries to increase their export focus in the more skill- and capital-intensive sectors, such as machinery and transport equipment (presumably in the more "medium-tech" subsectors). In labor-intensive sectors such as apparel, the labor-abundant giants China, India, and Indonesia retain high (though gradually declining) specialization, while middle-income Brazil and the economies in transition reduce their exposure in labor-intensive sectors more quickly. In resource-intensive sectors such as agriculture and energy the situation is reversed, with China and India further reducing their

exposure, while the other, more resource-abundant countries are able to retain or improve their position in one or another resource-intensive sector. The economies in transition, for example, improve their advantage in primary agriculture exports, while also increasing their presence in skill-intensive sectors, such as machinery and transport equipment and heavy manufactures.

Patterns of specialization among other developing countries are even more mixed. The increasing concentration of the Big 5 countries on various manufactures will create opportunities for other developing economies to exploit comparative advantages in resource-intensive sectors. Regions such as Sub-Saharan Africa, the rest of Latin America, and the Middle East and North Africa maintain or increase their revealed comparative advantage in one or more of the agricultural, energy, or other natural resource sectors. As shown by the experience of countries such as Argentina, Australia, Canada, Chile, Malaysia, New Zealand, and Thailand, efficient, well-functioning natural-resource-based sectors can provide an important source of income and a foundation for diversification and industrialization.

The Big 5 countries increase their specialization in machinery and transport equipment

Table 1-9 Patterns of specialization for selected product categories, 1992 and 2020
(Revealed comparative advantage indexes)

Country or group	Primary agriculture 1992	Primary agriculture 2020	Apparel 1992	Apparel 2020	Machinery and transport equipment 1992	Machinery and transport equipment 2020	Other services 1992	Other services 2020
High-income OECD	0.85	1.12	0.35	0.07	1.21	1.04	1.11	2.00
Newly industrialized economies	0.27	0.49	1.40	0.10	1.22	1.00	0.64	0.32
Big 5	1.52	0.84	3.11	2.60	0.42	1.13	0.69	0.28
China	1.55	0.22	5.61	4.33	0.48	1.48	0.68	0.39
India	1.73	0.74	3.88	1.67	0.21	1.13	0.77	0.15
Brazil	2.07	2.20	0.29	0.09	0.61	1.02	0.37	0.16
Indonesia	1.69	1.70	2.69	2.63	0.13	0.43	0.35	0.08
Economies in transition	1.14	1.29	1.65	0.17	0.45	0.75	0.93	0.34
Other developing countries	1.87	1.19	1.96	1.45	0.30	0.80	0.79	0.34

Note: The revealed comparative advantage index is a measure of international specialization described in note 17 to the text.
Source: Global Trade Analysis Project; World Bank data and staff estimates.

The scenario confirms that the advance of Big 5 countries such as China, India, and Indonesia will generate significant competitive pressures in unskilled labor-intensive sectors. Apart from other ASEAN (Association of Southeast Asian Nations) countries, which have already made big advances in manufacturing, few other developing regions will increase their specialization in these sectors by 2020. This does not mean that developing regions will be unable to develop a wide variety of lucrative manufacturing activities. Far from it. But it does suggest that they will have incentives to seek out and develop specialized, niche manufacturing lines where they can demonstrate comparative advantage in highly competitive world markets. Achieving such success will in turn place high demands on policymakers to create the necessary supporting conditions. These will include an open, competitive environment that allows and encourages entrepreneurs to search out and undertake large (and often risky) investments in new product lines, transparent and nonarbitrary governance and regulation, and measures to foster investment in education and infrastructure.

This discussion has looked at the implications of changes in world resource allocation resulting from changes in policies, factor accumulation, and technological change in all countries. Shifts in relative prices in response to these underlying policy and supply changes will also affect countries' terms of trade and incomes. Broadly speaking, there will tend to be an excess supply of products exported by fast-growing economies and an excess demand for products they import—imbalances that are eliminated by lower

prices for exports and higher prices for imports; in short, a terms of trade deterioration.

The scenario confirms this broad expectation, with industrial countries sharing in the benefits of fast growth in developing countries through terms of trade gains of roughly 0.4 percent a year. World prices for unskilled labor-intensive products exported by China, India, and Indonesia (textiles, apparel, and so on) fall relative to average world export prices. The phaseout of quotas under the Multifibre Arrangement also intensifies competitive pressures in the textile and apparel sector and contributes to lower prices. Real primary product prices fall too partly because of a combination of relatively rapid productivity growth and low income elasticity of demand for these commodities.[18] Prices for tradable services, which the fast-growing developing countries import and advanced countries export, show the largest real increases.

The scenario does not entail a worsening in the conditions of unskilled workers in either the developing or industrial countries. Quite the reverse. The rapid pace of capital accumulation and productivity growth in the scenario ensures substantial increases in the wages of unskilled workers in all countries and regions.

Effects of trade frictions and slower growth of the Big 5: an alternative scenario

In this scenario mounting trade frictions between the Big 5 countries and their trading partners result in more protectionism: import tariffs between the Big 5 and their trading partners in 2020 are assumed to be 50 percent higher than in the baseline (a mild assumption that still leaves 2020 tariffs for most developing countries below 1992 levels). More significant, in this less-welcoming external environment the domestic reform momentum in the Big 5 loses steam, and this is assumed to be reflected in a halving of total factor productivity growth rates and a slowdown in physical capital accumulation. As a result, growth in China, India, and Indonesia is reduced by roughly 2 percentage points a year and that in Brazil and the transition economies by about 1 percentage point. Rather than crafting a full-fledged "low-case" scenario, the object is to gain an understanding of the pattern of impacts on the outside world. It is important to note that the scenario will underestimate these impacts to the extent that growth in the Big 5 has dynamic effects on growth elsewhere, for example, through economies of scale, competition, or effects on innovation.

As a result of the change in growth assumptions, Big 5 GDP is about 27 percent lower relative to the baseline in 2020, while Big 5 exports and imports are 35–40 percent lower. (Even with these big dips relative to the baseline, the Big 5 shares in world GDP and trade still rise from 8–9 percent in 1992 to 12 percent and 14–15 percent, respectively, by 2020.) In the rest of the world, export and import volumes fall relative to the baseline by 2–3 percent because of slower growth in the Big 5. In the absence of dynamic effects, the principal effects on the rest of the world occur through changes in resource allocation and in the terms of trade.

As a result of slower demand growth in the Big 5, other countries and regions have less opportunity to specialize in the sectors in which they have the greatest comparative advantage. Thus, for example, OECD countries export fewer services and more apparel relative to the baseline. Indeed, most regions export more apparel and other light manufactures, the sectors in which China, India, and Indonesia have the greatest comparative advantage, while exporting less in one or more product areas in which the Big 5 have less advantage. In addition, most regions suffer lower terms of trade relative to the baseline because slower growth in Big 5 export supply and import demand generates smaller declines in their export prices and smaller increases in the prices of goods they import (table 1-10).

Aggregate losses for the rest of the world, largely from static resource allocation and terms of trade effects, amount to $109 billion in 1992 dollars, or 0.3 percent of these countries' baseline GDP in 2020. The pattern of welfare effects varies considerably, however. Hong Kong (China) suffers the largest loss—almost 4 percent of GDP. The Middle East and North Africa suffers the next largest loss, around 2 percent of GDP, as slow growth in the Big 5 results in lower world oil prices. As would be expected, regions with a structure of factor endowments similar to that of labor-abundant Big 5 countries (China, India, Indonesia) score welfare gains. The aggregate of three ASEAN countries[19] and the rest of South Asia have welfare gains of 0.3–0.4 percent of GDP, as competitive pressures from Big 5 countries in labor-intensive sectors such as apparel ease relative to the baseline. Conversely, it is these regions that in the baseline would have the largest need to take policy measures to upgrade the skills of their labor forces and otherwise raise productivity in response to competition from Big 5 countries.

Slow growth in the Big 5 reduces welfare in the rest of the world

Table 1-10 Alternative scenario: welfare effects in 2020
(Billions of 1992 U.S. dollars)

Economy or group	Allocative effects	Terms of trade effects	Residual	Total	Percentage of baseline 2020 GDP
World excluding Big 5	−60.7	−55.6	6.9	−109.4	−0.3
High-income OECD	−38.1	−17.6	2.5	−53.2	−0.2
Newly industrialized economies	−1.7	−9.5	1.1	−10.1	−0.5
Hong Kong (China)	0.3	−9.6	0.8	−8.5	−3.8
Developing countries excluding Big 5	−21.2	−18.9	2.5	−37.5	−0.7
ASEAN 3[a]	−4.2	7.5	0.7	3.3	0.3
Rest of South Asia	0.5	0.7	−0.1	1.1	0.4
Rest of Latin America and the Caribbean	−3.3	−4.1	0.6	−6.7	−0.5
Sub-Saharan Africa	−1.5	−3.8	0.3	−5.0	−0.6
Middle East and North Africa	−7.7	−20.4	1.2	−26.9	−1.7

a. Malaysia, Philippines, and Thailand.
Source: Global Trade Analysis Project; World Bank data and staff estimates.

Reversing the logic and moving from the alternative to the baseline scenario, it can also be deduced that most regions of the world experience aggregate welfare gains from faster growth and integration of the Big 5 countries. Concerns remain, however, that specific groups in society, particularly unskilled workers in industrial countries, will be hurt by the expansion of free trade assumed in the baseline scenario. But the comparison of the two scenarios does not provide much support for this possibility: unskilled wages in 2020 under the baseline scenario, where there is more trade with the Big 5, are higher by varying small amounts in most regions than in the alternative scenario. In other words, unskilled workers in most regions gain from the emergence of the Big 5, mainly through the improvement in these regions' terms of trade. In the Middle East and North Africa, for example, unskilled workers in the baseline gain not only from cheaper imports from the Big 5, but also through higher prices for oil and other Middle East and North Africa region exports due to strong demand in the Big 5. Again, it is only in the ASEAN 3 and the rest of South Asia, with a structure of endowments most similar to that in China and others, that unskilled wages are slightly lower in the baseline than in the alternative scenario.

Although the ratio of unskilled to skilled wages is slightly lower in the baseline than in the alternative scenario, the size of this relative wage effect is small: the ratio in industrial countries is only negligibly lower, about 0.1 percent in most cases. The impact of trade with developing countries on wages in industrial countries is the subject of a large and fast-growing body of literature (box 1-4).

The Big 5 countries and the world grain market

Concern is sometimes expressed that the combination of a large population and rapid income growth in countries such as China and India will generate intense demand pressures on limited global natural resources and major increases in prices of resource-intensive products. The rise in grain prices after 1993 has been proposed as a justification for such concerns. Lester Brown (1995) argues that China could have a major adverse effect on world grain markets as declining soil fertility, shrinking cropland, and stagnating yields reduce grain production by 1 percent a year. With demand rising quickly, in part as feed grain to supply rising meat demand, Brown projects China's net grain imports soaring to 368 million tons by 2030 from 21 million tons in 1995.

The Big 5 countries did indeed account for a hefty 45 percent of world grain consumption in 1990–95, up from 33 percent in 1960 (table 1-11). Given the substantial grain production in these countries, however, their impact on world markets has been more limited, with net imports of grain averaging only 15 percent of world grain trade in this period. Indeed, some of the Big 5 countries have enjoyed remarkable success in increasing food and other agricultural production over the past decades, supporting substantial increases in calorie supply and nutrition for hundreds of millions of people. In evaluating Brown's analysis of China, other researchers (Ingco, Mitchell, and McCalla 1996) reckon that it is not consistent with recent trends in land usage or land reclamation. Further, current yields may be overstated because cropland is underreported for tax reasons, and there is considerable scope for efficiency improvements in the use of fertilizer, water, land, and ancillary services, such as transportation and storage. Rozelle, Huang, and Rosegrant (1996) stress that declining investment in agricultural research in China could affect production, but given the country's concern over the issue, such a decline is unlikely. Their evaluation of soil erosion and rising salinity finds that only under extreme conditions would these be likely to result in sharply higher imports.

Model-based studies by the International Food Policy Research Institute, the FAO, and the World Bank looked at global grain balances through 2010 or 2020 and came to essentially similar conclusions. One such study to 2020 projects world grain output growth of 1.5 percent a year (Rosegrant, Agcaoili-Sombilla, and Perez 1995). This output growth, combined with slower growth in world population, leads to a projection of a 20 percent decline in real cereal prices between 1990 and 2020. This benign outcome assumes, however, that national and international public investment in agricultural research, extension, and infrastructure continues at the level of the late 1980s and early 1990s. An alternative scenario (eliminating funding by international donors for agricultural research in developing countries and international research centers) projects a fall in world grain production of about 6 percent, with grain prices 20–30 percent higher in real terms.

These studies underline the importance of maintaining yield growth. Developing and industrial countries have also promoted more efficient allocation of resources by reducing price controls, marketing monopolies, and subsidies. Much remains to be done, however. The Uruguay Round made a start on liberalizing agricultural trade but progress has been less than was hoped for. Trade liberalization can help ensure global food security in the long run by promoting specialization and allocation of resources to production in those parts of the world where productivity is highest. A corollary is that, in the long run, both industrial and developing countries will gain by placing less emphasis on self-sufficiency and more on relying on the world markets for cheap and plentiful food supplies.

Box 1-4 How trade with developing countries affects industrial country wages

Rapid growth of trade between industrial and low-wage developing countries since the mid-1970s has coincided with a period of deterioration in labor market conditions for unskilled workers in many industrial countries, providing apparent support for the argument that the first caused the second. A review of the literature on trade and wages (largely following Lawrence 1996) arrives at four major conclusions:

- International trade has played little part in slow real wage growth in the United States in recent decades. Real hourly wages in the U.S. business sector rose only 9 percent in 1973–94, but the slowdown is fully explained by lower productivity growth, especially in services. Trade might have reduced real wages if U.S. terms of trade had deteriorated, but this did not happen. Real earnings grew more quickly in other G-5 countries, and in most cases this was associated with healthy productivity growth in services. The rise in unemployment in Europe over the past twenty years is, as noted earlier, largely due to domestic labor market conditions. Krugman (1995) calculates that even on the extreme assumption of completely inflexible wages, only a little more than 1 percentage point of the 7–8 percent increase in European unemployment could be attributed to trade.

- The 1980s saw growing pay inequality along skill and education lines in the United States. Wages for workers with a high school education or less fell about 15 percent relative to remuneration for workers with a college education or more. How much of this was due to trade with low-wage countries? One way to answer that is to analyze how the factor content of a country's imports and exports change net demand for skilled and unskilled labor. Because manufactures imports from developing countries amount to only 2–3 percent of industrial country GDP, it is difficult to arrive at a large effect on wages: a median estimate from various studies suggests that about 10 percent of the deterioration in unskilled wages could be explained by international trade.[1] A second line of inquiry argues that if trade reduces the relative wages of unskilled workers, the relative prices of goods that use unskilled labor intensively should also fall. But there is little

evidence of that. The existing evidence is more consistent with a widespread bias in technological change toward more intensive use of skilled labor.

- The increase in international outsourcing by multinational enterprises (see chapter 2) is unlikely to provide a significant explanation for rising wage inequality. Rather than multinationals disproportionately shifting unskilled jobs abroad, the evidence suggests that they are raising the skill intensity of production in both headquarters and foreign affiliates in industrial and developing countries. Again the evidence is more consistent with a worldwide technological shock biased toward skilled labor.

- What of the future? Will adverse effects on unskilled wages not increase as trade with developing countries grows? Lawrence (1996) estimates the effects of an extreme scenario in which U.S. production of all unskilled-labor-intensive products is replaced by imports from developing countries, with U.S. exports of skilled-labor-intensive products rising by an equivalent amount. (Value added by unskilled-labor-intensive industries amounted to $550 billion in 1990, or 10 percent of U.S. GDP.) Unskilled wages are then calculated to fall relative to skilled wages on a one-off basis by a further 7.5 percent, or 4.5 percent or so in absolute terms. Although this could exacerbate the challenge for policymakers if unskilled workers also continue to be hit by biased technological change, on its own and spread over a fifteen-year adjustment period, the effect would be to only modestly reduce the rate of wage increase due to underlying productivity growth. Moreover, all workers would continue to benefit from lower import prices. The calculations also ignore the possible positive effects of trade liberalization on productivity through higher economies of scale and other dynamic effects. They also, however, ignore social adjustments costs—losses in output that occur as a result of transitional unemployment of unskilled workers.

---

1. Work by Wood (1994) suggests larger effects but these results have been criticized on several grounds, including the use of unrealistically low substitution elasticities between skilled and unskilled workers and between developing and industrial country goods.

The Big 5 countries and world energy markets

The Big 5 low- and middle-income countries consume 23 percent of the world's primary energy supplies, with China and Russia alone accounting for about 18 percent (table 1–12).[20] This share fell in the 1990s because of lower energy consumption accompanying the decline in economic output in Russia. Excluding Russia, however, energy consumption in Brazil, China, India, and Indonesia (the Big 4) grew at about

5 percent a year in the past ten years compared with 1.5 percent for the world as a whole, boosting their share in world demand to about 15 percent by 1994. Will the expected rapid economic growth in the big developing countries generate serious pressures on world energy markets and prices?

The Big 5's share of world energy demand is expected to rise from around a quarter to more than a third by 2020. Past experience shows that growth in electricity demand will outpace income growth in

Table 1-11 The Big 5 and world grain markets, 1990–95

	Grain consumption			Grain production			Net imports	
Country or group	Million tons (1990–95)	Percentage of world (1990–95)	Per capita growth (1985–95)	Million tons (1990–95)	Percentage of world (1990–95)	Per capita growth (1985–95)	Million tons (1990–95)	Percentage of world (1990–95)
Big 5	785	44.8	–0.5	746	39.1	–0.4	36.4	15.3
China	349	19.9	0.5	343	18.0	0.9	4.6	1.9
India	165	9.4	0.6	1,671	8.8	0.7	–1.4	–1.3
Indonesia	42	2.4	1.4	37	1.9	0.1	4.6	1.9
Brazil	50	2.8	2.2	42	2.2	0.6	7.6	3.2
Russia	180	10.3	–3.3	157	8.2	–3.4	21.0	8.8
World	1,752	100.0	–0.6	1,906	100.0	–1.1	238.2	100.0

Source: World Bank data and staff estimates.

many developing countries, generating increasing demand for coal as the dominant fuel for electricity, especially in India and China, though environmental concerns should encourage increased use of natural gas. Demand for oil will be boosted especially by rising automobile ownership, which is only around 3 per 1,000 people in India and China—it is 10 per 1,000 in Indonesia; 80–90 in Brazil, Russia, and Mexico; and 500 in Germany.

Other factors, however, will tend to dampen the growth of primary energy demand. The market-oriented policy reforms being implemented by the Big 5 and by many other developing countries are an important force promoting more efficient use of resources, including energy. Especially direct exam-

ples of such reforms are the removal of subsidies on fuel consumption or production. In China energy consumption per dollar of real GDP has fallen sharply since the start of reforms at the end of the 1970s. Energy demand growth in Russia is also expected to be well below income growth because of a huge potential for efficiency improvements. Russia and other transition economies have been energy intensive because of their concentration on heavy industry and because of the command system of supply and lack of pricing incentives under the former socialist economy. Energy use per unit of real GDP in the republics of the former Soviet Union is more than five times that in the OECD. Energy demand growth in these countries is expected to be moderate in

Table 1-12 The Big 5 and world primary energy production and consumption, 1994
(Percent, unless otherwise specified)

		Energy production			Energy consumption			Net imports[a]	
Country or group	GDP growth (1985–94)	Million tons oil equivalent	Share of world	Growth (1985–94)	Million tons oil equivalent	Share of world	Growth (1985–94)	Million tons oil equivalent	Share of world[b]
Big 4	6.1	1,200	14.7	5.0	1,200	15.0	5.1	1	0.0
China	10.0	799	9.8	3.8	791	9.9	4.8	–10	–0.3
India	5.2	180	2.2	5.0	227	2.8	6.4	48	1.6
Indonesia	7.4	153	1.9	5.1	70	0.9	7.6	–83	–2.9
Brazil	2.1	68	0.8	2.5	113	1.4	3.7	46	1.6
Russia	–4.4	911	11.2	–2.3	595	7.5	–4.6	–300	–10.4
Big 5	2.1	2,111	25.9	0.8	1,797	22.5	0.8	–299	–10.3
World	2.7	8,144	100.0	1.7	7,987	100.0	1.5	2,890[b]	—

a. Net imports differ from consumption less production by inventory changes and other adjustments.
b. As percentage of world gross imports of energy.
Source: IEA 1996.

coming years, with demand for oil actually decreasing by 0.3 percent a year through 2020 (Gately and Streifel 1997). Changes in industrial structure as countries shift to higher value added output are also likely to contribute to lower energy intensity. One study estimated that 80 percent of the expected decline in China's energy intensity between 1990 and 2020 would derive from such structural changes (World Bank 1995).

Supply trends in coming years will also tend to keep real energy prices down. Technological developments over the past decade have significantly reduced production costs for petroleum, natural gas, and coal. These trends are expected to continue, with renewable energy sources contributing additional resources at the margin. Further, energy production in the Big 5 exceeded their consumption by 300 million tons of oil equivalent in 1994, about 14 percent of production. Russia is the major net exporter; the other four produce and consume about the same amount in aggregate. All five have rich hydrocarbon resources and the potential to raise domestic production significantly, especially if they can reduce the heavy involvement of state enterprises and attract large amounts of private and foreign investment to introduce modern technologies. These demand and supply considerations together suggest that real oil prices will gradually decline over the period to 2020.

Environmental concerns

A rather different concern is that increases in energy consumption associated with sustained growth in developing countries will add to damage to the natural environment. In particular, the burning of fossil fuels is the main source of emissions of greenhouse gases such as carbon dioxide. The accumulation of these gases in the atmosphere threatens, over a long time span, to bring about substantial changes in the world climate. For example, if global carbon dioxide emissions from fossil fuel burning were maintained at just the present rate of 6.5 gigatons of carbon per year, atmospheric concentrations by 2100 would reach twice the preindustrial levels, a benchmark used by scientists to indicate the onset of serious climate change damage. Mid-range scenarios produced by the United Nations Intergovernmental Panel on Climate Change suggest that in the absence of specific climate change mitigation policies, such emissions would rise to over 11 gigatons per year by 2025. Stabilizing carbon concentrations in the atmosphere would require reducing annual emissions to around 2.5 gigatons, the planet's natural absorptive capacity (IPCC 1992 and 1995).

The global response to the threat of climate change is the United Nations Framework Convention on Climate Change, which came into force in 1994 and has been ratified by 165 countries. As a first step, the convention calls on industrial countries to stabilize their anthropogenic (human-caused) greenhouse gas emissions. It recognizes, however, that responses to climate change need to be integrated with achievement of social and economic development goals and that developing countries are the least able to bear the cost of greenhouse gas mitigation while being the most vulnerable to climate change effects. The convention does not prescribe greenhouse gas emission targets for developing countries, and the study of the Big 5 countries in this report does not assume that specific policies are undertaken to mitigate such emissions.[21]

Most researchers nevertheless agree that the bulk of future increases in emissions will come from developing countries. How these countries can help reach global mitigation objectives while achieving their development aims is thus a question likely to grow in importance over coming decades. Options under discussion at present include "win-win" policies that have economic value in their own right while contributing to mitigation goals—for example, elimination of fuel subsidies and other economic distortions that reduce economic efficiency while promoting greenhouse emissions. Another is the establishment of an international market for trade in carbon emission credits or permits, which could assist in undertaking mitigation in the most cost-effective way. The consensus of scientific opinion expressed in the Intergovernmental Panel and elsewhere is that, in the long run, the decisive factor in mitigation will be the development and transfer of new energy technologies. Thus appropriate public policies that facilitate this process merit further attention and research.

Risks to globalization: some lessons from integration in the nineteenth century

Similarities are often found between global integration today and that in the second half of the nineteenth and the early part of the twentieth century. Reductions in barriers to trade, rapid improvements in transport and communications, and increasing trade and capital flows all characterized the world economy then as now (figure 1-12). The earlier episode of integration came to an end with the first world war, followed by a period of rampant protectionism, capital and foreign exchange controls, and extreme macroeconomic and political instability. Surveying the period just after its close, Keynes (1919) noted that "very few of us realize with conviction the intensely unusual, unstable, complicated, unreliable, temporary nature of the economic organization by which Western Europe has lived for the last half century." Relevant questions might then be "Why did global integration in the nineteenth century fail?" and "Is the present wave different enough to avoid the same fate?"

Differences between integration then and now

To start with the differences, trade liberalization after the second world war has gone on longer, is more widespread, and has firmer institutional foundations. The period in the nineteenth century when trade barriers were coming down was relatively short, starting with the repeal of the Corn Laws in Britain in 1846 and climaxing in the 1860s and 1870s in the wake of the 1860 Cobden-Chevalier treaty between Britain and France (Bairoch 1993). The tide started to turn with Bismarck's sponsorship of a new German tariff in 1879, followed by increases in tariffs in France and other countries. These increases were not large enough to prevent continued growth in world trade up to the first world war, but the change in philosophy that had occurred was quickly built on when protectionism gained ground after the war. An industrial power as important as the United States had also moved in a protectionist direction, raising tariffs after the 1865 victory of the North in the Civil War. Finally, the movement toward free trade in the nineteenth century proceeded largely through bilateral treaties, without today's overarching multilateral institutional frameworks, such as the General Agreement on Tariffs and Trade (GATT) and WTO, which scrutinize and provide a check on moves toward protectionism.

The character of trade today also tends to generate closer and more intense ties between countries. World trade in the earlier period was dominated by primary commodities and interindustry trade between major economic sectors, while today the largest part is manufactures and intraindustry trade. Manufactures are more complex and finely differentiated and require more specialized components than in earlier times (Krugman 1995). International specialization now applies within the stages of manufacturing processes to a greater extent, with production of components and assembly conducted in different countries contributing to larger volumes of world trade relative to GDP. And while the achievements of the nineteenth century in physical transportation (railways, steamships) were perhaps even greater than today's in relative terms, the earlier period had little comparable to the information, computing, and telecommunications technologies of the present, which allow businesses to manage far-flung production operations on a much more closely integrated basis. These multinational enterprises, which conduct much of the modern international division of labor (see chapter 2), constitute a stronger and more vocal lobby in favor of free trade than any corporation 100 years ago.

Is integration irreversible?

Does all this mean that the current global integration is irreversible? Probably not, because economic activity now—as then—takes place in a web of political and social relationships that are not always well understood or managed. Here the history of the nineteenth century's global integration provides some obvious but still useful lessons. The revival of protectionism took place against a backdrop of mounting great-power rivalry, nationalism, and, ultimately, preparation for war. The efficiency losses from a bad trade policy will always seem of little account in such a climate. Indeed, many states at the time looked to larger tariff revenues as a way of paying for armaments, as well as for social spending thought necessary to build national cohesion. The swing to protection in Germany in 1878–79, for example, was associated with both the introduction of accident insurance and other social legislation and a sharp rise in military spending in the following decade (Stern 1977; Witt 1987).

Earlier experience also shows the importance of addressing the political economy and adjustment cost issues raised by global integration. While the benefits of integration tend to be widespread, the costs are

Trade ratios fell in the interwar period

Figure 1-12 Merchandise exports from various countries, 1820–1992

Percentage of GDP

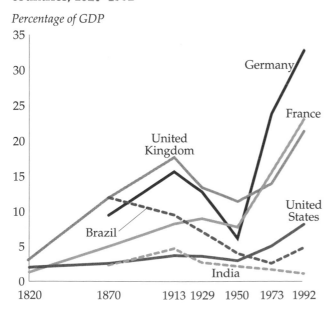

Note: Exports and GDP calculated using 1990 prices.
Source: Maddison 1995.

often highly concentrated, leading to coordinated political action by adversely affected groups (see chapter 3). In the 1879 German example the landed interest, suffering from an influx of cheap foreign grain, was at the forefront of the campaign for the "tariff of iron and rye," together with important industrial interests. In our own day the commitment to freer trade has sometimes proved vulnerable to erosion through the use of nontariff barriers such as the Multifibre Arrangement, antidumping, voluntary export restraints, and subsidies to protect specific groups hurt by foreign trade. Because the pressure from special interest groups for protection is likely to be a constant, it will likely be important to maintain a broad social coalition or consensus in support of outward-oriented policies. A case can be made for well-designed systems of adjustment assistance to help the most vulnerable groups adapt to new circumstances. Finally, macroeconomic stability is a crucial support for global integration. The clearest example of the failure of this condition is, of course, the Great Depression of the 1930s, but it may also have been a factor in the earlier period, when long-running stagnation in European business conditions in the 1870s (also called a great depression) brought many manufacturing groups to the side of protection.

Notes

1. Important recent domestic initiatives include the 1996 U.S. Telecommunications Act, planned regulatory reforms in the European airlines and telecommunications sectors in 1997–98, and a broad range of reform proposals in Japan, including a financial big bang by 2001. See also the discussion of services trade liberalization in this chapter.

2. Hoj, Kato, and Pilat 1995; Ito 1996 for Japan. In manufacturing Pilat (1997) estimates the proportion of productivity differences with the United States explained by differences in physical and human capital per worker at 45 percent for Japan, 20 percent for the United Kingdom, and virtually zero for Germany and France. Productivity gaps are, however, found to be significantly associated with measures of lack of competition, such as high industry concentration, low entry rates, low export intensity, and high import protection.

3. Basic telecommunications services provide end-to-end transmission of customer-supplied information, such as the relay of voice or data from sender to receiver. They usually exclude value added services, where suppliers add value to a customer's information by enhancing its form or content or providing for its storage or retrieval. (Examples of value added services are on-line data processing, storage or retrieval, electronic data interchange, e-mail, and voice mail.)

4. Counting the European Union as one. The earlier reference to sixty-nine countries counted EU members separately.

5. ITU 1997 and staff estimates. The output of the telecommunications industry as a whole, comprising telecom services and equipment, was $788 billion in 1995, making it the third largest industrial sector in the world, after health care and finance. The information-communications market, defined as the sum of telecommunications and computer hardware, software, and services, totaled $1.37 trillion in 1995.

6. Some of this evidence is summarized in Saunders, Warford, and Wellenius 1994. In a cross-section study of growth in the fifty U.S. states, Dhalokia and Harlam (1994) find this association to be more important than that with other elements of infrastructure, such as education or highways.

7. Voice and data transmission costs have fallen by factors of 10 and 1,000, respectively, over this period.

8. Petrazzini (1996), who also presents evidence on the impact of competition on prices and service quality.

9. Other important initiatives include the recently completed Information Technology Agreement among thirty-nine (mostly industrial) countries to eliminate tariffs on telecom equipment and computer hardware and software by 2000 or 2005. The Multilateral Agreement on Investment currently being negotiated among OECD members seeks to establish a more comprehensive multilateral framework for rules on market access and legal security for international investors.

10. World Bank 1997a. The picture for 1996 is distorted by early repayment of U.S. Treasury loans by Mexico. Excluding the prepayment, official development finance increased by $5 billion. Nonetheless, grants and other concessional finance fell by $1 billion to levels close to those of 1990—a sharp decline in real terms.

11. Long-term trends in cereal and energy markets are further reviewed in the discussion of the large developing countries.

12. In particular, no attempt is made to explicitly model the potential "dynamic effects" on growth of more open trade policies or faster growth abroad operating through effects on economies of scale or the pace of technological progress. Rates of growth of factor supplies and of technological change are exogenously assumed, with technological change also assumed to be neutral with respect to factors of production. The model is solved as a comparative static exercise under the assumption of full employment of factors, thus excluding the transitional adjustment costs of global integration discussed in chapter 3. Technical descriptions of the GTAP model are provided in Hertel 1996.

13. This analysis was conducted in parallel with the OECD study "Globalization and Linkages to 2020: Challenges and Opportunities for OECD Countries" (OECD Development Centre 1997) and has benefited from discussions with OECD researchers. Compared with the OECD study, this analysis focuses more on the impact of the Big 5 on other developing countries and regions, and on estimating the specific impact of the Big 5 as the difference between a baseline and a low-case scenario.

14. Assumptions on labor force and human capital growth derived from World Bank population projections and staff estimates are not included.

15. Historical total factor productivity and capital stock growth rates in this discussion are from Collins and Bosworth 1996; productivity growth rates in China are from Borensztein and Ostry 1996.

16. Historical growth estimates are from Maddison 1995.

17. A country's revealed comparative advantage index for a given product is defined as its market share in world exports of that product divided by its market share in total world exports of all products. An index value over 1 indicates a specialization or revealed comparative advantage in that product.

18. Prices of food and energy are set exogeneously on the basis of specialized analysis by the World Bank's Development Prospects Group. The GTAP model is used to equate world supply and demand at these set prices.

19. The effects in ASEAN countries are likely to be concentrated in Thailand and the Philippines, which have significantly lower per capita incomes than Malaysia.

20. Total primary energy supply refers to total domestic demand for primary fuels before transformation to electricity and other products.

21. Economies in transition are subject to stabilization targets under the convention, but with greater flexibility than industrial countries.

References

Bairoch, Paul. 1993. *Economics and World History: Myths and Paradoxes*. Chicago: University of Chicago Press.

Borensztein, E., and J. Ostry. 1996. "Accounting for China's Growth Performance." *American Economic Review Papers and Proceedings*. May.

Brown, Lester R. 1995. *Who Will Feed China? Wake-Up Call for a Small Planet*. Washington, D.C.: Worldwatch Institute.

Brown, Lester R., and Hal Kane. 1994. *Full House: Reassessing the Earth's Population Carrying Capacity*. Washington, D.C.: Worldwatch Institute.

Collins, S., and B. Bosworth. 1996. "Economic Growth in East Asia: Accumulation versus Assimilation." In *Brookings Papers on Economic Activity 2*. Washington, D.C.: Brookings Institution.

Dhalokia, R., and B. Harlam. 1994. "Telecommunications and Economic Development: Econometric Analysis of the U.S. Experience." *Telecommunications Policy* 18(6).

Gately, Dermot, and Shane S. Streifel. 1997. *The Demand for Oil Products in Developing Countries*. World Bank Discussion Paper 359. Washington, D.C.

Hertel, Thomas, ed. 1996. *Global Trade Analysis: Modeling and Applications*. Cambridge: Cambridge University Press.

Hoj, Jens, Toshiyasu Kato, and Dirk Pilat. 1995. "Deregulation and Privatization in the Service Sector." *OECD Economic Studies* 25. OECD, Paris.

IEA (International Energy Agency). 1996. *Energy Statistics and Balances of Non-OECD Countries 1993–94*. Paris.

Ingco, Merlinda D., Donald O. Mitchell, and Alex F. McCalla. 1996. *Global Food Supply Prospects*. World Bank Technical Paper 353. Paper prepared for the World Food Summit, Rome, November 1996. Washington, D.C.

IPCC (Intergovernmental Panel on Climate Change). 1992. *Climate Change 1992: The Supplementary Report to the IPCC Scientific Assessment*. Cambridge: Cambridge University Press.

———. 1995. *Climate Change 1995: The Science of Climate Change*. Cambridge: Cambridge University Press.

Ito, Takatoshi. 1996. "Japan and the Asian Economies: A 'Miracle' in Transition." In *Brookings Papers on Economic Activity 2*. Washington, D.C.: Brookings Institution.

ITU (International Telecommunication Union). 1997. *World Telecommunication Development Report 1996/97*. Geneva.

Keynes, John Maynard. 1919. *The Economic Consequences of the Peace*. Reprint. London: Penguin Books, 1995.

Krugman, Paul. 1995. "Growing World Trade: Causes and Consequences." In *Brookings Papers on Economic Activity 1*. Washington, D.C.: Brookings Institution.

Lawrence, Robert Z. 1996. *Single World, Divided Nations? International Trade and OECD Labor Markets*. Washington, D.C.: Brookings Institution and OECD Development Centre.

Maddison, Angus. 1995. *Monitoring the World Economy 1820–1992*. Paris: OECD.

OECD (Organization for Economic Cooperation and Development). 1994. "The OECD Jobs Study." Paris.

———. 1996. *Economic Outlook*. December. Paris: OECD.

OECD Development Centre. 1997. "Globalization and Linkages to 2020: Challenges and Opportunities for OECD Countries." Paris.

Petrazzini, B. 1996. "Global Telecom Talks: A Trillion Dollar Deal." Policy Analyses in International Economics 44. Institute for International Economics, Washington, D.C.

Pilat, Dirk. 1996. "Labor Productivity Levels in OECD Countries: Estimates for Manufacturing and Selected Services Sectors." OECD Economics Department Working Paper 169. Paris.

———. Forthcoming. "Competition, Productivity and Efficiency." *OECD Economic Studies*. Paris: OECD.

Rojas-Suarez, L., and S. Weisbrod. 1995. "Financial Fragilities in Latin America: The 1980s and 1990s." Occasional Paper 132. International Monetary Fund, Washington, D.C.

Rosegrant, Mark W., Mercedita Agcaoili-Sombilla, and Nicostrato D. Perez. 1995. "Global Food Projections to 2020: Implications for Investment." Food, Agriculture, and the Environment Discussion Paper 5. International Food Policy Research Institute, Washington, D.C.

Rozelle, Scott, Jikun Huang, and Mark Rosegrant. 1996. "Why China Will Not Starve the World." *Choices* (first quarter).

Saunders, R., J. Warford, and B. Wellenius. 1994. *Telecommunications and Economic Development*. Baltimore: Johns Hopkins University Press.

Stern, Fritz. 1977. *Gold and Iron: Bismarck, Bleichroder and the Building of the German Empire.* New York: Knopf.

Stiglitz, J. 1997. "Reflections on the Natural Rate Hypothesis." *Journal of Economic Perspectives* 11(1): 3–10.

Witt, P. C. 1987. *Wealth and Taxation in Central Europe.* Cited in Volker R. Berghan, *Imperial Germany 1871–1914.* London: Oxford University Press.

Wood, Adrian. 1994. *North-South Trade, Employment and Inequality.* London: Oxford University Press.

World Bank. 1995. "The World Bank and the U.N. Framework Convention on Climate Change." Environment Department Paper 008, Climate Change Series. Environment Department, Washington, D.C.

———. 1997a. *Global Development Finance 1997.* Washington, D.C.

———. 1997b. *Private Capital Flows to Developing Countries: The Road to Financial Integration.* World Bank Policy and Research Report. New York: Oxford University Press.

WTO (World Trade Organization). 1997. "Ruggiero Congratulates Governments on Landmark Telecommunications Agreement." (Http://www.wto.org/Whats_new/press67.htm.) Geneva.

Developing countries and the globalization of production

An important trend in the world economy today is the globalization of production in developing countries. Global production is defined here as cross-border production by multinational enterprises and their networks of affiliates, subcontractors, and partners.[1] Production by multinational enterprises at home and abroad accounts for a fifth of world GDP, intrafirm trade by multinationals accounts for a third of world trade, and their parent firms account for much of world research and development.

- Worldwide reductions in policy barriers to international trade and investment and continuing declines in international transport and communications costs are making markets everywhere more contestable, increasing competitive pressures on firms. But the same forces also stimulate and facilitate firms' efforts to improve efficiency and gain access to new markets by reorganizing production processes on a global basis. Since the mid-1980s average import tariffs in developing countries and international transport and communications costs have both dropped by roughly a third. Perhaps even more fundamentally, the increasing importance of knowledge and other specialized, intangible assets in modern production and distribution also contributes to the expansion of cross-border production by multinationals and their partners.
- Global production networks are increasing the integration of developing countries into world markets. The share of world output produced by multinational affiliates is rising. In the 1990s the increase in developing countries has been especially marked, amounting to 2.5 percentage points of GDP. Production by multinational affiliates is increasingly oriented toward world export markets, and trade within multinationals is rising as a share of world trade. Firms are taking advantage of falling policy barriers and transport costs to disaggregate production processes, especially in manufacturing, into stages that are outsourced to different countries according to

their comparative advantage. This slicing up of the value chain is widening opportunities for developing countries to participate in international specialization and gains from trade.
- The benefits of global production for developing countries are potentially large. In many countries multinational operations have a substantial direct, positive impact on the growth of trade, output, and employment. In addition, a defining characteristic of multinational firms is their ownership of specialized intangible assets related to technological and management know-how, assets that create a basis for indirect, or spillover, benefits. These benefits include diffusion of management and labor skills, better information about world markets, introduction of new ideas and technologies, and, generally, a faster pace in catching up with best practices in the world economy. These effects can be especially important in the services sector. Thus, from China to Hungary and from India to Mexico, global production networks both help integrate developing countries into world markets and act as conduits of information and knowledge.
- The challenge for policymakers in developing countries is to establish conditions that help attract more global production and realize more of its benefits. These include political and macroeconomic stability, open trade and investment regimes, improvements in transport and communications infrastructure, adequate protection of property rights, and a predictable institutional environment without excessive red tape. An important condition for enhancing the benefits of global production is ensuring a high degree of competition in host country markets. Open international trade and investment policies and well-designed domestic competition and regulatory policies can contribute to maintaining high levels of competition in both goods and services industries.

What drives global production?

The growing importance of global production in world output is underpinned by several factors. These include widespread liberalization of international trade and investment policies in both industrial and developing countries, improvements in transportation and communications technologies, and the growing importance of knowledge and other specialized intangible assets in production and marketing.

Liberalization of trade and investment policies

World trade and investment barriers fell rapidly in the 1980s and early 1990s. Industrial country tariffs on industrial products were reduced in successive rounds of the GATT to 6–7 percent by the early 1990s and under the Uruguay Round will fall to under 4 percent. Average tariffs will be even lower when regional trading arrangements such as the European Union and the North American Free Trade Agreement (NAFTA) are accounted for. The coverage of industrial country nontariff measures on developing country exports is expected to drop from 18 percent to 4 percent. Restrictions on cross-border investment are falling, and the focus of trade liberalization is moving on to reducing "behind-the-border" barriers to international trade and investment through such measures as the Uruguay Round's General Agreement on Trade in services and agreement on Trade-Related Investment Measures and the EC '92 initiative of the European Union. Competition policies to deter restrictive business practices were strengthened in the European Union, while in the United States regulatory reforms aimed to enhance competition in several service and utility sectors (OECD 1996b; UNCTAD 1994d; Lawrence 1996; Low and Yeats 1994).

In developing countries the swing to greater reliance on markets and competition was even more evident. Average most-favored-nation import tariffs in developing countries fell from about 34 percent to 24 percent between 1984–87 and 1991–93 and are slated to fall to about 14 percent under the Uruguay Round. Nontariff barriers fell even more in most countries. Brazil and Mexico, for example, reduced mean import tariffs from 35–50 percent to 14–15 percent, and nontariff barriers from 12–40 to 1–2 percent. Barriers to foreign investment also came down swiftly. Indonesia and India, for example, now have far fewer sectors closed to foreign investment and have progressively dismantled restrictions on foreign ownership and divestiture. Regional agreements (Association of Southeast Asian Nations [ASEAN], Asia-Pacific Economic Cooperation [APEC], EU Association Agreements, Mercosur, and NAFTA among them) also contributed to lower trade and investment barriers in developing countries.

Falling transport and communications costs

Lower trade and investment barriers are increasing the contestability of markets by foreign firms while also spurring and facilitating cost reduction through reorganization of production processes on an international basis according to the comparative cost advantages of different locations. These trends are magnified by reductions in cost and improvements in the quality of transport and communications services. Lower transport costs have extended the reach of global production to labor-intensive manufacturing, allowing the dispersion of production stages over longer distances even for low value added products (box 2-1). Communications improvements have extended the scope of global production to more technologically complex, information-intensive, and time-sensitive products and services by allowing better information flows and improved monitoring and coordination of production and distribution in distant locations. Examples are the manufacture of electronics parts for just-in-time production, overnight electronic data processing, and the manufac-

---

Box 2-1 Transport, foreign know-how, and Colombian cut flower exports

Colombia is now the world's second largest exporter of cut flowers, accounting for about 10 percent of the world export market and directly employing about 70,000 workers in 1990, with another 50,000 in ancillary packaging and transport. Most exports are to the United States. Cut flower production in the United States began to relocate from the eastern to the western and southern states from as early as the 1950s and 1960s, and then, from the mid-1970s, to Colombia. In both cases air transportation freed cut flower production from areas close to consumers but with high land and labor costs. Two factors were key to Colombia's success. First, investment by Floramerica, a U.S. firm, supplied marketing and other know-how to get the cut flower industry started. The demonstration effects and diffusion of know-how from Floramerica led to rapid growth of locally-owned Colombian firms that hired Floramerica staff and followed its production and marketing methods. Second, critical transport and regulatory bottlenecks were removed. Many early shipments had been destroyed by delays in being loaded onto planes or inspected by Colombian customs. Neither the dominant airline nor customs was particularly responsive to these problems. A weak handling and distribution system at the entry point in the United States was another problem. Floramerica encouraged other airlines to enter and compete for the business, while a growers association established an efficient handling and distribution center in Miami.

Source: Mendez 1991.

ture of apparel and footwear in a world of designs and fashions that last only a season.

Key cost and quality improvements in transport and communications, and some of their major consequences, include the following:

- A decline in sea freight unit costs in real terms of almost 70 percent between the start of the 1980s and 1996. This decline was about equal to the fall in ocean freight costs for the United States in 1880–1910, another period of mounting global integration, but occurred in half the time. Air freight costs have fallen by 3–4 percent a year in real terms over a long period, as a result of technological advances, longer average trips, greater competition, and economies of scale (Peters 1993a; Lloyds *Shipping Economist*; North 1958; ICAO 1992).

- A fall in the per-minute cost of international phone calls in the 1990s in real terms of about 4 percent a year in developing countries and about 2 percent in industrial countries (ITU 1996a).

- An increase in the proportion of sea freight cargo carried in containers to about 80 percent from less than 20 percent in 1970, allowing better tracking of cargo, more efficient and reliable port services, and greater ease in switching to other modes of transportation (Pearson 1992).

- Increased use of electronic data interchange by airlines and specialized air-freight delivery firms to cut delivery times and improve tracking of cargo. These quality improvements are being pushed by and reinforce the adoption of just-in-time production and inventory management techniques.

- In telecommunications, gains in carrying capacity from optical fiber and satellite networks, making possible the low-cost transfer of vast amounts of data and creating new markets, such as computer software exports from India.

- Better control over costly inventories, more use of just-in-time concepts in purchasing and distribution, and shorter order cycles as widespread trends in virtually all markets. A U.S. toy manufacturer sets up a purchase contract with a firm in Hong Kong (China), which establishes a joint venture to manufacture labor-intensive toys elsewhere in China, using plastics shipped from Malaysia, and ships the finished product to the United States—all using just-in-time processes. Just-in-time purchases now account for almost half of all purchases in textiles, compared with a quarter in 1987 (figure 2-1). Order cycles in the U.S. electrical and electronics industry have been shaved from some five months in 1980 to seven weeks in 1990 to close to two weeks today (Peters 1996; Schware and Kimberly 1995).

Just-in-time purchases account for a rising share of purchases

Figure 2-1 Application of just-in-time methods in purchasing in North America and Europe, 1987, 1990, and 1995

Percentage of shipments

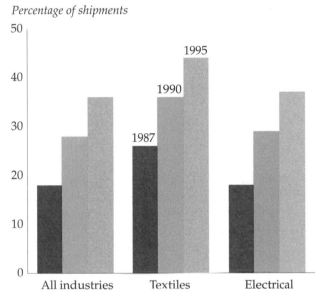

Source: Peters 1996.

Deregulation, lower entry barriers, and increased competition have been key factors in transport and communications improvements—in many cases playing a bigger role than technological advances alone. For example, the major factors behind the reduction of international sea freight rates in recent years were greater competition and deregulation that forced outflagging, labor cost savings, greater energy efficiency, and reduction of capital costs through extended use of ships. In Brazil the removal of freight reservation led to a dramatic reduction in sea freight costs to Europe. Deregulation and heightened competition have been a major source of cost reductions in both air cargo and telecommunications markets (Peters 1993a; ICAO 1992; ITU 1996a).

Growing importance of knowledge and other intangible assets in world production

While policy liberalization and falling transport and communications costs increase competition in domestic and foreign markets, not all these trends necessarily imply more cross-border production by multinationals. For example, while falling trade and transport barriers encourage greater subdivision of production processes across countries according to comparative advantage, this subdivision could occur through arm's length trade between independent firms in some industries. But that is less likely in the kind of technologically sophisticated and differentiated products that are becoming steadily more important in world demand, output, and trade. For such products the competitive strength of firms tends to lie in the possession of highly specialized, intangible assets, such as knowledge about how to produce cheaper or better-quality products at given input prices, ability to innovate, special skills in design, styling, promotion, marketing, or sales, or possession of a trademark or brand with a strong customer following. For a variety of reasons firms tend to find it easier and more profitable to use these intangible assets, usually developed over many years, in-house, rather than selling or licensing them to other firms at arm's length.[2] In these circumstances a firm may find that the best way to exploit the locational advantages of production in a foreign country is to establish a foreign affiliate that retains access to the firm's specialized assets—in short, become a multinational.

The increasing importance of knowledge capital in world production is evident from a number of trends. The real measured stock of intangible capital in the United States in the form of formal education, training, and research and development (R&D), among other items, equaled its physical capital stock by the mid-1970s and exceeded it by 15 percent in 1990 (Abramovitz and David 1996). Investment in information technology overtook other capital expenditures in the United States in the 1990s, and there is little reason to think that these trends are not reflected in most industrial and some developing countries. Several studies document the growth in the share of knowledge- or information-producing industries in output and employment in all OECD countries. Business expenditure on R&D as a share of GDP in the OECD continues to rise (figure 2-2). In most OECD countries studied, the technology intensity of production, accounting for both direct and indirect (or embodied) technology, increased significantly between the 1970s and early 1990s, with especially marked increases for Japan and Germany (OECD 1997).[3]

Modern theories of the multinational enterprise view it as essentially an institutional device that allows intangible assets, such as knowledge, which are not otherwise easily transferred, to be deployed in a number of countries so as to undertake production with complementary local factors of production. Thus it is not surprising that multinationals undertake most of the world's private R&D expenditure. The parent firms of U.S. multinationals undertook 58 percent of all R&D performed in the United States in 1989, public or private. R&D spending in turn is found to be a robust predictor of foreign direct investment (FDI) by a firm or industry (figure 2-3).[4] Technology transfer by multinationals takes place principally to their own affiliates: more than 80 percent of registered receipts for technology sales (royalties, licenses, and patent rights) by U.S. multinationals were from their foreign affiliates; the share is 90 percent for Germany and more than 60 percent for Japan. Technology transfer is also embodied in goods, and intrafirm trade between multinationals and their affiliates accounts for large shares of high-tech exports and imports. The growing importance of knowledge and other intangible assets in production therefore suggests an important underlying reason for the growth of global production.

Developing country firms also seek to upgrade production and marketing technologies to remain competitive in domestic and world export markets. A clothing manufacturer in Bangladesh or the Czech Republic is not immune to the impact of more advanced production and marketing methods in the world garment industry. Indeed, in sectors where economies of scale in R&D, marketing, and global brand-name development are most significant, participation by developing country firms in global production networks through joint ventures and other alliances with multinationals may be a precondition

---

Business R&D spending continues to rise

Figure 2-2 Research and development expenditures in OECD countries

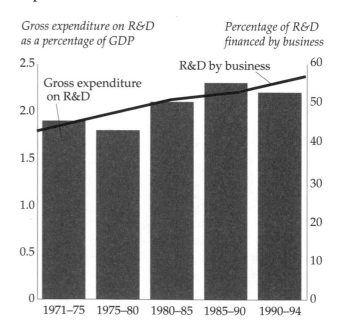

Gross expenditure on R&D as a percentage of GDP

Percentage of R&D financed by business

Source: OECD 1997.

for entry and participation in world markets. Case studies suggest that even large developing countries, such as India, represent too small a part of the world market for, say, autos to support the R&D outlays required to stay abreast of technology. Participation in the world car market, or even in basic automotive components, may require collaboration with foreign principals providing access to technology and marketing channels. Similarly, participation in the world athletic footwear market may require marketing and production alliances with companies that have global brand recognition (Gereffi and Korzeniewicz 1994).

Growth in global production

Growth in cross-border production by multinational enterprises and their networks of associated firms— global production for short—is deepening the economic integration of countries. This section reviews and presents evidence on key aspects of the rise in global production:
- New estimates of the rising share of world and developing country output produced by multinationals and their affiliates.

R&D spending is a good predictor of foreign direct investment

Figure 2-3 U.S. foreign direct investment and research and development expenditures, 1994

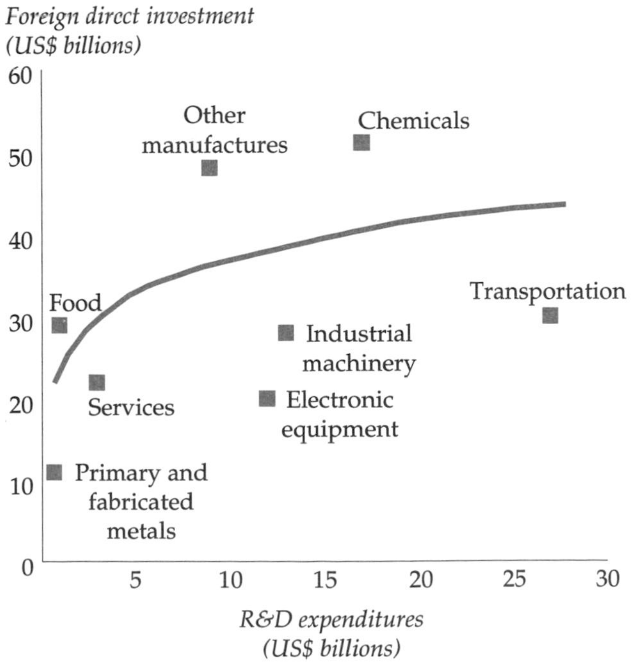

Foreign direct investment
(US$ billions)

Source: U.S. Bureau of Economic Analysis data.

- The greater outward orientation of multinational affiliates and the increasing importance of intrafirm trade in world trade: rather than aiming to primarily serve protected domestic markets, global production is increasingly integrating host countries into the world economy.
- The increasing role of international outsourcing.

There is no systematic or standard source of data on global production. Rather, information must be pieced together from many sources, such as surveys or censuses in a handful of industrial countries covering production by home firms in foreign markets, data collected in a few host countries on production or sales by foreign firms in home markets, balance-of-payments data on capital flows, and commodity-specific international trade data. The result should be seen as a series of snapshots that attempt to highlight important aspects of the phenomenon of global production rather than as a comprehensive picture of the whole.

Rising share of global production in world output

Cross-border production by multinational affiliates constitutes an increasing share of world output. Recent estimates of the value added output of multinational affiliates abroad (that is, excluding the output of parent firms in their home countries) as a share of world GDP[5] show a rise of 2 percentage points over twenty years to reach 6.4 percent in 1990. An acceleration in the 1990s resulted in a 7.5 percent share by 1995 (table 2-1). (Multinational production at home and abroad in 1990 is estimated at about 22 percent of world GDP.)

In the 1990s the most rapid increase in global production occurred in developing countries

Table 2-1 Share of multinational affiliates in world output, selected years, 1970–95
(Percent)

	Share in world output			Share in developing country GDP
Year	GDP	Manufacturing	Services	
1970	4.5	—	—	—
1977	5.4	11.5	2.3	—
1982	5.8	12.7	2.5	4.4[a]
1988	6.3	15.6[b]	3.1[b]	—
1990	6.4	16.5	3.4	3.9
1992	6.2	17.6	3.7	4.3
1995	7.5	—	—	6.3

— Not available.
a. 1983.
b. 1989.
Source: Lipsey 1997; Lipsey, Blomstrom, and Ramstetter 1995.

At present some 60 percent of multinational affiliate output is concentrated in manufacturing (accounting for about a fifth of world manufacturing output). But affiliate output in 1990 was only 3–4 percent of services, which account for more than 60 percent of global output. Services include government, however, as well as transport, communications, utilities, and finance, where until recently foreign investment was frequently excluded, even in industrial countries. But with the worldwide deregulation and opening of services in recent years, future increases in global production may be highest in this sector. Global production is also negligible in agriculture, which represents about 5 percent of world output (though undoubtedly more significant in related manufacturing and service sectors, such as agricultural processing, farm machinery, fertilizers, pesticides, storage, packaging, transportation, distribution, and marketing).

The geographical distribution of multinational affiliate production has also been uneven. Until recently it was much more extensive in industrial than developing or transition economies, few of which had adopted outward-oriented policies before the late 1980s. The share of multinational affiliate output in developing country output in 1990 was only just over half the share in industrial countries, after falling in the 1980s, the decade of the debt crisis (see table 2-1). The boom in FDI to developing countries in the first half of the 1990s contributed to a reversal of this trend, however: affiliate output increased almost 2.5 percentage points of GDP in 1990–95, bringing its share nearer the world average (see table 2-1).

Data inadequacies prevent a more detailed calculation of the distribution of affiliate production across developing countries. But some indication is provided by data on FDI, an indirect indicator showing financial flows associated with establishing production capacity in foreign countries. Such data are available in greater detail than other sources of information on multinational operations. Over the past twenty-five years FDI flows to both industrial and developing countries have followed a rising though highly cyclical trend (figure 2-4). Flows to developing countries in particular showed an unprecedented surge in the 1990s. As a share of gross domestic investment, FDI flows to developing countries averaged more than 5 percent in 1990–95, up from less than 1 percent in the 1970s and less than 2 percent in the 1980s.

As discussed in *Global Economic Prospects 1996*, FDI flows suggest large disparities in the participation of developing countries and regions in global production. Nine countries accounted for almost 90 percent of the increase in FDI flows to developing countries in 1990–95. Many developing countries, however, saw a significant increase in FDI inflows,

especially relative to GDP, even though their shares in total inflows were small. The simple average of FDI to GDP ratios for low- and middle-income countries (LMICs) doubled between 1990 and 1994 (table 2-2). This ratio rose in every region except East Asia, where it was already high. Dispersion of FDI to GDP ratios fell in the first half of the 1990s, as shown by lower coefficients of variation for all LMICs and most regions. The spread of global production capacity—as revealed by analysis of FDI—appears to be broadening.

Global production can be viewed more broadly than in terms of affiliates established through FDI and controlled by parent firms. Multinationals participate in an array of collaborative ventures with host country firms or affiliates of other multinationals, including joint ventures, equity participation, marketing tie-ups, and subcontracting and component supply arrangements involving close coordination between the parties. Joint ventures and other forms of collaboration are important because they combine the differing strengths of domestic and foreign partners (Caves 1996). The more unique, firm-specific, and proprietary the assets deployed in production, however, the more likely they are to be retained in a majority-owned or -controlled affiliate. Systematic data on collaborative ventures between firms are even more limited than are data on multinational affiliates. The range of cross-border corporate alliances that may be formed is wide, however

---

FDI flows are rising but highly cyclical

Figure 2-4 Foreign direct investment in different parts of the world, 1970–95

Percentage of GDP

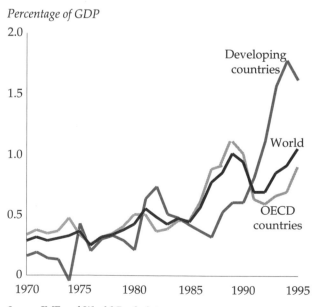

Source: IMF and World Bank data.

Table 2-2 Distribution of FDI in developing countries, 1990 and 1994

	1990			1994		
Country group or region	*US$ billions*	*Percentage of GDP[a]*	*Coefficient of variation*	*US$ billions*	*Percentage of GDP[a]*	*Coefficient of variation*
Low- and middle-income countries	27.7	0.85 (0.45)	2.68	84.8	1.80 (0.99)	1.92
East Asia	10.9	2.80 (2.02)	0.81	44.1	2.64 (1.84)	0.98
South Asia	0.3	0.26 (0.21)	1.17	1.9	0.68 (0.62)	0.87
Latin America and the Caribbean	7.6	0.26 (0.93)	12.57	24.5	2.50 (1.78)	2.18
Sub-Saharan Africa	0.9	0.93 (0.14)	2.13	3.4	1.55 (0.23)	1.87
Middle East and North Africa	2.9	0.49 (0.62)	2.23	2.8	0.84 (0.42)	1.43
Europe and Central Asia	4.6	0.94 (0.45)	1.40	8.1	1.80 (1.46)	0.63
Middle-income countries	21.8	0.91 (0.93)	2.89	44.5	1.80 (1.20)	1.89
Low-income countries (excl. China)	2.0	0.76 (0.08)	2.23	5.8	1.67 (0.41)	2.12

a. Simple averages. Median values are in parentheses.
Source: IMF data; World Bank data and staff estimates.

(figure 2-5). Such growing cross-border alliances are evident in many sectors, including clothing, chemicals, construction, electronics, footwear, semi-conductors, and telecommunications (OECD 1994; Zampetti 1994; Cowhey and Aronson 1993; Gereffi and Korzeniewicz 1994).

Increasing international trade orientation of global production

There is some evidence that overseas production by multinational affiliates is becoming more oriented toward exports rather than the domestic market of the host country. This is especially evident in technologically complex products. In addition, intrafirm international trade (that is, trade within multinationals, between parents and affiliates or between different affiliates of the same parent) appears to be gaining ground relative to overall world trade. Both these trends suggest that multinational firms can serve as important conduits to international markets for developing countries. Since a large part of world trade is intrafirm or, in services, occurs principally through the presence of a foreign firm in the local market, it is evident that restrictions on foreign investment will hurt international trade as well. So efforts to liberalize trade also need to consider the liberalization of investment codes.[6]

The share of exports in sales of U.S. majority-owned foreign affiliates has more than doubled, from less than 20 percent in 1966 to more than 40 percent in 1993.[7] The rise has been largest for foreign affiliates in developing countries, where barriers to trade were previously the highest and have since fallen the most in relative terms (figure 2-6). Regional and country

variations in trade barriers and economic policy also affect the picture. The greater inward orientation of Latin America and India until recently provided foreign affiliates with strong incentives to orient sales to the domestic market, while in more outward-oriented

Figure 2-5 Automotive corporate alliances within and between different regions, 1992

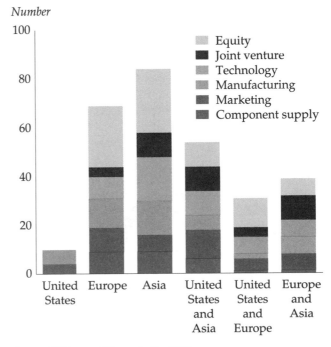

Source: O'Brien and Karmokolias 1994.

Figure 2-6 Exports of U.S. majority-owned foreign affiliates in manufacturing, 1966–93

Percentage of total sales

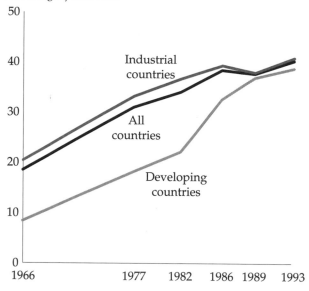

Source: U.S. Bureau of Economic Analysis data.

Figure 2-7 Exports from U.S. majority-owned foreign affiliates in selected host countries, 1966–93

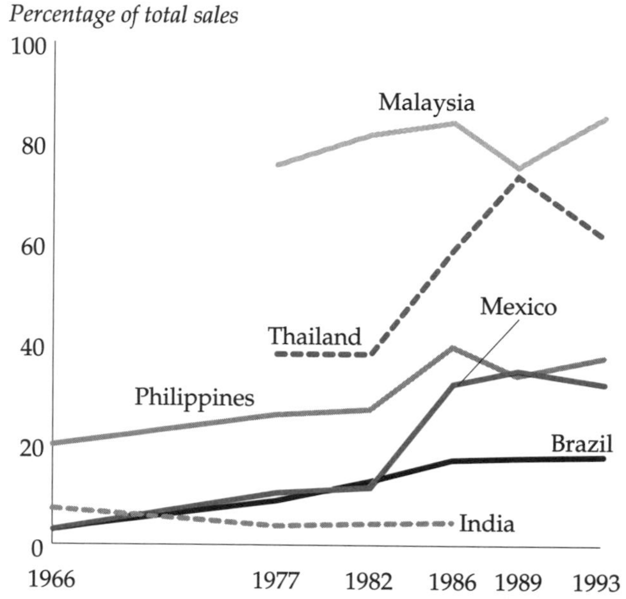

Percentage of total sales

Source: U.S. Bureau of Economic Analysis data.

East Asia the propensity to export was high and rising (figure 2-7). The most striking increases in export to sales ratios were for technologically sophisticated sectors such as machinery, office and computing machines, electric and electronic equipment, and transportation.

Trends for Japanese manufacturing foreign affiliates are similar, but export propensities vary more by region, being much higher for affiliates in Asia and in Europe than for those operating in the United States. The relocation of labor-intensive manufacturing by firms from the Republic of Korea, Taiwan (China), Hong Kong (China), and Singapore to their affiliates in China, Indonesia, the Philippines, and Thailand also contributed to the large increase in intraregional trade in East Asia over the last decade.

Intrafirm trade has also risen as a share of international trade in many industrial countries in recent years (figure 2-8). In the United States the industries with the highest levels of intrafirm exports relative to total industry exports in 1993 were those with high research and development and significant firm-level economies of scale: machinery (84 percent), office and computing machines (94 percent), electronic components (85 percent), and transportation (87 percent). Trade with affiliates is highest in industries that use specialized knowledge (OECD 1996a; UNCTAD 1996).

Growing international outsourcing

Falling trade and transport barriers tend to encourage firms to separate production processes (especially in manufacturing) into stages that can be outsourced to different countries according to their comparative advantage. This trend can significantly broaden the opportunities for international trade available to developing countries (box 2-2).

A more systematic source of evidence is the growing importance of trade in parts and components in the machinery and transport equipment sector (SITC 7).[8] This trend reflects both the import of components from low-cost production locations abroad and their export to overseas assembly or processing locations. Machinery and transport equipment is the fastest-growing segment of world trade, containing such technologically dynamic sectors as computers, telecommunications equipment, and other electronic products and parts. It accounts for roughly 50 percent of world trade in manufactures. The OECD countries (excluding recent members such as the Republic of Korea and Mexico) exported $440 billion of machinery and transport equipment components in 1995—about 30 percent of all shipments in this sector, up from 26 percent in 1978. The United States has had the highest proportion of components

Intrafirm trade is on the rise

Figure 2-8 International intrafirm trade's share in total country trade, 1982–83, 1989, and 1992

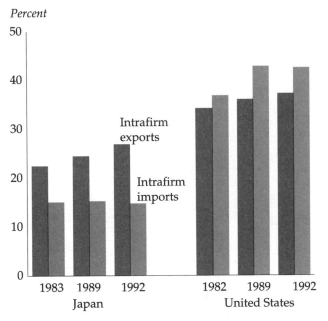

Percent

Intrafirm exports

Intrafirm imports

Note: Data for Japan exclude firms engaged in commerce.
Source: UNCTAD 1996.

exports in the past twenty years, while Japan has experienced the most dramatic increase since 1978 (figure 2-9). These trade data do not differentiate between intrafirm trade (or trade between closely associated firms) and arm's length trade. However, it is precisely in the technologically sophisticated machinery and transport equipment sector that intrafirm trade is found to make up the highest proportion of overall trade.

Some present (or former) developing countries have been among the fastest-growing destinations for OECD components exports. Exports to the ten largest developing country importers totaled $81 billion in 1995, or 18 percent of all components exports, up from 10 percent in 1978. The bulk of component exports went to East Asian countries, including China, which has experienced the most rapid increase since 1978 and was also the single largest East Asian destination in 1995 (figure 2-10). Newly industrializing economies and developing countries exported about $100 billion of these products in 1995. Although data limitations do not allow the tracking of trends in developing countries' exports of these products over the 1980s, available information indicates they were of major importance by the beginning of the 1990s. Components exports from Singapore

exceeded $20 billion, while Taiwan (China), the Republic of Korea, Malaysia, and Mexico all had exports in excess of $10 billion each. These trends signal the increasing interdependence of production sharing operations in the machinery and transport sectors—in which industries in one country become increasingly reliant on suppliers in another for essential manufacturing inputs.

The trend toward outsourcing is also seen in the growth of offshore purchases as a proportion of total

Figure 2-9 Components share of OECD machinery and transport equipment exports to world, 1978 and 1995

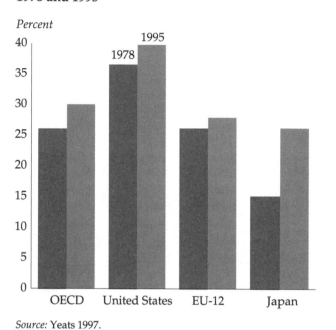

Percent

Source: Yeats 1997.

Figure 2-10 Components exports to developing countries as share of total machinery and transport equipment components exports, 1978 and 1995

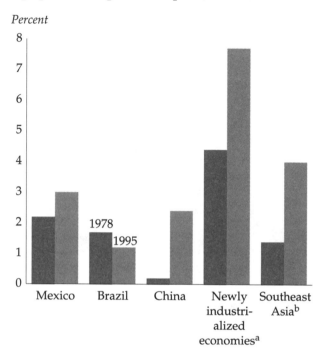

Percent

a. Hong Kong (China), Republic of Korea, Singapore, and Taiwan (China).
b. Indonesia, Malaysia, and Thailand.
Source: Yeats 1997.

purchases of inputs by industrial country firms. A World Bank survey of 628 North American and 240 European industrial groups or firms found that their offshore outsourcing rose about 30 percent between 1987 and 1995 in response to growing cost competition and restructuring of businesses.

As much as 12 percent of total nonenergy purchases by U. S. manufacturing firms were offshore by 1990, compared with less than half that level in the early 1970s (table 2-3). The average figure masks wide variation among sectors. In sectors where production can be broken into self-contained stages that are relatively easy to transport and that vary considerably in their use of different types of labor skill (footwear, electronics, instruments, and toys, for instance), the share of outsourcing in purchases is much higher—about 18–22 percent.[9]

Impact of global production in developing countries

The direct impact of multinational operations on trade, capital formation, and production in many developing countries became significant in the 1990s. In principle countries can now participate in global production by mastering a slice of the value added chain in a given industry rather than waiting to mas-

ter all the different stages, resulting in a wider range of options for production and trade. Multinational firms tend to differ markedly from local firms in their technologies, management quality, and knowledge about and access to foreign markets, features often reflected in a higher level of productivity. Such differences and the growing dimensions of global production create the potential for indirect, or spillover, benefits, which strengthen the general know-how and skills of local residents and firms.

Direct effects of global production

The direct effects of global production on economic activity in a developing country can be substantial, even in a country as large as China. Here foreign-invested firms generate from a quarter to a third of all investment and exports and 10–15 percent of industrial production and taxes (table 2-4).

FDI was 5–6 percent of aggregate investment in developing countries in the early 1990s, well above

Table 2-3 Offshore outsourcing by the United States in selected years

Year	Imported inputs	
	Value (US$ billions)	*As percentage of nonenergy purchases*
1972	48.8	5.3
1979	143.7	7.7
1987	356.0	11.5
1990	407.0	11.6

Source: Feenstra and Hanson 1996.

the 1–2 percent of the previous fifteen years. It has sometimes been argued that FDI will tend to substitute for domestic investment, so that, in extreme cases, the host country's capital stock does not change. Recent work shows that such offset effects may not be particularly significant. One study concluded that FDI inflows and outflows tended to raise or lower overall investment dollar for dollar; that is, without any offset in domestic investment (Feldstein 1994). Indeed, in a cross-country analysis of growth and investment, Borenzstein, De Gregorio, and Lee (1995) find that FDI inflows to developing countries are associated with larger increases in overall investment, suggesting that FDI crowds in domestic investment. They estimate that a dollar of FDI in developing countries is associated with $0.50–$1.30 of additional domestic investment.[10] In an undistorted policy regime inflows of foreign capital will also tend to move into labor-intensive sectors, where many developing countries' comparative advantage lies, having a further positive effect on employment and wages.

Because of access to superior know-how and other intangible assets, multinational affiliates tend to have a higher level of productivity than local firms. In Venezuela, for example, foreign-invested firms were more productive, paid higher wages, and conducted more international trade than local firms (table 2-5).

Indirect benefits or spillovers

Spillovers refer to benefits arising from the presence of multinationals that are not fully captured by them in their market transactions with customers and suppliers. Such benefits can arise when multinationals lead to diffusion of information about the existence and profitability of new technologies, production methods, management and marketing techniques, or export market opportunities. Some important channels:

- *Labor market spillovers.* Training of local employees is important because new skills are transferable as managers and employees move—as studies in Kenya, Hong Kong (China), the Philippines, and Latin America show.[11]
- *Market access and demonstration effects.* Foreign firms, with their greater knowledge of world markets and access to international marketing channels, tend to be more involved in international trade. In one study multinational affiliates in Mexico were twice as likely to export as local firms. But, more important, multinational exports in a particular industry and region in Mexico significantly increased the probability of exports by local firms. Studies of the development of exports in Hong Kong and Taiwan (China) in the 1960s have also argued for strong demonstration effects from the operations of multinationals.[12]
- *Supplier spillovers.* Foreign firms collaborate with local suppliers, and spillover benefits occur as these suppliers use their improved capabilities

Table 2-4 Effects of FDI in China, 1991–95

Item	1991	1992	1993	1994	1995
Actual FDI flows (US$ billions)	4.4	11.2	27.5	33.8	37.5
Average amount per project (US$ millions)	0.9	1.2	1.3	1.8	2.5
FDI as a ratio to gross domestic investment (percent)	4.5	8.0	13.6	18.3	25.0
Volume of exports by foreign affiliates (US$ billions)	12.1	17.4	25.2	34.7	—
Share of foreign affiliates in exports (percent)	17.0	20.4	27.5	28.7	31.3
Share of foreign affiliates in industrial output (percent)	5.0	6.0	9.0	11.0	13.0
Number of employees in FDI projects (millions)	4.8	6.0	10.0	14.0	16.0
Tax contribution as share of total (percent)	—	4.1	—	—	10.0

— Not available.
Source: UNCTAD 1996; World Bank data.

Table 2-5 Performance characteristics of foreign-invested and domestic firms in Venezuelan manufacturing, 1976–89
(Ratio of foreign firm performance to domestic firm performance)

Sector	Output per worker	Real wages	Exports as percentage of sales	Imported inputs as percentage of sales	Net exports as percentage of sales	Total factor productivity differential[a]
All sectors	1.7	1.6	8.4	2.9	6.9	8.5
Machinery, metal products	1.7	1.4	10.9	3.2	–10.3	7.7
Textiles, apparel, leather	1.4	1.2	3.5	1.6	–0.2	9.9
Chemicals	1.4	1.4	3.5	1.6	–7.1	—
Food, beverages	2.0	2.0	0.7	4.4	10.2	9.1
Basic metals	1.6	1.3	8.3	2.6	18.8	0.0

— Not available.
a. Percentage difference between foreign and domestic firms.
Source: Aitken and Harrison 1994.

to supply other customers (box 2-3). A survey by the International Labour Organization indicates the importance of such subcontracting by multinational affiliates. Of particular interest was the prevalence of more or less intensive consultation and support between multinationals and their domestic subcontractors, especially in product design, blueprints, technical support, production process planning, and, above all, quality control. Some 70–100 percent of multinational affiliates reported providing this kind of technical support and quality control assistance to suppliers (Halbach 1989). Among formal studies Wolff and Nadiri (1993) find a significant positive association between technological progress in U.S. manufacturing industries and that in sectors that supply them.

Indirect evidence of the benefits of international firms is provided by cross-country studies of aggregate growth. These typically find aggregate FDI to be significantly associated with higher per capita GDP growth, although they do not establish the causality between more FDI and faster growth. In a cross-country growth study of both industrial and developing countries conducted for this report (Wacziarg 1997), each percentage point share of FDI in GDP was found to be associated with 0.3–0.4 percentage point higher per capita GDP growth. This estimate is consistent with the findings of other studies.[13]

Evidence of the effects of foreign firms on the rest of the economy also comes from microeconomic studies using plant data. Blomstrom and Wolff (1989) find evidence of intra-industry spillovers in Mexico, while Haddad and Harrison (1993) find that local Moroccan firms tend to be nearer best-practice productivity lev-

els in sectors with more foreign investment. A recent study finds subcontracting relations and joint ventures to have been an especially potent source of productivity spillovers in the Czech Republic (box 2-4). Aitken and Harrison (1994) find a negative association with multinational presence in Venezuela, however, possibly as competition from foreign firms forces local firms to forgo scale economies. These mixed results are not unexpected, only in part because of the statistical difficulties in capturing the subtle effects involved. Foreign firms have a direct interest in pre-

---

Box 2-3 Technological spillovers in the sewing machine industry in Taiwan (China)

An important early case study of links between multinationals and their local suppliers is provided by Taiwan, China. In 1963 the Singer company was allowed to set up a subsidiary to produce sewing machines, overriding strong opposition from the domestic industry, whose output was small in scale and poor in quality. The Singer subsidiary grew rapidly, particularly in the export market. It also steadily increased local purchases and conducted an extensive program of training and technical support for its parts suppliers in production techniques, measurement, inspection, quality control, and management. Far from being hurt by the arrival of Singer, local sewing machine assembly firms benefited greatly from the improvement in the competence of the local parts supply industry. While Singer's exports increased by a factor of around eight in 1966–76, the exports of the industry as a whole rose by a factor of more than twenty.

Source: Schive 1990.

venting spillovers of proprietary technology to competing firms in the same industry. But the extent of spillovers is also likely to depend on economic policies prevailing in host countries.

Potential and benefits of global production in services

Services play a crucial role in the world economy, contributing an estimated 63 percent of world output in 1995. Differences in service sector efficiency often lie at the heart of differences in standards of living between countries (box 2-5).

Two characteristics have tended to set the service sector apart and cut it off from foreign channels of competition and productivity gains. First, many services are not easily traded internationally because they are intangible, cannot be stored, or require immediate use or close contact between producers and consumers. Although technological change is making more services tradable over time (a process described in *Global Economic Prospects 1995*), the share of services in world trade—about 20 percent in 1995—remains far below its share in world GDP. This is also why the provision of services by foreign suppliers often entails direct investment rather than cross-border trade.[14] Second, foreign enterprises have often been excluded from or tightly controlled in providing services. From the mid-1980s, however, policy reforms to open up the service sectors to foreign investment have contributed to faster growth in FDI in this sector than in any other sector in both high-income and developing countries. Policies to privatize and increase competition in key service sectors such as transport, telecommunications, utilities, and finance have been especially important.

Does liberalization of investment barriers induce much growth in FDI in services? A look at the EU, whose members have made far-reaching service liberalization commitments with each other, suggests that the answer is yes. The EU became the single most important destination for services FDI in the second half of the 1980s. The share of services in total FDI inflows into the EU rose to 60–65 percent (compared with half that share in outflows of FDI from the EU). Furthermore, within the EU, it is FDI rather than trade that is the preferred way of contesting markets (Hoekman 1997).

What are the main benefits of global production in services?

- Liberalization of trade and investment regimes in infrastructure services can bring large efficiency gains. More competition in the provision of port services in Veracruz, Mexico reduced their cost by some 30 percent in one year, while container turnover went up almost 50 percent. Labor productivity at Aeromexico and Mexicana airlines increased 50–100 percent following privatization and participation by foreign equity. Privatization and associated inward FDI in Argentina's telecommunications industry in the early 1990s resulted in significant improvements in the quantity and quality of services (Hoekman and Primo Braga 1997).
- The high skill level needed in many service sectors and the invariably high local labor content suggest that transfer and diffusion of knowledge and know-how may be a vital aspect of the gains from FDI in services. Case studies for the insurance and hotel industries reveal that multinationals engage in substantial in-house training of local personnel (UNCTAD 1994d).
- Although more hamstrung than manufacturing, service firms also build global production networks. Communications technology increasingly

---

Box 2-4 Global production and technological catch-up in the Czech Republic

A recent study finds that subcontracting and joint ventures with Western firms make a significant contribution to productivity gains by local firms in the Czech Republic.

An analysis of 706 firms that account for 64 percent of manufacturing output in the Czech Republic suggests that growth in these firms' total factor productivity in 1992–95—more than 4 percent a year—was higher than in any other Central and Eastern European country for which enterprise data are available. What were the sources of rapid productivity gains in the Czech Republic? The study suggests that:

- Firm productivity growth appears to have been driven by privatization, greater financial market discipline, and initial conditions such as the size of the firm and the sector it operated in.
- Foreign investment and trade associated with multinationals were other important factors. Joint ventures with foreign firms had a larger and more significant association with productivity growth than even privatization. Imports of intermediate inputs from OECD countries were also significant—but only for imports that were part of subcontracting arrangements with Western firms, not for arm's length imports.
- Simple equity flows (FDI that is not a joint venture) showed no significant correlation with growth in total factor productivity, perhaps because such flows are very recent. Finally, a large fraction of gains in total factor productivity remains statistically unexplained, which may be due to unobserved managerial effects too subtle to capture.

Source: Djankov and Hoekman 1997.

The productivity of capital invested in the telecommunications sector in Germany and Japan is less than half that in the United States. The reasons? State ownership, poor incentives, and less competition. This may help explain why, despite similar per capita incomes, the United States has 60 telephone lines for every 100 people compared with 48 in Japan and Germany (McKinsey Global Institute 1996).

The number of telephones per person worldwide varies enormously, from nearly 70 per 100 in Sweden (the world's highest) to 0.09 in the Democratic Republic of Congo, formerly Zaire (the world's lowest). Differences in per capita incomes explain less than half the differences in telephone density. A cross-country econometric study points to the low productivity in services typical of most state-owned monopolies, high prices to consumers (if they can get a phone), demand-insensitive supply of services, and poor management and employee skills (Bowles 1995). The waiting time for a telephone in Bangladesh, Ghana, or Haiti is ten years or more (ITU 1996a). On the demand side, relative openness to trade also appears to play an important role. This may help to explain why Brazil has 7 telephone lines per 100 people compared with 11 for Chile and 15 for Malaysia; and why Argentina has 14 lines per 100 people compared with 40 for the Republic of Korea—despite similar per capita incomes.

Other examples of how productivity in services matters:

- Singapore serves as a maritime hub for Asia. Underlying this position is the efficiency of its port, which has the world's fastest ship turnaround times and is the busiest in the world, serving more than 700 shipping lines from eighty countries.
- Just outside Taipei is an automated warehouse and distribution center run by a private company (Contract Distribution Services), which handles all aspects of logistics for imported sea freight consignments. It can receive, load, and deliver an order within twenty-four hours.
- Hong Kong Air Cargo Terminal Limited handles air cargo for sixty-plus international airlines. It serves 280 flights and 3,500 tons of cargo a day. Its mishandling rate is 1 in 6,500, far superior to the 1 in 20 rate for most airlines. The company's dwell time is nineteen hours for exports, one of the best in the world.

Source: Hanna, Boyson, and Gunaratne 1996; Reinfeld 1994.

allows service firms to split and disperse parts of service production to foreign affiliates or outsource labor-intensive activities, such as data entry in the Caribbean or software writing in India, generating substantial employment benefits in supplier countries. These spin-offs can generate other benefits, for example, the increased use of computers in Indian businesses.

- Services provide critical linkages in an economy. The most obvious examples are transportation and telecommunications, but business services (such as finance, insurance, and accounting) also allow other industries (both goods and service producing) to operate more efficiently.[15]

Policy implications

Global production is generating important benefits for many developing countries. That raises two broad policy issues. First, for countries that already participate in global production, what policies might increase the benefits they draw from it? Second, for those developing countries that are not attracting much global investment, what policies might improve flows?

Enhancing the benefits of global production

Policies that enhance competition force firms to seek improvements in efficiency and are also likely to be helpful in maximizing the benefits countries derive from global production. More open trade and investment frameworks are among the best channels for introducing such competitive pressures in traded sectors. In nontraded services sectors encouragement of foreign investment and well-designed regulatory policies to enhance competition need special emphasis.

Some recent studies provide evidence that more competition in host country markets increases the pressures and incentives for multinationals to transfer more and better-quality technology to affiliates. In Mexico, for example, affiliate technology imports (as measured by payments per employee for patents, royalties, and trademarks) were significantly associated with various measures of competition in the host country's market (Blomstrom, Kokko, and Zejan 1992). The effect was found to be much stronger in consumer goods, where it is arguably easier for local firms to compete because the technology level they need to reach is lower. This finding runs against policies in some developing countries to restrict FDI to high-tech industries—where, it is argued, "we have more to learn"—because multinationals will, in any case, face less competitive pressure to transfer their best technologies to affiliates in these sectors.

Kokko and Blomstrom (1995) replicate some of these findings for technology imports by U.S. majority-owned foreign affiliates in thirty-three host countries. In addition, they find that U.S. foreign affiliates' technology imports have no association with formal technology transfer requirements in host countries, such as using the most advanced technology available, performing R&D locally, providing access to parent patents, or transferring skills to local staff. They have a significant negative association with various other formal performance requirements, such as minimum local content and employment rules and import restrictions. Indeed, as more and more developing countries open up and compete to attract FDI, onerous performance requirements are more likely to drive away than to attract investors.

Measures to increase competition could include reducing regulations, obstructions, and red tape that serve as barriers to entry into sectors and markets. They could include eliminating of major distortions in labor, capital, land, and other factor markets that raise costs and increase risks for firms (such as restrictions preventing firms from reducing workforces when needed). They should certainly include reducing trade barriers and maintaining a transparent and open FDI regime, so that, rather than one or two politically well-connected multinationals carving out protected monopolistic enclaves, there are multiple firms facing serious competition both from direct imports and from other multinationals. Balasubramaniam, Salisu, and Sapsford (1996) provide evidence that the growth impact of FDI increases with the openness of the trade regime. Developing countries with more open trade policies tend to have a closer positive association between the presence of foreign firms (proxied by FDI to GDP ratios) and total factor productivity growth, countries with closed trade regimes, where the effect is weaker (and sometimes negative; figure 2-11). Developing countries with more open trade regimes also tend to have a higher positive correlation between FDI to GDP ratios and the share of high-technology products in exports (figure 2-12).[16]

With respect to the absorptive capacity of host countries, Borensztein, De Gregorio, and Lee (1995) find that FDI has a positive effect on growth once countries have a minimum level of education. For the average level of secondary schooling in the sample (about 0.9 year), they find every percentage point of FDI to GDP to be associated with around 0.5 percent faster growth. Many policies aimed at increasing the degree of competition in host countries would also tend to increase absorptive capacity. For example, flexible labor markets could stimulate spillovers by both encouraging multinationals to adopt more labor-intensive methods and allowing more mobility of workers between foreign and local firms. Low regulatory and bureaucratic overhead costs would help local firms compete for multinational subcontracts and so expand the scope for supplier linkages.

Increasing competition in service sectors

While the importance of competition in services is increasingly accepted, implementation has tended to lag. For example, commitments by developing countries to liberalize services under the World Trade Organization's recent General Agreement on Trade in Services were relatively limited. The share of commitments by developing countries that retained no restrictions on either market access or national treatment was about 7 percent of the maximum possible. The share for high-income countries was 25 percent. (Hoekman 1996). Given the substantial potential gains from liberalization of FDI and trade in services, why do many countries choose to maintain protection in services? The principal factors seem to be a desire to protect employees in overstaffed, state-owned enterprises, fears of unemployment from computerization in labor-intensive service sectors (banking, public services), and concerns about the impact on small businesses (for example, the impact of foreign wholesale dis-

---

The growth impact of FDI increases with openness . . .

Figure 2-11 Correlation between foreign direct investment and total factor productivity growth, 1975–90

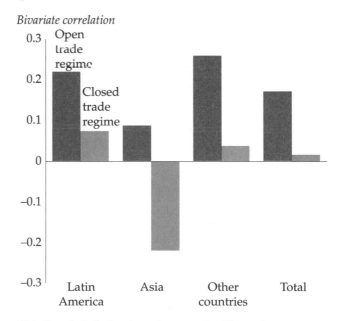

Bivariate correlation

Note: Sample includes sixty-nine countries. Figure shows bivariate correlation between the foreign direct investment to GDP ratio (quinquennially averaged for 1971–75, 1976–80, 1981–85, and 1986–90) and total factor productivity growth (five-year averages ending in 1975, 1980, 1985, and 1990).
Source: IMF data; Coe, Helpman, and Hoffmeister 1995; Sachs and Warner 1995; World Bank data and staff estimates.

. . . as does the positive association of FDI and high-tech exports

Figure 2-12 Correlation between foreign direct investment and the share of high-tech exports, 1975–90

Bivariate correlation

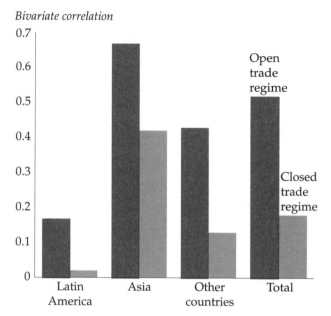

Open trade regime

Closed trade regime

Note: Sample includes fifty countries. Figure shows bivariate correlation between foreign direct investment and the share of high-technology exports in total exports.
Source: IMF data; Sachs and Warner 1995; World Bank data and staff estimates.

tributors on small retailers in Indonesia). Issues of labor market adjustment are prominent (see chapter 3). However, in most cases of liberalization of services in developing countries, the eventual benefits from faster growth are likely to outweigh possible short-run negative effects.

One reason why liberalization in services may be slower is the need to establish an adequate regulatory framework (World Bank 1997). Privatization of state monopolies and entry by private providers in infrastructure sectors that are nontraded and have natural monopoly characteristics present difficult institutional challenges. In such cases the absence of an efficient regulatory framework that ensures adequate competition means there is no guarantee that privatized services will necessarily be more efficient than publicly delivered services. For example, in Indonesia the price of electricity from new private power plants was driven down to about $0.06 per kilowatt-hour from $0.09 only after competition was improved through competitive bidding and clearer allocation of risk.

Improving the climate for global production

More than half of all developing countries do not participate to a significant extent in global production. Most are in Sub-Saharan Africa, South Asia, and the Middle East and North Africa. In 1994 only a quarter or so of the countries in these regions had FDI inflows above 1 percent of GDP, not much better than the proportion of countries in the 1970s. Factors that appear to be relevant in explaining FDI flows to countries that receive a relatively high level of FDI do not work well for countries that receive less (Singh and Jun 1995). Countries that receive little FDI do have some common features, however (figure 2-13). Of forty-nine developing countries receiving FDI of less than 1 percent of GDP in 1990–94, around a quarter suffered war or intense civil strife—conditions that largely preclude receipt of significant FDI. Of the remainder, some three-quarters were afflicted by serious macroeconomic instability, defined as budget deficits averaging more than 5 percent of GDP or inflation of 50 percent a year. Others saw negative output growth over the period covered by the analysis. One or more of these conditions affected four-fifths of countries receiving little FDI.[17]

Among these countries the building blocks for more FDI are therefore much the same as for economic activity in general—peace, basic macroeconomic stability, and institutional credibility (World Bank 1997). Encouragingly, some Sub-Saharan African countries that have made progress on some of these problems are starting to attract FDI inflows (box 2-6). Given these preconditions, what other factors are important to attract more FDI? The literature on the determinants of FDI inflows is vast and often inconclusive. No attempt is made to summarize it here.[18] Rather, taking these preconditions as given, some common features of countries participating in global production are noted.

- *Attractiveness as a base for exports to world markets will gain in importance.* The size of the domestic market has typically been found to be among the more important determinants of FDI. Newer findings suggest that a country's attractiveness as a base for exporting to world markets is gaining in importance, a trend consistent with the declines in trade barriers and transport costs described earlier (Lucas 1993; Singh and Jun 1996). This finding is encouraging for small economies—Hong Kong (China) and Singapore have shown that smallness need not be a handicap in drawing foreign investment.

- *Openness to trade is important.* More open economies get more FDI (Edwards 1990; Balasubramanyam and Salisu 1991). Using panel data on U.S. multinational affiliates in

Figure 2-13 Developing countries and foreign direct investment: factors associated with low FDI to GDP ratios, 1990–94

Number of countries

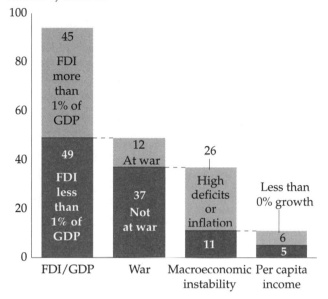

Source: World Bank data and staff estimates.

developing countries in 1977–94, Slaughter (1997) finds that direct measures of global production such as affiliate employment, assets, and capital stock were consistently greater in more open economies.

- *Private provision of basic infrastructure is growing in importance.* The quality of infrastructure is an important consideration for global manufacturing and marketing systems that are reliant on just-in-time processes, total quality management, and flexible manufacturing systems (Wheeler and Mody 1992). Improvements in the transport and logistics infrastructure—roads, telecommunications, ports, customs management—play a vital role. Deregulation to allow entry by private (including foreign) providers in a competitive environment will be important in achieving such improvements. Port deregulation in Argentina shows the large gains that are possible (figure 2-14; World Bank 1996a). The price of a telephone call from Chile to the United States in 1996 was one fourth and one seventh, respectively, of the price of calls from Brazil and Argentina (Petrazzini 1997).
- *The effect of special tax advantages can be overestimated.* Studies have consistently suggested

Box 2-6 Is Sub-Saharan Africa starting to re-attract foreign investors?

Many countries in Africa have improved their economic policies in recent years. Most have undertaken some degree of macroeconomic stabilization and structural adjustment (see chapter 1). Most have eased restrictions on FDI and liberalized foreign currency markets. Some countries also provide fiscal incentives—lower corporate taxes, tax holidays, and import duty exemptions (for example, in labor-intensive manufacturing in Lesotho and export processing zones in Mauritius). Most are members or signatories to multilateral investment conventions, such as the Multilateral Investment Guarantee Agency, the International Center for Settlement of Investment Disputes, the New York Convention on Recognition and Enforcement of Foreign Arbitration Awards, and the Convention on Protection of Industrial Property.

Annual FDI inflows doubled from about $1.5 billion in 1984–89 to about $3 billion in 1994–95. But the share of Africa in flows to all developing countries still dropped from about 6 percent to 3 percent. Almost two-thirds of inflows were accounted for by one oil exporter, Nigeria. In one recent study (using panel data for 1980–95 on thirty-one Sub-Saharan countries) the explanation for low flows of FDI to Africa appeared to lie in three factors—low GDP growth, low trade openness, and high variability of real effective exchange rates (Bhattacharya, Montiel, and Sharma 1996).

Nevertheless, more Sub-Saharan African countries are starting to attract FDI, even if it is still concentrated in natural resources. Countries as diverse as Angola, Ghana, Lesotho, Mozambique, Namibia, Tanzania, and Uganda saw substantial increases in FDI. Two groups of African countries did poorly in attracting FDI in 1980–95: the CFA countries before their exchange rate adjustment in 1994, and countries bedeviled by civil conflict or negative economic growth. Another study stresses five actions as important in enhancing FDI potential in Africa: reduce bureaucratic procedures and assure property rights and transparency; treat foreign and domestic investors equally; expand privatization, especially in infrastructure; establish efficient business tax systems with low rates; and ease access to foreign exchange and expatriate employment and reattract skilled labor (UNCTAD 1995; Pearce, Islam, and Sauvant 1996).

that special tax and other fiscal incentives have little influence on FDI, though harmonization of corporate tax systems to best-practice standards is important.[19] Indeed, it is possible that beggar-thy-neighbor competition between countries to attract more FDI by offering larger tax breaks could lead to suboptimal outcomes for all countries. To guard against such adverse outcomes (or where there are concerns about issues such

Figure 2-14 Effects of deregulation on port costs and performance in Buenos Aires, Argentina, 1991 and 1995

Index (1991 = 100)

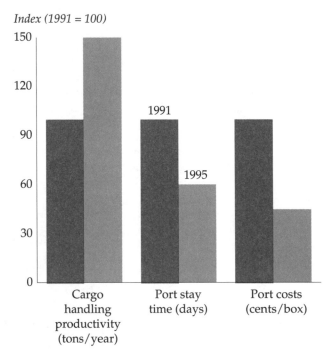

Source: World Bank 1996a.

as the impact of transfer pricing on tax revenues), policymakers may wish to consider the possibility of greater international coordination in setting national policies and standards (Graham 1996).

Conclusion

Several trends in the world today are contributing to the expansion of cross-border production by multinational enterprises and their networks of closely associated firms. These include the liberalization of economic policies in most countries, continued reductions in the cost of transport and communications, and the growing importance of knowledge and other intangible assets in modern production and distribution. The expansion of global production provides developing countries with opportunities to enhance the benefits they draw from greater integration with the world economy. The "slicing up of the value chain" by multinationals in their global production networks broadens opportunities for developing countries to participate in international specialization and other gains from trade. And the presence of these firms improves the scope for a

readier diffusion in developing countries of international information, know-how, and best practices. Maintenance of a high level of competition between firms is likely to be an important precondition for making the most of the potential benefits of global production. Other important conditions for both attracting foreign investment and enhancing its benefits include a stable political and macroeconomic climate, open trade and investment policies, adequate transport and communications infrastructure, and the maintenance of a predictable and effective institutional environment.

Notes

1. The simplest definition of the multinational enterprise is a firm with plants in more than one country.

2. The nature of the informational and other market failures that hamper arm's length transfers of intangible proprietary assets are discussed in Caves (1996). For example, firm A cannot tell firm B about the nature of a piece of knowledge it wishes to sell firm B because it fears losing the secret, while firm B does not want to buy sight unseen for fear of being hoodwinked.

3. Studies of information industry output are summarized in Foray and Lundvall 1996. See also World Bank 1996b.

4. See, for example, Caves 1996; Graham 1996; Blomstrom and Kokko 1997.

5. These estimates are based on data on value added or sales by foreign affiliates of multinationals based in Germany, Japan, Sweden, and the United States, the only home countries publishing such data. Data sources and estimation methods are described in Lipsey (1997) and Lipsey, Blomstrom, and Ramstetter (1995).

6. Links between trade and foreign investment and their implications for policy are discussed in WTO (1996).

7. The most detailed data on multinational activities are widely recognized to be those on U.S. multinational enterprises maintained by the U.S. Bureau of Economic Analysis. On many specialized questions, therefore, analysis in this area is often restricted to consideration of U.S. multinationals alone.

8. Changes in the Standard International Trade Classification (SITC) system (Revision 2) differentiate trade in components and parts from trade in finished goods for the machinery and transportation equipment (SITC 7) group. This differentiation is not available, at least to the same extent, in other major categories of international trade.

9. Peters 1996; Feenstra and Hanson 1996; Slaughter 1995; Yeats 1997.

10. Although, like other forms of external finance, FDI inflows need to be serviced with a stream of payments to foreign residents, these dividends are paid on a sustainable basis out of additional output and foreign exchange earned by the enterprise. In addition, there is evidence that FDI

inflows provide a more stable form of external financing than portfolio or some other types of flows (Chuhan, Perez-Quiros, and Popper 1996).

11. Gerschenberg 1987; Katz 1987; Chen 1983.

12. Aitken, Hanson, and Harrison 1994, on Mexico; Reidel 1975 on East Asian newly industrialized economies.

13. Blomstrom, Lipsey, and Zejan (1992) find that a 1 percent increase in the FDI to GDP ratio is associated with a 0.3 percentage point increase in per capita growth, though, interestingly, they find that this effect is significant only for the half of sample developing countries with higher incomes.

14. The importance of services in the process of global integration is perhaps best exemplified by the extent to which they are embodied in merchandise exports and imports. For high-income countries services (including both externally purchased and in-house services) account for 60–80 percent of the value of merchandise exports. For low-income economies the figure is only 20 percent (François and Reinert 1996).

15. Indeed, input-output analysis reveals that the dependence of the manufacturing sector on service inputs increases with per capita income. The relative importance of producer services in high-income countries is three times higher on average than in low-income countries (Park and Chan 1989).

16. High-technology exports are the share of differentiated and science-based goods in manufacturing exports. The classification is based on Lall (1996) and OECD (1987).

17. The median budget deficit for the whole sample was around 4 percent of GDP. The median for countries with significant FDI flows was less than 2 percent, while that for the low-FDI group was nearly 8 percent. The mean inflation rate for the whole sample was about 14 percent. Only three countries had inflation rates exceeding the 50 percent cutoff in the low-FDI sample. Differences in relative openness (using the openness index in Sachs and Warner 1996) were not significant in distinguishing low- from high-FDI countries.

18. See Dunning 1993, Caves 1996, or Pearce, Islam, and Sauvant 1992 for surveys.

19. See, for example, Root and Ahmed 1979; Lim 1983; Contractor 1991; Li and Guisinger 1992; Head, Ries, and Swenson 1994; Shah and Slemrod 1991; Koechlin 1993.

References

Abramovitz, M., and P. A. David. 1996. "Technological Change and the Rise of Intangible Investments: The U.S. Economy's Growth Path in the Twentieth Century." In OECD, Employment and Growth in the Knowledge-Based Economy. Paris.

Aitken, Brian, Gordon Hanson, and Ann Harrison. 1994. "Spillovers, Foreign Investment, and Export Behavior." NBER Working Paper 4967. National Bureau of Economic Research, Cambridge, Mass.

Aitken, Brian, and Ann Harrison. 1994. "Do Domestic Firms Benefit from Foreign Direct Investment? Evidence from Panel Data." Policy Research Working Paper 1248. World Bank, Washington, D.C.

Alexander, L. S. 1996. "Technology, Economic Growth, and Employment: New Research from the U.S. Department of Commerce." In OECD, Employment and Growth in the Knowledge-Based Economy. Paris.

Australia Bureau of Transport and Communications. 1994. International Aviation, Report 86. Canberra.

Balasubramanyam, V. N., and M. Salisu. 1991. "Export Promotion, Import Substitution, and Direct Foreign Investment in Less Developed Countries." In A. Koekkok and L. B. M. Mennes, eds., International Trade and Global Development: Essays in Honour of Jagdish Bhagwati. London: Routledge.

Balasubramanyam, V. N., M. Salisu, and D. Sapsford. 1996. "Foreign Direct Investment and Growth in EP and IS Countries." The Economic Journal 106 (January).

Bhattacharya, A., P. J. Montiel, and S. Sharma. 1996. "Private Capital Flows to Sub-Saharan Africa: An Overview of Trends and Determinants." World Bank, International Economics Department, Washington, D.C.

Blomstrom, Magnus, and A. Kokko. 1997. "How Foreign Investment Affects Host Countries." Policy Research Working Paper 1745. World Bank, International Economics Department, Washington, D.C.

Blomstrom, Magnus, A. Kokko, and M. Zejan. 1992. "Host Country Competition and Technology Transfer by Multinationals." NBER Working Paper 4131. National Bureau of Economic Research, Cambridge, Mass.

Blomstrom, Magnus, and Robert Lipsey. 1989. "U.S. Multinationals in Latin American Service Industries." World Development (U.K.) 17: 1769–76.

Blomstrom, Magnus, R. Lipsey, and M. Zejan. 1992. "What Explains the Growth of Developing Countries?" NBER Working Paper 4132. National Bureau of Economic Research, Cambridge, Mass.

Blomstrom, Magnus, and E. Wolff. 1989. "Multinational Corporations and Productivity Convergence in Mexico." NBER Working Paper 3141. National Bureau of Economic Research, Cambridge, Mass.

Borensztein, Eduardo, J. De Gregorio, and Jong-Wha Lee. 1995. "How Does FDI Affect Economic Growth?" NBER Working Paper 5057. National Bureau of Economic Research, Cambridge, Mass.

Bowles, D. 1995. "Telephone Penetration: Industrial Countries vs. LDCs." In D. Lamberton., ed., Beyond Competition: The Future of Telecommunications. New Yor: Elsevier Science.

Caves, Richard E. 1996. Multinational Enterprise and Economic Analysis. Cambridge: Cambridge University Press.

Chen, E. K. Y. 1983. Multinational Corporations, Technology and Employment. New York: Macmillan.

Chuhan, P., G. Perez-Quiros, and H. Popper. 1996. International Capital Flows: Do Short-term Investment and Direct Investment Differ? Washington, D.C.: World Bank and International Finance Corporation.

Coe, D. T., and E. Helpman. 1993. "International R&D Spillovers." NBER Working Paper 4444. National Bureau of Economic Research, Cambridge, Mass.

Coe, D. T., E. Helpman, and A. W. Hoffmeister. 1995. "North-South R&D Spillovers." NBER Working Paper 5048. National Bureau of Economic Research, Cambridge, Mass.

Contractor, F. J. 1991. "Ownership Patterns of U.S. Joint Ventures Abroad and the Liberalization of Foreign Government Regulation in the 1980s: Evidence from the Benchmark Surveys." *Journal of International Business Studies* 21.

Cowhey, P. F., and J. D. Aronson. 1993. *Managing the World Economy: The Consequences of Corporate Alliances.* New York: Council on Foreign Relations.

Djankov, Simeon, and Bernard Hoekman. 1997. "Avenues of Technology Transfer: Foreign Linkages and Productivity Change in the Czech Republic." Paper prepared for a Conference on Trade and Technology Diffusion: The Evidence with Implications for Developing Countries, April 18–19, Fondazione Mattei, Milan.

Dunning, John H. 1993. *Multinational Enterprises and the Global Economy.* Wokingham: Addison-Wesley.

Edwards, Sebastian. 1990. "Capital Flow, Foreign Direct Investment and Debt-Equity Swaps in Developing Countries." NBER Working Paper 3497. National Bureau of Economic Research, Cambridge, Mass.

Feenstra, Robert C., and Gordon H. Hanson. 1996. "Globalization, Outsourcing and Wage Inequality." NBER Working Paper 5424. National Bureau of Economic Research, Cambridge, Mass.

Feldstein, M. 1994. "Effects of Outbound Foreign Direct Investment on the Domestic Capital Stock." NBER Working Paper 4668. National Bureau of Economic Research, Cambridge, Mass.

Foray, Dominique, and Bengt-Ake Lundvall. 1996. "The Knowledge-Based Economy: From the Economics of Knowledge to the Learning Economy." In OECD, *Employment and Growth in the Knowledge-Based Economy.* Paris.

François, Joe, and Kenneth Reinert. 1996. "The Role of Services in the Structure of Production and Trade: Stylized Facts from a Cross-Country Analysis." *Asia-Pacific Economic Review* 2: 35–43.

Gereffi, G., and M. Korzeniewicz. 1994. *Commodity Chains and Global Capitalism.* Hartford, Conn.: Praeger.

Gerschenberg, I. 1987. "The Training and Spread of Managerial Know-How: A Comparative Analysis of Multinational and Other Firms in Kenya." *World Development* 15: 931–39.

Graham, Edward. 1996. *Global Corporations and National Governments.* Washington, D.C.: Institute for International Economics.

Haddad, Mona, and Ann Harrison. 1993. "Are There Positive Spillovers from Direct Foreign Investment? Evidence from Panel Data for Morocco." *Journal of Development Economics* 42: 51–74.

Halbach, Axel J. 1989. *Multinational Enterprises and Subcontracting in the Third World: A Study on Inter-industrial Linkages.* Working Paper 58. Geneva: International Labour Office.

Hanna, Nagy, Sandor Boyson, and Shakuntala Gunaratne. 1996. *The East Asian Miracle and Information Technology.* World Bank Discussion Paper 326. Washington, D.C.

Harvard Business School. 1985. *Nike in China.* Cambridge, Mass.: Harvard University Press.

Head, C. Keith, John C. Ries, and Deborah L. Swenson. 1994. "The Attraction of Foreign Manufacturing Investments: Investment Promotion and Agglomeration Economies." NBER Working Paper 4878. National Bureau of Economic Research, Cambridge, Mass.

Hoekman, Bernard. 1996. "An Assessment of the General Agreement on Trade in Services." In Will Martin and L. Alan Winters, eds., *The Uruguay Round and the Developing Economies.* Cambridge: Cambridge University Press.

———. 1997. "Globalization of Services." Background paper prepared for *Global Economic Prospects 1997.* World Bank, Washington, D.C.

Hoekman, Bernard, and Carlos A. Primo Braga. 1997. "Trade and Protection in Services: A Survey." Policy Research Working Paper 1747. World Bank, International Economics Department, Washington, D.C.

ICAO (International Civil Aviation Organization). 1992. "Outlook for Air Transport to the Year 2001." Circular 237-AT/96. Montreal.

ILO (International Labour Organization). 1990. *Structure Changes in Civil Aviation: Implications for Airline Management and Personnel.* Geneva.

IMF (International Monetary Fund). Various years. *International Financial Statistics.* Washington, D.C.

ITU (International Telecommunication Union). 1995. *World Telecommunication Development Report.* Geneva.

———. 1996a. *Direction of Trade.* Geneva.

———. 1996b. *World Telecommunication Development Report.* Geneva.

———. 1997. *World Telecommunication Development Report.* Geneva.

Katz, J. M. 1987. *Technology Creation in Latin American Manufacturing Industries.* New York: St. Martin's Press.

Koechlin, Timothy. 1993. "The Determinants of the Location of USA Direct Foreign Investment." *International Review of Applied Economics* 6(2): 203–16.

Kokko, A., and M. Blomstrom. 1995. "Policies to Encourage Inflows of Technology through Foreign Multinationals." *World Development* 23(3).

Lall, S. 1996. "Implication of New Technologies for Emerging Asia." Background paper prepared for Asian Development Bank's *Emerging Asia.* Manila.

Li, Jiato, and Stephen Guisinger. 1992. "Globalization of Service Multinationals in the 'Triad' Regions." *Journal of International Business Studies* 23(4): 675–96.

Lim, D. 1983. "Fiscal Incentives and Direct Foreign Investment in Less Developed Countries." *Journal of Development Studies* 19: 207–12.

Lipsey, R. E. 1996. "Internationalization of US MNEs and Impact on Developing Countries." Paper prepared for UNU/Intech Workshop, November 15–16.

———. 1997. "Globalized Production in World Output." Background paper prepared for *Global Economic Prospects 1997*. World Bank, Washington, D.C.

Lipsey, R. E., M. Blomstrom, and E. Ramsetter. 1995. "Internationalized Production in World Output." NBER Working Paper 5385. National Bureau of Economic Research, Cambridge, Mass.

Low, Patrick, and Alexander Yeats. 1994. "Nontariff Measures and Developing Countries." Policy Research Working Paper 1353. World Bank, Washington, D.C.

Lloyds. Various issues. *Shipping Economist*. London.

Lucas, Robert E. B. 1993. "On the Determinants of Direct Foreign Investment: Evidence from East and Southeast Asia." *World Development* 21(3): 391–406.

McKinsey Global Institute. 1996. "Capital Productivity." Washington, D.C.

Mendez, Jose A. 1991. "The Development of the Colombian Cut Flower Industry." Policy Research Working Paper 660. World Bank, Washington, D.C.

North, Douglas. 1958. "Ocean Freight Rates and Economic Development 1750–1913." *Journal of Economic History* 18.

O'Brien, Peter, and Yannis Karmokolias. 1994. "Radical Reforms in the Automotive Industry: Policies in Emerging Markets." International Finance Corporation Discussion Paper 21. World Bank, Washington, D.C.

OECD (Organization for Economic Cooperation and Development). 1987. *Structural Adjustment And Economic Performance*. Paris.

———. 1994. "Globalisation of Industrial Activities: A Case Study of the Clothing Industry." *OECD Working Papers* (international) 2(60): 1–53.

———. 1996a. *Employment and Growth in the Knowledge-Based Economy*. Paris.

———. 1996b. *Indicators of Tariff and Non-Tariff Barriers*. Paris.

———. 1997. *Technology and Industrial Performance*. Paris.

Park, Se-Hark, and Kenneth Chan. 1989. "A Cross-country Input-Output Analysis of Intersectoral Relationships between Manufacturing and Services." *World Development* 17(2): 199–212.

Pearce, R., A. Islam, and K. Sauvant. 1992. *The Determinants of Foreign Direct Investment: A Survey of Empirical Evidence*. New York: United Nations Centre on Transnational Corporations.

Pearson, Roy. 1992. *Container Ships and Shipping*. London: Fairplay Publications.

Peters, Hans. 1993a. "The International Ocean Transport Industry in Crisis." Policy Research Working Paper 1128. World Bank, Washington, D.C.

———. 1993b. "Service: The New Focus in International Manufacturing and Trade." Policy Research Working Paper 950. World Bank, Washington, D.C.

———. 1996. *Facing the Challenge of Trade and Industry Logistics Management*. Washington, D.C.: World Bank.

Petrazzini, B. 1997. *Global Telecom Talks*. Washington, D.C.: Institute for International Economics.

Reidel, J. 1975. "The Nature and Determinants of Export-Oriented Direct Foreign Investment in a Developing Country: A Case Study of Taiwan." *Weltwirtschaftliches Archiv* 3(3): 505–28.

Reinfeld, William. 1994. "Advanced Infrastructure and Its Role in Asian Economies." Background paper prepared for *World Development Report 1993*. World Bank, Washington, D.C.

Root, F. R,. and A. A. Ahmed. 1979. "Empirical Determinants of Manufacturing Direct Foreign Investment in Developing Countries." *Economic Development and Cultural Change* 27(4): 751–67.

Sachs, Jeffrey, and Andrew Warner. 1995. "Economic Reform and the Process of Global Integration." In *Brookings Papers on Economic Activity 1*. Washington, D.C.: Brookings Institution.

Schive, Chi. 1990. *The Foreign Factor: The Multinational Corporation's Contribution to the Economic Modernization of the Republic of China*. Stanford, Calif.: The Hoover Institution.

Schware, Robert, and Paul Kimberly. 1995. *Information Technology and National Trade Facilitation: Making the Most of Global Trade*. World Bank Technical Paper 316. Washington, D.C.

Shah, Anwar, and Joel Slemrod. 1991. "Do Taxes Matter for Foreign Direct Investment?" *World Bank Economic Review* 5(3): 473–91.

Singh, H., and K. Jun. 1995. "Some New Evidence on Determinants of Foreign Direct Investment in Developing Countries." Policy Research Working Paper 1531. World Bank, International Economics Department, Washington, D.C.

Slaughter, Matthew J. 1995. "Multinational Corporations, Outsourcing and American Wage Divergence." NBER Working Paper 5253. National Bureau of Economic Research, Cambridge, Mass.

———. 1997. "Measuring the Globalization of Production." Background paper prepared for *Global Economic Prospects 1997*. World Bank, Washington, D.C.

UNCTAD (United Nations Conference on Trade and Development). 1994a. *Liberalizing International Transactions in Services: A Handbook*. Geneva.

———. 1994b. *Multimodal Transport and Trading Opportunities* Report by the Secretariat. Geneva.

———. 1994c. *Review of Maritime Transport*. Various issues. Geneva.

———. 1994d. "Transnational Service Corporations and Developing Countries: Impacts and Policy Options." Geneva.

————. 1995. *World Investment Report*. New York.

————. 1996. *World Investment Report*. New York.

U.S. Bureau of Economic Analysis, U.S. Department of Commerce. "Survey Data (1977–94)." Washington, D.C.

Wacziarg, Romain. 1997. "Measuring the Dynamic Gains from Trade." Background paper prepared for *Global Economic Prospects 1997*. World Bank, Washington, D.C.

Wei, Shang-Jin. 1995. "Attracting Foreign Direct Investment: Has China Reached Its Potential?" *China Economic Review* 6(2): 1871–99.

Wheeler, David, and Ashoka Mody. 1992. "International Investment Location Decisions: The Case of U.S. Firms." *Journal of International Economics* 33(8): 57–76.

Wolff, Edward, and M. Ishaq Nadiri. 1993. "Spillover Effects, Linkages Structure and Research and Development." *Structural Change and Economic Dynamics* 4(12): 315–31.

World Bank. 1992. *Export Processing Zones*. Policy and Research Series 20. Washington, D.C.

————. 1993. *Latin America and the Caribbean: A Decade after the Debt Crisis*. Washington, D.C.

————. 1995. *Global Economic Prospects and the Developing Countries 1995*. Washington, D.C.

————. 1996a. "Competing Private Ports; Lessons from Argentina." Private Sector Development Department Note 100. Washington, D.C.

————. 1996b. *Harnessing Information for Development*. Washington, D.C.

————. 1997. *World Development Report 1997: The State in a Changing World*. New York: Oxford University Press.

WTO (World Trade Organization). 1996. *Trade and Foreign Direct Investment: A New Report by the WTO*. Geneva.

Yeats, Alexander. 1997. "Just How Big Is Global Production Sharing?" Background paper prepared for *Global Economic Prospects 1997*. World Bank, Washington, D.C.

Yi, Kei-Mu. 1996. "Outsourcing and the Growth in World Trade: Evidence and Explanations." *IMF Seminar Series* (international) 14: 145.

Zampetti, Americo Beviglia. 1994. "Globalisation of Industrial Activities: A Case Study of the Consumer Electronics Sector." *OECD Working Papers* (international) 2(44): 1–53.

3

Adjusting to trade liberalization

Policymakers in developing countries now widely recognize that opening economies to the outside world can bring many long-term benefits—more efficient resource use, increased technology transfer, and greater productive efficiency spurred by the discipline of world markets. Yet while many developing countries have liberalized trade policies, others have made only limited progress. One reason is concern that the costs of adjustment associated with trade liberalization might be high relative to its benefits, in particular, that they may be high enough in the short term to cause a reversal of trade liberalization before its long-run benefits can be reached. This chapter reviews what is known about the adjustment costs of trade reform and considers the circumstances and policies that may affect the size of these costs. It explores the following key points:

- Redeployment of resources induced by trade liberalization is not without friction. Workers in import-competing industries may become unemployed for a period before finding jobs in expanding export industries. Output losses suffered by the economy as a result of such unemployment are the social adjustment costs of trade liberalization. Their size will be linked to the rigidities or distortions affecting the movement of resources in the economy, as well as to the degree of macroeconomic stability and other factors affecting new investment. These costs are, however, usually limited in magnitude and duration, while the gains from a more efficient allocation of resources should grow with the economy. The empirical evidence suggests that the social costs of trade liberalization tend to be small relative to its benefits.
- The speed of adjustment to trade reform will be affected by the flexibility of labor and other factor markets. In the absence of extensive government intervention, labor markets in developing countries tend to work relatively efficiently, partly because of the importance of informal and agricultural labor markets. Stringent and strictly

enforced government interventions in formal labor markets (for example, extensive restrictions on dismissal of workers) can, however, delay adjustment and exacerbate its costs. In some countries, employment practices of state-owned enterprises, such as over-staffing, unrealistically high wages, or excessive job security, can constitute an important source of labor market inflexibility. The potential adverse effect of trade reforms on the finances of state enterprises can also cause governments to hold back from trade liberalization. Reforms of restrictive labor market practices and adjustment in state enterprises can therefore be important policies complementing trade liberalization.

- Adjustment costs will be minimized if there is a strong private investment response to liberalization, particularly in newly profitable export sectors. Macroeconomic stability is critical in securing such a response. Where investment is irreversible or entails significant sunk costs, high uncertainty about future business conditions because of macroeconomic instability may prevent new opportunities from being grasped. Large fiscal deficits will also make it more difficult to secure a real exchange rate depreciation—an important condition for offsetting possible adverse effects of liberalization on the external trade balance. Reforms that lack credibility because they are seen not to be sustainable in the long run will not evoke a sustained investment response. Although concerns about the adverse effect of trade reforms on government finances may be overdone when they relate to abolition of quotas or the reduction of very high tariffs, governments may need to enhance the efficiency and coverage of tax systems in the longer term to tap new areas of economic activity stimulated by trade liberalization as sources of revenue.
- While trade reforms are likely to have significant net social gains and contribute substantially to growth and poverty reduction in the long run,

the private costs of trade liberalization for some groups and individuals can be large. These include not only the costs of moving from one sector to another, but also permanent declines in returns to particular factors of production and destruction of rents shared between firms and workers in highly protected sectors. Private costs raise at least two important issues. First, losers from trade liberalization, who tend to be more concentrated and better organized than gainers, will strive to undermine and reverse reforms. Attention to the strategy and political economy of reforms may therefore be essential to their sustainability in the long run. Second, it may be desirable for equity reasons to set up a social safety net to help the most vulnerable groups adversely affected by trade reforms.

The adjustment costs of trade liberalization

After decades in which most developing countries pursued restrictive trade policies based on a program of import substitution, the 1980s saw a broad turn toward trade liberalization. Even so, as last year's *Global Economic Prospects* reported, there are major disparities in the extent of opening up by different developing countries and regions. A study of trade regimes in fifty-nine developing countries estimated that substantial progress has been made in reducing nontariff barriers but that opportunities for further liberalization remain, especially with respect to tariffs (IMF 1994; figure 3.1). Using a combined measure of tariff and nontariff barriers, the report noted that the number of countries with restrictive trade policies fell from forty-four in 1990 (of fifty-nine studied) to twenty-nine in 1993, but that most of the improvement was in Latin America and transition economies. The number of countries in Africa, the Middle East, and Asia (which in this study included mainly South Asian countries) classified as having restrictive trade policies fell only marginally.

Social and private adjustment costs

Like any other major policy change, trade reform generates both benefits and social and private costs. The social costs of trade liberalization refer to the value of output that is lost due to resources idled by liberalization. Sectors of the economy that had been protected by tariffs, quotas, and other governmental interventions may not be able to sustain output, capacity utilization, and employment once trade is liberalized. Firms in these sectors may shed workers faster than they can be absorbed in other expanding sectors of the economy. With idle resources, output will temporarily fall below its level before liberaliza-

tion. This shortfall is a measure of the social adjustment cost. The size of the gap depends on the number of workers unemployed due to liberalization, the speed at which the economy can absorb them, and the wage that they earn once they become re-employed.[1]

The size of social adjustment costs relative to efficiency gains will determine the welfare effects of trade liberalization, although it is unlikely that these costs would exceed the benefits. That is because the efficiency gains from trade liberalization are permanent and grow along with the economy.[2] By contrast, adjustment costs are limited to the output lost when resources become unemployed because of trade reform. These costs will be temporary to the extent that these resources are applied in new or expanding sectors of the economy in a reasonable time. In fact, there are good reasons to think that, in the medium to long run, trade reform will increase demand for labor in developing countries that have abundant labor and a comparative advantage in labor-intensive production.

Private costs of adjustment arise not only as a result of transitional unemployment but also when some workers and entrepreneurs—particularly those in once protected import-competing sectors—find their skills, talents, and investments worth less after liberalization than before because of permanent changes in returns to factors of production brought about by trade liberalization. Specific groups of workers and

---

Progress has been made, but there is still room for improvement

Figure 3-1 Countries with restrictive trade policies, 1990 and 1993

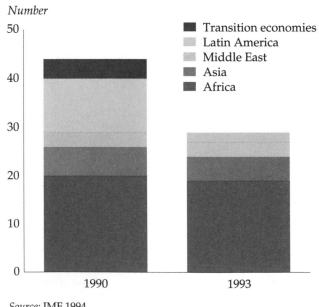

Source: IMF 1994.

firms also suffer from the destruction of rents they had previously shared in protected sectors. These private costs are virtually inevitable and can be large for the individuals who bear them. The reverse side, of course, is that other workers and entrepreneurs—particularly those in export sectors—find their skills, talents, and investments worth more after reform. These redistributive aspects of trade liberalization are likely to be important in determining the political feasibility and sustainability of reforms. There may also be equity reasons for adopting carefully designed social safety net programs to assist vulnerable groups adversely affected by reforms.

The chapter turns next to an overview of empirical work on the size of social adjustment costs. The number of studies attempting to quantify the adjustment costs of trade liberalization is small, and most focus on industrial countries and provide only indirect evidence for developing countries. An effort is made to summarize the results of most studies that apply to developing countries, the more important studies on industrial countries, and other studies of developing countries that provide indirect evidence of adjustment costs.

Trade liberalization and employment in developing countries

Several studies suggest that, in the absence of severe macroeconomic crisis, trade reform is consistent with continued growth in employment—even in the short term. One study of trade reforms in developing countries found that in all but one of twelve countries for which data were available, manufacturing employment was higher during the reform and a year after its completion than in the prereform period (figure 3-2). Countries that adopted the strongest liberalization reforms included those with the strongest employment performance, such as Brazil and Singapore. Indeed Chile was the only country that experienced lower manufacturing employment after strong liberalization, although this is widely recognized to have been due to macroeconomic factors such as extreme overvaluation of the real exchange rate and the impact of the world recession in 1982.[3]

These results are broadly confirmed in studies of several African countries (table 3-1). Employment growth among existing firms in five African countries remained mostly positive after trade reform, with

In most cases manufacturing employment rose during and after trade reform

Figure 3-2 Manufacturing employment before, during, and after liberalization

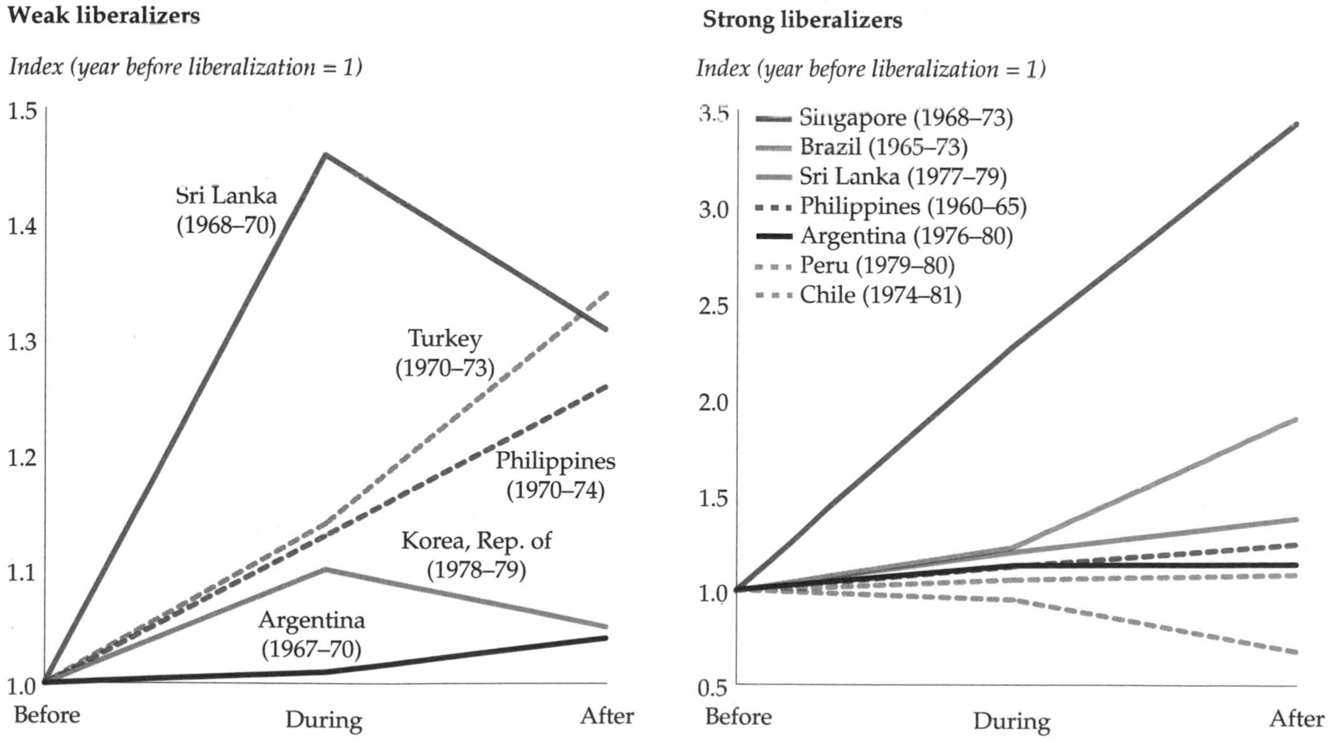

Weak liberalizers
Index (year before liberalization = 1)
1.5
1.4
1.3
1.2
1.1
1.0
Sri Lanka (1968–70)
Turkey (1970–73)
Philippines (1970–74)
Korea, Rep. of (1978–79)
Argentina (1967–70)
Before
During
After
Strong liberalizers
Index (year before liberalization = 1)
3.5
3.0
2.5
2.0
1.5
1.0
0.5
Singapore (1968–73)
Brazil (1965–73)
Sri Lanka (1977–79)
Philippines (1960–65)
Argentina (1976–80)
Peru (1979–80)
Chile (1974–81)
Before
During
After

Note: Years indicate liberalization period.
Source: Papageorgiou, Choksi, and Michaely 1990.

Table 3-1 Annual labor growth of firms after liberalization in five African countries
(Percentage change)

Number of employees[a]	All five countries	Ghana	Malawi	Mali	Senegal	Tanzania
1–5	+18	+10	+19	+24	+7	+20
6–20	+11	+6	–3	+20	+12	+10
21–49	+3	+3	+2	+2	0	+3
50+	+1	–9	—	+10	0	+17
All sizes	+5	–1	+5	+13	+2	+9

— Not available.
a. Total employment of the firm at the time of reforms.
Source: Parker, Riopelle, and Steel 1995 (table 6.2).

much growth coming from especially buoyant employment growth in micro- and small-scale enterprises. In Mauritius unemployment fell from 21 percent to 17.5 percent between 1985 and 1989, a period of relatively intense trade liberalization. By contrast, employment in the modern sector in Senegal fell 10 percent over the three years subsequent to reforms.[4]

A study of employment in six countries that underwent trade liberalization over the past fifteen years found that in Costa Rica, Peru, and Uruguay employment increased before, during, and after reforms. The same could not be said for the former Czechoslovakia, Poland, and Romania. The rise in unemployment in the transition economies of Central and Eastern Europe and the Commonwealth of Independent States (CIS)

has, however, been due to systemic reforms that go well beyond trade liberalization (Harrison and Revenga 1995; see box 3-1).

The conclusions to be drawn from these studies are limited. They do not suggest what the level or growth of employment and output would have been without liberalization. Without controlling for other factors that affect employment, it is not possible to say whether the number of jobs would have grown at an even faster pace or would have stagnated had trade not been liberalized. It is also difficult to gauge the impact of reforms on unemployment because joblessness could have risen if employment growth had fallen below labor force growth. However this does not seem to be the case in Costa Rica, Peru, and

---

Box 3-1 Trade liberalization and adjustment costs in transition economies

After the breakup of the former Soviet Union in September 1991, the fifteen newly independent states were faced with enormous adjustment problems, which included adjusting to a radically different trade regime. Trade among the fifteen states suffered a dramatic decline, which contributed to their output decline. Clearly, however, large adjustment costs should not deter these economies from moving toward a market economy and integrating into the global economy.

On the contrary, the evidence suggests that some newly independent states such as Estonia, Latvia, and Lithuania that implemented trade reforms most rapidly experienced the lowest adjustment costs. Output in Estonia began expanding in 1993, while output in the other two Baltic countries started to grow by late 1994. Slow reformers such as Belarus, Georgia, Ukraine, and Uzbekistan faced declining output for a longer period and still had much of their adjustment costs ahead of them (Michalopoulos and Tarr 1994, 1996).

Rapid reform has had such a positive impact partly because of the removal of previously extensive export controls. In many cases, the export tax equivalent of export quotas on raw materials was more than 200 percent. Removing export restrictions allowed enterprises to sell output in markets where they could obtain hard currencies and encouraged the efficient reorientation of production toward industries that were internationally competitive. In turn, earnings were used to purchase needed inputs for various industries, thus arresting the decline in output.

More generally, trade reform in transition countries has typically been part of broader reforms aimed at liberalization, macroeconomic stabilization, and systemic change. *World Development Report 1996* showed that in countries where liberalization has been stronger, output losses have been on average smaller and the difference has increased over time. Thus policymakers in transition economies will maximize people's incomes by liberalizing as much as possible within the range left open by country-specific constraints.

Uruguay, three countries for which unemployment rates are available. Here unemployment during trade reforms either fell or did not show a clear trend. Even with these qualifications, however, there is little evidence of employment falling after trade reform, except where there were other factors at play, such as severe macroeconomic instability or major systemic reforms.

Some recent studies analyze the links between trade liberalization and labor markets more explicitly. One study of the impact of the Mexican trade liberalization of 1985–87 on plant-level employment and wages concluded that each 10 percentage point reduction in tariff levels was associated with a 2–3 percent reduction in firm-level employment. Similar results were found for Uruguay.[5] In Morocco, however, substantial trade liberalization was found to have had little effect on employment in most firms, though the effects were large in some sectors. For example, employment in the clothing sector grew by 250 percent after reforms.[6] These results are suggestive, but do not really say anything about the effect of trade on aggregate employment. Because these stud-

ies are conducted at the plant level rather than the worker level, the authors cannot say what happened to dismissed workers—whether they suffered a spell of unemployment or quickly found employment elsewhere (box 3.2).[7] Of course, liberalization can result in substantial shifts of employment among narrowly defined sectors even when aggregate employment is unchanged. One simulation of the labor market effects of trade liberalization in Bangladesh (a country with powerful labor unions) projected widely divergent effects on labor demand. Under one scenario, trade reform could be expected to reduce labor demand by almost 11 percent in basic metals, but increase labor demand by more than 30 percent in leather.[8]

Measures of adjustment costs

Some analysts have tried to explicitly measure the adjustment cost of trade liberalization. Virtually all such studies have focused on industrial countries, but they provide some insight on adjustment costs in developing countries.

Box 3-2 Trade liberalization and wages in developing countries

Opening an economy to trade can be expected to result in a redistribution of income. Neoclassical trade theory says that countries tend to export goods that make intensive use of the economy's relatively abundant factors and import goods that make intensive use of the economy's relatively scarce factors. As such, the demand for the economy's abundant factors rises to meet export needs, while the demand for scarce factors falls because of competition from imports. Given the relative abundance of unskilled labor in many developing countries, trade liberalization could be expected to raise the wages of the least skilled relative to those of skilled workers. Because skilled wages are higher than unskilled wages, trade reform presumably creates a more equal distribution of income. What is the evidence?

Information on wage inequality in developing countries is sparse and mixed. Evidence from East Asia—particularly Hong Kong (China), the Republic of Korea, Singapore, and Taiwan (China)—supports the view that greater openness in countries with an abundance of unskilled labor benefits this type of labor. Indeed, this is why the development experience of these countries from the 1960s to the 1980s is described as the "growth with equity miracle." Even for these countries, however, the picture of relative wages is more complex, reflecting the interplay of the increase in relative demand for unskilled labor and the supply of skilled labor.

The generally favorable verdict on East Asia in the 1960s and 1970s has been brought into question by analysis of experience in Latin America in the 1980s. In some

countries (including Argentina, Chile, Colombia, Costa Rica, Mexico, and Uruguay) increased openness has been associated with widening wage differentials. However, studies of Chile have shown that poverty was dramatically reduced in the 1980s, despite little change in income distribution, and that the wages of unskilled labor increased relative to the wages of skilled labor in the 1990s.

One explanation: unlike East Asia, Latin America has abundant natural resources, so that greater openness favors production of resource-intensive commodities such as minerals. If, in turn, skilled labor and natural resources are complementary inputs, this could increase the relative demand for skilled workers. Another possibility is that openness has facilitated greater capital flows to the region and that capital and skills are complementary in production. This argument would be further strengthened if capital embodied skill-intensive technologies and if there were a skill bias in technologies developed in richer countries. Empirical work, however, has not as yet come down decisively in favor of one mechanism or the other.

Africa might also be characterized as having a comparative advantage in resource-intensive production but, to the extent that this is in smallholder agriculture rather than minerals, the advantage should favor the unskilled rural labor force. There is little hard evidence for Africa, but what does exist seems to suggest that greater openness and policy changes in the 1980s and 1990s are associated with recovery in growth and some reduction in poverty—but with an increase in inequality in some cases.

Source: Demery and Squire 1996; Robbins 1996a; Wood 1997; World Bank 1997a.

In the first study of this kind, Magee (1972) considered the costs and benefits of the United States completely liberalizing its trade with the rest of the world, explicitly accounting for permanent benefits of liberalization and temporary adjustment costs.[9] Adjustment costs are estimated by taking account of the number of workers who lose their jobs due to elimination of import barriers multiplied by their average wage, adjusted for the expected duration of unemployment (assuming that all adjustments are completed within five years).[10] The present discounted value of adjustment costs is compared with efficiency gains from liberalization, assuming different rates of discount. After only one year U.S. trade reform would create $5.70 of present value benefits for every $1 of adjustment costs. By the end of five years, trade reform would result in more than $8 of benefit for every $1 of adjustment cost. Even when the future is heavily discounted, for every $1 of adjustment cost the reforms generate more than $19 of benefit by the end of the fifteenth year and $26.50 when summed over an indefinitely long horizon.

This study focused on economywide adjustments, but others have looked at individual industries. For example, one study using data on voluntary separations in the British footwear industry concluded that the average displaced worker regained employment within seven weeks (Winters and Takacs 1991). This rapid speed of adjustment implies a huge ratio of benefits to costs. A number of other studies have also tried to quantify the adjustment costs of liberalization. While the details vary from study to study, the general findings are easily summarized, suggesting that the amount of resource reallocation likely to result from substantial liberalization will be small relative to the natural flows into (and out of) employment and that the social costs of adjustment are likely to be small relative to the social benefits (appendix 2).

What do these studies say about adjustment in developing economies? First, marginal benefits of trade liberalization are highest when trade barriers are large. A 50 percent reduction in protection should generate a larger benefit for a highly protected economy (such as India) than for a country where protection is relatively small (such as the United States). In addition, given that there is no well-accepted theory or empirical evidence characterizing the relationship between marginal adjustment costs and liberalization, it may not be unreasonable to expect that the ratio of benefits to costs in developing countries will also be higher than in industrial countries. A second point is that there are dynamic gains to liberalization that go beyond the static efficiency gains. The 1996 edition of *Global Economic Prospects* explored the links between freer trade and economic growth. Adding these dynamic considerations would further increase the ratio of benefits to costs. Adjustment costs, how-

ever, could be significantly higher if factor markets in developing countries adjust more slowly than those in industrial countries, implying lengthier spells of unemployment.

Speed of adjustment and labor market flexibility

The costs of trade liberalization are likely to depend on the flexibility of factor markets. In particular, inflexible or poorly functioning labor markets will slow the movement of labor from import-competing to export sectors and generate other adverse effects.[11] Most studies of adjustment costs explicitly account for the speed of adjustment by incorporating data on periods of unemployment or job turnover. Unfortunately, these measures are not typically available for most developing countries. The evidence seems to indicate a wide variety of country-specific experience. A survey of civil service workers laid off by the government of Ghana between 1987 and 1992 revealed that two-thirds experienced no spell of unemployment after retrenchment and that another 20 percent found work within a year. At the other end of the spectrum, the average length of unemployment for 1.7 million workers (almost 9 percent of the labor force) dismissed from Hungarian state enterprises in 1990–92 was estimated at 50 months.[12]

Role of labor market distortions . . .

Surveys of labor markets in developing countries have generally concluded that, in the absence of heavy government intervention, they tend be relatively efficient. For one thing, many workers in developing countries are in the informal and agricultural sectors, which are relatively flexible. This means that firms in expanding sectors may be able to draw on the pool of workers in those sectors, though the higher costs imposed by inflexibility in the formal sector will continue to discourage new investment. Minimum wage laws or other labor-market regulations are frequently evaded in many developing countries. Thus, in Morocco, despite minimum wage laws and restrictions on firings, firms adjust employment to changes in labor demand within a year, about the same pace as firms in North America. In practice, average wages in at least half the firms surveyed were below the minimum, and restrictions on dismissals were often skirted by hiring workers on temporary contracts. Noncompliance, however, may impose costs of its own (bribery, evasion, discouraging creation of firms above a certain size, and so on), which may still act as disincentives to investment in the wake of trade reform.[13]

Significant labor market distortions are often found to be closely associated with high trade protection. Banerji and Ghanem (1997) show this association in a sample of ninety developing countries and argue that governments that adopt high trade protection also tend to adopt restrictive labor market policies that allow workers in protected industries to share rents, usually at the expense of outsiders. Rama (1994b) makes a similar case for Uruguay, noting that unionization across sectors tends to rise with trade protection. In this view, trade liberalization will naturally generate pressures for the dissolution or dismantling of labor-market distortions.[14] An alternative interpretation is that high labor market distortions require governments to maintain high trade protection. Whatever the interpretation, labor market imperfections that outlast the product market imperfections that gave rise to them are likely to add to the problems of adjustment.

In particular, policies that prohibit firms from dismissing any employees without explicit government approval can slow adjustment to a crawl, if not stop it altogether. If firms are subject to foreign competition but are unable to reduce their work forces because of job security legislation, they may be forced into bankruptcy. This may have contributed to the reversal of Peruvian reforms in the 1980s. Rising import penetration ratios across industrial sectors were found to be strongly associated with falling output value but to have only a weak association with employment. The weak adjustment of employment in the face of falling output could have been due to strict enforcement of Peru's Labor Stability Law and may have contributed significantly to a fall in profits.[15]

While nominally designed to protect workers, regulations that make it costly to fire employees may result in lower labor demand, employment, and wages and hold back growth in expanding sectors. Research on India and Zimbabwe found that labor demand was depressed by the need to obtain government permission before dismissing any employee. Low exit rates out of unemployment in Sri Lanka are largely due to the Termination of Employment Act, which prevents firms from laying off workers without their written consent. Trade reform in Madagascar in the 1980s may have been hampered by labor regulations so severe that firms were not allowed to close if that meant firing permanent employees. In these circumstances, even though trade reform may create incentives for expansion of export-oriented sectors, firms may remain cautious about undertaking new investment because they risk being saddled with an unnecessarily large and expensive labor force. Thus reforms of labor market regulations may be an important complementary policy for successful trade reforms.[16]

. . . and of state-owned enterprises

The presence of a large state-owned enterprise sector is a significant source of labor market distortions in many developing countries. The state-owned enterprise share in total employment was particularly important in Africa, rising to 35–45 percent in countries such as Niger, Senegal, and Zambia in 1986–91. The state sector also played a significant role in formal sector labor markets in other countries such as Brazil, China, and India. Whereas private firms sometimes do not comply with regulations, state enterprises are often required to maintain or increase real wages independent of productivity trends or to act as employers of last resort, especially for graduates and the educated, resulting in considerable overstaffing. In Egypt, public employment rose 25 percent in 1976–86, four times the growth in private employment. Overstaffing is estimated to run as high as 93 percent in the spinning industry in Egypt, 91 percent in the port of Bombay in India, and 40 percent in Turkish railways. In some countries such as the former centrally planned economies, state-owned enterprises are important providers of fringe benefits, such as health care, education, and housing (Squire and Suthiwart-Narueput 1997).

These characteristics of state enterprise employment contribute to segmentation of labor markets, hamper labor market flexibility, and reduce the speed of adjustment to reforms by making workers reluctant to leave their jobs (and managers to fire them) or to take up new positions in the private sector. Or, as happened in Morocco in the late 1980s and early 1990s, state enterprises may serve as employers of last resort and increase employment while trade reforms are under way (Currie and Harrison forthcoming). In that case trade liberalization will often worsen the already poor financial condition of state enterprises (or of highly regulated formal sector private firms and, in some cases, of banks that make loans to these firms). Faced with losses in the state enterprise sector, governments may elect to increase subsidies, a policy that will frustrate the resource reallocation required by trade liberalization, aggravate fiscal deficits, and contribute to a reversal of reforms (as occurred in Turkey in the mid-1980s; World Bank 1995).

A better approach is to undertake reforms that encourage increased efficiency and flexibility in these firms, such as hardening budget constraints, privatizing, and increasing competition to reduce labor market and other distortions affecting these sectors. For example, Chile in the late 1970s and Estonia and the Czech Republic in the 1990s liberalized trade while simultaneously restructuring or privatizing state enterprises. Given the rents accruing to many workers and managers in state enterprises, it is not surprising that public sector labor unions are sometimes among the most vehement opponents of trade and investment liberalization. Nevertheless, the productivity of workers in state enterprises is often below their wages, so that the social adjustment costs of state enterprise reforms necessitated by trade liberalization will be less than the private costs they generate.[17]

Speed of adjustment and private investment response

If labor-market flexibility is a vital element in how quickly workers are able to redeploy from one sector to another, the conditions governing new (particularly private) investment are likely to be crucial in determining how quickly and extensively firms generate new jobs in export sectors.

Macroeconomic stability and credibility of reforms

Macroeconomic stabilization (in the first place the reduction of large and chronic fiscal deficits) is fundamental to ensuring the success of trade reforms for several reasons. First, macroeconomic instability—frequently reflected in high and volatile inflation and real exchange rates—will tend to generate uncertainty about the future, while also degrading the information content of relative price signals, the mechanism through which trade liberalization has its effect. In such an environment firms are likely to adopt a wait-and-see attitude before making largely irreversible new investments in the export sector. In analyzing the anatomy of export booms in developing countries, researchers have found that in most cases the greater part of export growth comes from firms becoming exporters for the first time, rather than from existing exporters expanding their operations. New exporters have to commit to significant start-up costs, including marketing, adapting products and packaging for foreign markets, and mastering bureaucratic procedures related to foreign trade. The more uncertain are the expected profits from exporting, the less likely are these investments to be made.[18]

Second, the reduction of large fiscal deficits is likely to be an important element in supporting depreciation of the real exchange rate, itself a significant condition for sustaining trade reforms. A real depreciation (in effect an increase in the price of tradables relative to the price of nontradables) will improve incentives for exports, while easing adjustment in import-competing sectors affected by the removal of protection during trade reform. However, devaluation of the exchange rate is unlikely to be translated into a real devaluation in the long run unless backed by restrictive fiscal policies that reduce demand for nontradables and allow a shift of resources into tradables. In the absence of a real devaluation, trade reform will likely increase the external trade deficit, which in turn will increase the skepticism of forward-looking economic agents about the credibility and long-run sustainability of the trade

reform. If firms expect trade reforms to be reversed, they are unlikely to undertake the investment in the export sector necessary for trade reforms to succeed. Similarly, expectations of a reversal of trade reform may induce consumers to borrow abroad and step up purchases of temporarily cheaper imports, behavior that could worsen balance of payments difficulties and bring on the collapse of trade reform.

Among the trade reforms studied by Thomas, Nash, and others (1991), the most substantial reformers also achieved the most significant reductions in fiscal deficits (figure 3-3). Papageorgiou, Choksi, and Michaely (1990) also note that of thirteen episodes in which trade reforms were sustained, only one was characterized by an expansionary fiscal policy. In most cases where trade reform was sustained, it began with an initial depreciation of the real exchange rate, and in no case in this study did a successful episode begin with an appreciation of the real exchange rate. Fiscal reforms and macroeconomic stabilization are thus important complementary measures to trade liberalization. However, it needs to be noted that the appropriate sequence of reforms will often be contingent on circumstances. From a political economy perspective, there is sometimes a "window of opportunity" to carry through trade liberalization, when opposition to it is weak. This opportunity often occurs in the midst of a macroeconomic crisis. Many countries have therefore conducted trade and fiscal reforms simultaneously.

There is also some support for the view that opening of the capital account should come after fiscal and trade reforms are in place. The reasoning is that macroeconomic stabilization may induce higher interest rates, that, with an open capital account, lead to large inflows that contribute to real exchange rate appreciation, erosion of export incentives, and increasing pressure to reverse trade reforms. The collapse of structural reforms in Latin America's Southern Cone countries at the end of the 1970s and in the early 1980s is often given as a case in point. In Argentina, for example, capital account opening before fiscal adjustment led to a sharp real exchange rate appreciation and a loss of competitiveness that precluded even the launching of trade reforms. More recent experience in some developing countries that conducted extensive liberalization of trade and investment regimes alongside exchange rate-based stabilization has also been the subject of much study. The short-run effect of such a policy mix is often a consumption boom, big capital inflows, and real exchange rate appreciation. In the longer term, it can lead to unsustainable increases in the external deficit unless steps are taken to correct the appreciation and to moderate demand. In this model, the costs of adjustment may be muted in the early boom phase but are likely to be larger in the later adjustment phase.[19]

Figure 3-3 Macroeconomic balances before and after reforms for twenty-four countries

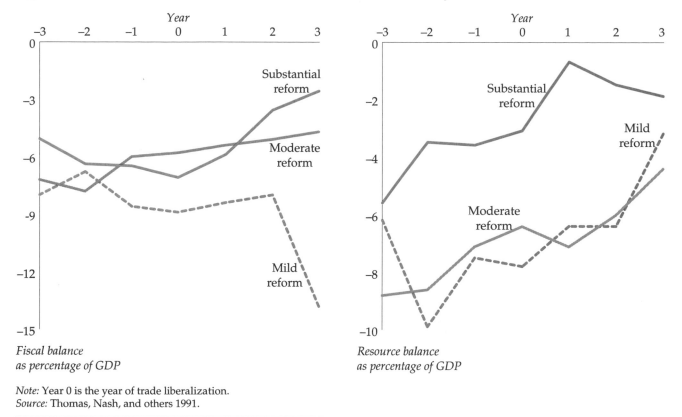

*Fiscal balance
as percentage of GDP*

*Resource balance
as percentage of GDP*

Note: Year 0 is the year of trade liberalization.
Source: Thomas, Nash, and others 1991.

There is also evidence that once factors such as macroeconomic conditions are controlled for, trade liberalization itself is associated with higher investment. In a study of the robustness of empirical relationships associated with long-run cross-country growth performance (so-called growth regressions), Levine and Renelt (1992) found only two relationships that could be described as empirically robust— first, the positive association between growth and the share of investment in GDP and, second, the positive association between the investment share and trade openness, measured as the share of trade in GDP. Baldwin and Seghezza (1996) provide further empirical evidence of the second link and spell out economic mechanisms that may plausibly underlie it. One is that the production of investment goods uses internationally traded intermediate inputs (electronic components, say) so that trade liberalization reduces the price of investment goods and triggers faster capital accumulation. Another is that the production of investment goods may be subject to scale economies, resulting in an imperfectly competitive market structure. Trade liberalization is likely to increase the degree of competition in investment

goods production, again leading to lower prices for those goods and a higher investment rate. Openness can also be assumed to increase the efficiency of investment, contribute to obsolescence of the existing capital stock, and increase demand for capital in the emerging export sectors. There is, moreover, further new evidence on the link between trade liberalization and investment (box 3-3). (Chapter 2 notes evidence linking trade liberalization with higher inflows of foreign direct investment.)

Impact of trade reform on government finances

Governments in developing countries tend to derive more revenues from taxes on trade than do governments in industrial countries, largely because of the greater ease with which international trade can be controlled and taxed. Developing countries are therefore more likely to be concerned that trade reforms may reduce revenues and increase fiscal deficits. The dependence of government revenues on trade taxes remains high, particularly, in countries in Sub-Saharan Africa, South Asia, and the Middle East and North Africa (figure 3-4).[20]

Box 3-3 Trade liberalization and investment

In an empirical study of the impact of trade liberalization on economic growth, Wacziarg (1997) calculates that a one standard deviation increase in an index of trade policy openness is associated with a 0.9 percentage point higher per capita GDP growth. The positive impact of trade policy openness on growth can be separated into different components, one of which is the impact on investment. Other channels are improvements in policies induced by greater openness and increased technology transfer. About half of the positive effect of trade policy openness on growth is due to its effect on the investment rate (see table).

Effect on per capita GDP growth of one standard deviation increase in the trade policy openness index
(Percentage points)

Variable	Direct effects	Indirect effects[a]	Total effects
Overall effect on per capita GDP growth	0.78 (6.7)	0.15 (5.4)	0.93 (7.8)
Factor accumulation			
Gross domestic investment	0.36 (4.5)	0.06[b]	0.42
Induced policy improvements			
Macroeconomic policy quality	0.18 (2.8)	0.05 (3.1)	0.23
Black market premium	0.04 (2.7)	0.02 (3.3)	0.06
Government size	0.05 (2.2)		0.05
Technology transfer			
Foreign direct investment	0.09 (2.2)	0.03[b]	0.12
Manufactured exports	0.08 (2.5)		0.08

a. Impact of trade policy openness on one channel through another channel.
b. Sum of several indirect channel effects, each with a t-statistic higher than 2.4.
Note: Numbers in parenthesis are t-statistics based on heteroskedastic-consistent standard errors (White-robust) and linear approximations around nonlinear functions of the initial parameters.
Source: Wacziarg 1997.

Trade reforms affect government finances in many ways. The most obvious is the direct effect of lower import tariffs on government revenues in the short run. Trade reform in developing countries, however, frequently includes substituting tariffs for quantitative import restrictions, a change that boosts government revenues. An examination of trade reforms in 1980–87 reveals that quota reformers, primarily countries that replaced quantitative restrictions with tariffs, experienced an increase in import taxes relative to GDP; tariff reformers, which concentrated on reducing tariffs, experienced lower import taxes relative to GDP (figure 3-5; Thomas, Nash, and others 1991). A World Bank (1992) study of nine countries undertaking trade-oriented adjustment programs in the 1980s concluded that trade taxes relative to GDP increased in Côte d'Ivoire, Ghana, Jamaica, Pakistan, and Turkey; fell in Indonesia, Mexico, and Morocco and remained constant in Colombia.

A second qualification: reducing high tariffs may reduce the incentive to smuggle, thus increasing the share of official transactions in imports. In addition, import volumes tend to rise as tariff rates fall, offsetting the loss of revenue arising directly from lower tariffs. Finally, a study of Jamaica, Kenya, and Pakistan suggests that actual tariff collection rates (the ratio of import taxes to import value) are generally much lower than official tariff rates due to extensive exemptions granted by governments, often on an ad hoc basis in response to lobbying (Pritchett and Sethi 1994). In Kenya, for example, collection rates averaged about 30 percent for products subject to a statutory tariff of 80 percent. Furthermore, the higher the official tariff, the less collections increased in response to a rise in official tariff rates (figure 3-6). Especially at high levels, official tariffs could be substantially reduced without simultaneously reducing collections. Furthermore, even when reductions in official tariff rates tend to reduce revenues, the effect can be offset by reductions in exemptions.

Nevertheless, these effects cannot always be relied on, especially when trade reforms move on from removal of the most extreme trade restrictions (such as quotas and high tariff rates) to reductions of more moderate tariff rates. Trade reform will also have indirect effects on government finances by changing the size and composition of the tax base and affecting aspects of government expenditures. In the short run domestic tax collections may fall if income and spending decline during the adjustment to trade liberalization. In the longer run the gains from trade reform are substantially larger than adjustment costs and should

Figure 3-4 Taxes on international trade in various income groups and regions, 1980 and 1994

*Percentage of central
government current revenues*

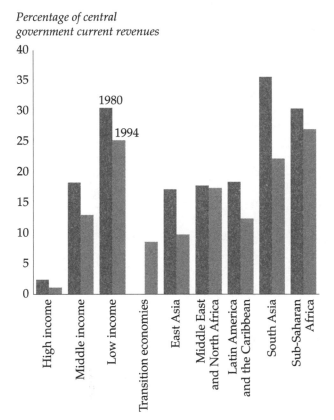

Source: World Bank 1997b and staff estimates.

Figure 3-5 Import taxes in tariff-reforming and quota-reforming countries

Percentage of GDP

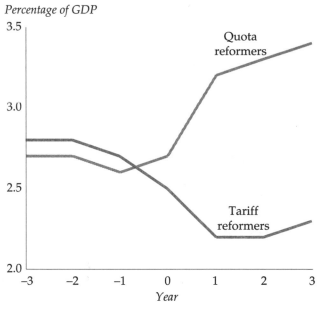

Note: Year 0 is the year of trade liberalization.
Source: Thomas, Nash, and others 1991.

*Raising already high tariffs has only
a small effect on revenue*

Figure 3-6 Official and collected tariffs in Pakistan and Kenya

Collected rate (percent)

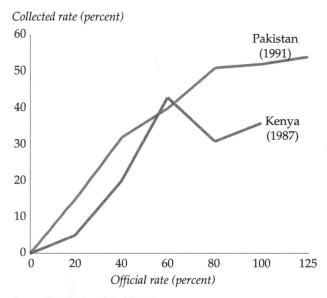

Source: Pritchett and Sethi 1994.

therefore yield a significantly higher domestic tax base and potential tax revenue. There may, however, be a temporary worsening in the fiscal deficit before new income sources and tax revenues kick in. A simulation of fiscal impacts of substantial trade reform in Kenya suggests that in the first three years after liberalization the fiscal deficit might average 0.5 percent of GDP higher but would converge to a level 0.5 percent of GDP smaller than before liberalization. This suggests a rationale for foreign assistance to help reforming countries cover temporary increases in fiscal deficits.[21]

To tap new areas of long-term income and spending generated by trade reforms, governments may need to improve coverage of the domestic tax base by improving tax administration and collection, raising rates or increasing the coverage of existing consumption or income taxes, or introducing new measures, such as a value added tax (VAT). In the case of Mexico, for example, a VAT was introduced some years before trade reforms, so that trade taxes were already a small part of government revenues when reforms began. For many countries, however, implementing such changes will take time and investment to build up the necessary skills, information, and institutions. Trade reform may also have indirect effects on government spending—for example, the cost of safety net programs to assist workers in transition to new jobs. In the absence of significant restructuring or privatization, losses of noncompetitive state-owned enterprises in import-substituting industries will tend to increase as competition from imports rises. These losses will increase the need for government subsidies, while restructuring of state enterprises or other government agencies may also impose a cost to the treasury in financial incentives offered to employees to induce them to quit voluntarily (box 3-4).[22]

Although there is little reason to believe that liberalization has a negative long-run impact on the fiscal budget, increased short-term financing may be needed. In addition, governments may need to undertake longer-term policies to complement trade reforms, including enhancing the efficiency and coverage of the tax system, and reform of loss-making state enterprises.

Dynamic role of micro- and small-scale enterprises

In considering the investment response to trade reforms, micro- and small-scale enterprises (fewer than fifty employees) can play a significant role in easing adjustment costs. In one sample of countries these enterprises accounted for 20–25 percent of employment in the 15–64 year age group. Their dynamic character—shown in an annual rate of new formations generally in excess of 20 percent, much higher than the 10 percent or so start-up rates typical in industrial countries—suggests that entrepreneurs in these countries are quick to respond to new opportunities, making speedy adjustment to trade reform likely (table 3-2).[23]

The adaptability of micro- and small-scale enterprises is confirmed by the findings of a survey of eighty-two small manufacturing firms in Ghana after trade reforms in 1983 (Steel and Webster 1992). The study investigated the view that industrialization in African countries is inhibited by a shortage of entrepreneurs. It found that the number of firms in which production rose after liberalization was about the same as the number in which it fell. Some firms benefited from access to imported inputs that were unavail-

---

Box 3-4 Designing efficient compensation schemes for public sector downsizing

The design of efficient compensation schemes for public sector retrenchment is the focus of a current study, indirectly supported by the World Bank, reviewing forty-one public sector downsizing operations. Detailed case studies are being conducted for Algeria, Argentina, Ecuador, Egypt, India, Kazakstan, and Turkey.

In many countries severance pay is required to induce workers to quit voluntarily, because of legal or political constraints. For example, a court ruling in Brazil forced the government to rehire 100,000 dismissed civil servants. In some cases trade unions may block any restructuring if members are not properly compensated.

One of the difficulties in designing severance packages that are economically efficient is to create incentives so that individuals choose to work where they are most productive. This is difficult for several reasons. First, productivity in the public sector is difficult to measure. While there may be some correlation between observable worker characteristics (such as education) and productivity, the correlation is not perfect. Moreover, it is difficult to determine who works hard and who shirks. Severance packages that are overly generous and offered to all employees might induce the most productive workers to leave. If this happens, public sector output may collapse, leading to rehiring of the same workers. In fact, such rehiring occurred in about 25 percent of the forty-one operations studied.

To appropriately target severance pay, it is important to identify both the services to be terminated and the occupational categories that are in excess. Mechanisms designed to eliminate ghost workers should also be implemented, because many workers who receive severance pay were working for the public sector on paper, but for the private sector in practice. Once targeting is complete, severance pay should be offered only to the workers who are targeted to leave. Moreover, the costs of downsizing can be reduced if the amount of severance pay is tied to observable characteristics such as age, education, number of dependents, and so on.

The cost of severance should be borne by the restructuring agency, not the general budget. If the agency pays the cost, it will fire an employee only if the lost output of the worker is smaller than the compensation needed to make up the worker's lost salary and adjustment costs. If funds come from the general budget or an outside agency, workers will be fired if their salary is higher than the value of their output, with no consideration of adjustment costs.

Finally, downsizing should include restructuring of public sector pay scales. Decompressing the wage structure may be a way to retain the most qualified civil servants. Civil servants could be given a menu of choices, including leaving with severance pay, staying where they are, or staying in the public sector at a higher wage but with a fixed-term contract. This choice should help retain hard-working civil servants who would choose the higher wage because they have good outside alternatives.

*High startup rates show the dynamism
of small enterprises*

**Table 3-2 Annual new startup rates for micro-
and small-scale enterprises**
(Percent)

Country	Year	Enterprise size (number of workers)			
		1	2–9	10+	Average
Botswana	1991	32.9	11.5	4.2	25.2
Dominican					
Republic	1993	—	—	—	20.6
Kenya	1992	33.7	10.3	1.6	21.2
Malawi	1991	26.9	14.1	13.1	21.7
Swaziland	1990	26.3	10.8	2.4	21.7
Zimbabwe	1990	22.8	10.6	18.7	19.3

— Not available.
Source: Liedholm and Meade 1995 (table 3.1).

able or expensive before liberalization. Many firms adapted by changing their product mix to specialized, nontraditional items, such as freezers and water coolers. Metal workers began producing gates and burglar alarms to supply the revitalized construction industry. A chalk producer who could no longer compete with imports began producing starch for the textile industry. Overall, 34 percent of firms surveyed changed their product mix after liberalization. The study found that the most severe constraint facing small firms was lack of access to finance for new investments, suggesting the importance of finding efficient ways of expanding access to capital markets. Reducing bureaucratic red tape and overregulation, which often bear heaviest on small firms, is also likely to be helpful.

Private adjustment costs: political economy and social policy issues

The limited evidence suggests that the social costs of trade liberalization may be small. But as with any significant policy change, trade reform creates winners and losers, and the private costs to specific individuals or groups could be large. Such costs may arise not only from the transitional costs of moving from one sector to another. They may also arise from the permanent changes in returns to factors of production that result from the changes in relative product prices accompanying trade liberalization, as well as from elimination of rents shared between firms and workers in highly protected sectors.

Discussion of the policy issues associated with private costs is important for at least two reasons. First, the losers from trade liberalization will almost invariably include politically well connected and influential

beneficiaries of protection who will strive to undermine the reforms. Attention to the strategy of reforms, taking proper account of their political economy dimensions, may therefore be essential to sustainability in the long run.[24] Second, policymakers will need to consider equity implications if reforms that are beneficial overall hurt the poorest or most vulnerable members of society. It may then be desirable to implement complementary social policies to soften the losses for this group or to assist them in making the transition to better opportunities.

Political economy aspects of trade reforms

The political difficulties arising from trade liberalization are exacerbated because the gains from liberalization are dispersed across many consumers and producers, whereas losses tend to be concentrated among just a few groups. This creates an asymmetry in the incentives for political action, with the opponents of reform likely to be the most active lobbyists. Moreover, complex economic interactions and incomplete information may make it difficult to identify the winners and losers in advance. Fernandez and Rodrik (1991) argue that this uncertainty could lead a majority to oppose change because they do not wish to take the perceived risk, even though it is known that most people will benefit.[25]

Although the evidence does not allow for many firm or unqualified conclusions, studies of experience with structural reforms, including trade reforms, in many countries over the past 30–40 years provide a wealth of details and many hypotheses about the successful political implementation of reforms. One of the most common findings (for example, by Williamson and Haggard 1994) is the necessity (though not the sufficiency) of having a coherent and united economic team in charge of reforms, something that, for example, precludes having people with conflicting views appointed in order to "let the president have the benefit of competing views." Summarizing case studies of reforms in eight countries, Haggard and Webb (1994) say that "one of the most consistent findings is the crucial role of bureaucratic organizations in both initiating and consolidating reform efforts. In every successful reform effort, politicians delegated decisionmaking authority to units within the government that were insulated from routine bureaucratic processes, from legislative and interest group pressures, and even from executive pressure."

They also note that in some cases taking this approach meant conducting administrative or institutional reforms to insulate and strengthen the position of the economic team relative to competing ministries traditionally tied to protectionist interest groups. For example, in Turkey the new democratic government transferred key powers to a new ministry reporting directly to the prime minister. In most cases of successful reforms studied by Williamson and Haggard (1994), the economic team also had the confidence of strong executives with a vision of where they wanted their country to go (see Nabli 1990 for a similar view). Commitment to reform of governments in Armenia and Estonia led them to persevere with reforms starting in 1992 despite having some of the highest adjustment cost of any reform program, whereas governments in some other transition economies, daunted by possibly smaller adjustment costs, resisted reforms (see box 3-1).

Even though the gains from reforms tend to be dispersed across many winners, who are usually less well organized and less motivated than losers, there are nevertheless actions politicians can take to foster the development of a broad coalition for reform. Thomas, Nash, and others (1991) note that if producers are organized in large umbrella bodies (including both winners and losers) both gains and costs will accrue within these bodies, which may deflect opposition. In Chile an influx of exporters gradually transformed the traditionally protectionist industry association into one favoring trade liberalization. In Mexico and other countries support for trade reforms was enhanced through regular consultations with the business associations representing the broadest range of industry associations. In Senegal, however, the technocratic reformers failed to consult with (or build ties to) potential private sector supporters, unlike the opponents of reform inside and outside the government, a failing that played a large role in the subsequent reversal of reforms.[26] As in Chile, Indonesia, and Mexico, reformers can also do much to win the battle of ideas by using the media to educate the public, through well-prepared presentations and arguments highlighting the ill effects of protection and rebutting media attacks on reform.

The design and implementation of trade reform programs can also affect their political sustainability. An important issue here is the speed with which reform is implemented. While there is broad consensus that macroeconomic stabilization and domestic price reforms should be conducted as quickly as possible, there is a range of views on the appropriate speed for trade liberalization. Rapid reforms, it is argued, may deprive opponents of the time they need to organize lobbying efforts. Speed can also signal the government's commitment to reform where economic agents are uncertain about the government's resolve, thereby increasing the credibility of reforms. In favor of more gradual reforms, it is argued that if firms are given more time to restructure, adjustment costs may be lower. By allowing more time to demonstrate positive results, a gradual approach may also favor the building of pro-reform coalitions.[27]

Another issue associated with design is that simpler rules are likely to be more effective in implementing reforms than are complex ones. For example, a strong political economy case can be made for moving to a uniform tariff, because it eliminates opportunities for rent-seeking and lobbying and throws the onus on interest groups to show why they should enjoy a different tariff.[28] Opposition to reforms can sometimes be assuaged by packaging complementary measures necessary to improve economic efficiency in such a way that losers from one aspect of reforms gain from another. Losers from import liberalization, for example, may be at least partly compensated by a supporting depreciation of the real exchange rate or labor market reforms. Haggard and Webb (1994) note that this kind of compensation was important in Chile, Mexico, Spain, and Thailand, but there was little evidence that direct compensation of losers played a role in securing the success of reforms. The direct compensation approach would raise concerns not only about efficiency losses but also about reviving the kind of rent-seeking behavior that trade liberalization discourages. Finally, the credibility of trade reforms may be greatly enhanced by embedding them in multilateral or other international trade agreements. However, firms or industries may still seek renewed protection by arguing for the use of antidumping regulations against supposed "unfair competition" from imports, a trend that has gained ground in developing countries in recent years (box 3-5).

Private costs and social policy measures

Even though trade liberalization is likely to yield significant net benefits to society and the poor, there may still be equity grounds for social policy measures to help specific lower-income groups that may be adversely affected by reforms to adjust to new circumstances (box 3-6). Private adjustment costs for specific groups can be high. American workers displaced from their jobs between 1980 and 1986 were still earning on average 25 percent less than they did in 1979. After fifteen months, employees displaced from their jobs at the Ecuadorian Central Bank in 1994 were earning on average only 55 percent of their pre-displacement income. There was no indication of any recovery in income despite low unemployment rates. One reason is that the central bank paid more than the private sector. Earnings losses for Turkish workers laid off from privatized cement firms and state-owned petrochemical firms amounted to 61 and 57 percent, respectively.[29]

In considering appropriate social policy responses to these difficulties, some points should be kept in mind. In most of these examples, earnings losses were industry specific and associated with the size of rents accru-

Box 3-5 Why developing countries should not introduce antidumping

In 1996 developing countries accounted for more than half the antidumping actions reported to the WTO (see figure). Sixty-one developing and transition countries have notified the WTO of antidumping legislation. Yet while antidumping provides a politically attractive cover for industries seeking protection, its costs to the country using it tend to be even higher than those of ordinary protection through tariffs. And in the infrequent cases in which there is a genuine problem of predatory pricing or an exceptional need to provide temporary protection, there are always less costly methods than antidumping.

Antidumping is costly because it gives the importing country leverage to force foreign exporters to raise their prices. Exporters have to choose between having a tariff applied on their export sales or agreeing to raise prices (a *price undertaking*) or to limit sales (a *voluntary export restraint*). Since exporters can typically increase their profits they usually prefer a settled agreement to the imposition of an antidumping duty. These agreements do not provide tariff revenue to the government. The effect on the importing country is similar to that of a foreign cartel: the exporting countries charge higher prices to the importing countries through an agreed limitation on sales or minimum prices. The costs to the U.S. economy of its own antidumping actions in the 1980s are estimated at about half the cost of the 1974 OPEC price increase (Finger 1991).

Indeed, it is the realization that antidumping hurts the national interest that is chiefly behind its reduced use by industrial countries since the mid-1990s. For several years after the start of liberalization Australia initiated more antidumping cases than any other country. Realizing that antidumping was vitiating its reform program, the government revised the law to allow it to determine antidumping actions on the basis of its general trade policy principles. In the United States, industries that rely on imported inputs, such as the computer industry, have brought increasing pressure on the government to take their interests into account in any decision to restrict imports. Antidumping initiations in the United States fell from more than 60 a year in 1992–93 to only 16 in 1996. In the EU, pressures from domestic industries that pay the cost of antidumping protection have combined with foreign policy interests to bring about a similar reduction.

Given the high costs of antidumping, why is it so popular?

- The rhetoric of antidumping, accusing foreigners of unfairness or predatory pricing to drive out domestic competitors, provides a vehicle to build a political case for protection.
- Special antidumping procedures allow discrimination against foreign firms when identical practices by local firms would not be considered unfair under domestic competition laws.
- The legal and administrative cost of the investigation process itself tends to curb imports.
- The action is unilateral, permitted by GATT and WTO rules, and requires no compensation.
- Particular foreign exporters can be picked out.
- In industries with few producers, antidumping can be used to enforce cartel pricing.
- The threat of antidumping action provides leverage to force an exporter to accept a voluntary export restraint.
- Governments effectively delegate trade policy to industries. Cases are typically initiated by petitions from industries and move forward in a technical and mechanical manner.

Antidumping's purported policing of predatory actions by foreigners is a major part of its emotional power. In reality studies find that predatory pricing is never an issue in the vast majority of antidumping cases (Palmeter 1988; OECD 1996). Antidumping is ordinary protection with a good public relations program. Nonetheless, political leaders may need to assure domestic interests that competition is "fair" and that predatory pricing will not be permitted. The appropriate policy tool for this purpose is domestic competition law, which applies to domestic and foreign firms alike. Domestic competition law rather than antidumping is the right way to create the "level playing field" often demanded by protectionist lobbies.

If antidumping is not the way to go, how should government evaluate requests for exceptions to liberalization? Here are some general guidelines:

Developing countries accounted for more than half the antidumping actions in 1996

Antidumping initiations reported to GATT/WTO

Box continues on next page.

71

- *Identify the costs and the losers.* The benefits of protection for import-competing firms should be compared with the costs to users of imports. Procedures should bring out the costs of the requested exception and the identities of those who will bear them, including the losses in employment and output in industries that use imported inputs. These costs and the people who will bear them should have the same standing in law and administrative practice as the other side already enjoys.
- *Be clear that the action is an exception* to the principles underlying liberalization. Applying protection multilaterally will encourage such actions to be exceptions.
- *Don't sanctify the criteria for the action.* Procedures should not imply that there is some moral reason

for an exception or compare the situation of the petitioner with pre-established criteria for granting an exception. Firms seeking protection will usually find clever ways to describe their situation so that it fits the criteria. Procedures should instead stress the function of the review as identifying the costs and benefits of the requested action.

When protection is offered, it should adhere to the "safeguard" procedures of Article XIX of GATT/WTO. Under Article XIX the protection must be multilateral and temporary. It requires (unless the action is for less than three years) a country that raises tariffs above its bound levels to provide compensation to its trading partners by lowering other tariffs or allowing retaliation against its exports. These costs are such that a country would only want to apply temporary protection in exceptional cases.

Source: Finger 1991, 1996; OECD 1996; Palmeter 1988.

---

ing in the original job. It was workers who, for given skills, were earning above-market wages in a protected industry who lost the most—the above-market wage premium having, in effect, been a transfer from workers in unprotected industries, which imposed efficiency losses on the rest of the economy. It is therefore difficult to rationalize a policy that would compensate for all earnings losses since this implies continuing transfers from workers in less protected industries. Moreover, not all displaced workers fare poorly. More than two-thirds of displaced Slovenian workers who found new jobs earned wages higher than before (Mills and Sahn 1995). Similarly, more than half the retrenched public-sector workers in Guinea who found new jobs did so at higher wages, though the average duration of unemployment for this group was roughly two and a half years and 30 percent of those who were retrenched between 1985 and 1988 were still unemployed in 1992 (Orazem, Vodopivec, and Wu 1995).

The private costs borne by dislocated workers and entrepreneurs need not coincide with social costs. Some workers may enjoy high wages due to distortions in the labor market, such as excessive union power or inflexible government wage scales. In those cases there is substantial private cost but few social costs as competitive pressures from trade reform force a reduction in the size of distorted sectors. Similarly, trade liberalization might induce changes in the market value of various forms of human capital. Workers who have accumulated significant amounts of firm-specific or sector-specific human capital may suffer a substantial private loss as the demand for skills declines. But these are no more a social cost than is the change in any price induced by changing market conditions.

With these qualifications in mind, social safety net programs may be important in helping the most vulnerable groups adversely affected by reforms. Important policy issues and problems arise in the design of such programs, and for some of these satisfactory solutions may not yet exist. How should programs be designed to deliver benefits only to target groups—the adversely affected poor—and avoid turning into an expensive welfare program? And how should benefits be designed to avoid sapping incentives for job-search or work? Some industrial countries use means testing to target assistance to the needy, but high administrative requirements may make this less feasible in developing countries. Partial solutions may include geographical targeting or self-targeting, in which benefits are designed to attract only those they are intended to help—for example, a subsidy on an inferior good consumed only by the poorest, or public works programs at below market wages. Examples include Zambia's targeted subsidy on roller meal (a coarse grain consumed only by the poorest), Jordan's use of coupons for purchase of subsidized basic items in fixed quantities equal to the consumption of the poorest 10 percent, and Chile's use of large-scale public works, a program that at the height of the economic crisis in 1982 provided work for 13 percent of the labor force. Where unemployment benefits are used, they need to be at a level and duration that minimize adverse effects on work incentives.[30]

Other policies involve equipping workers for change, from providing basic literacy and numeracy skills to helping workers take advantage of new job opportunities. In other instances, retraining programs may be useful in reducing social and private adjustment costs if they help shorten periods of unemploy-

Box 3-6 Trade liberalization and poverty

The effect of any policy on the poor is important, not only for local policymakers but also for the international community. Indeed, because the poor are frequently marginalized politically and socially (as well as economically), they may be under-represented in decisionmaking locally and rely disproportionately on outside agencies to look after their interests.

What is the effect of liberalization on poverty? First, experience suggests that rapid economic growth translates into sustainable reductions in poverty. Evidence also shows a significant association between trade liberalization and long-run improvements in economic growth. Thus, there is likely to be a positive link between liberalization and eradication of poverty in the long run. Second, it is probably too simplistic to talk about "the poor" without further qualification because the circumstances and causes of poverty vary greatly. Some poor people may be excluded even when there is a general reduction in poverty. Thus, generalizations about the effect of liberalization are likely to be scarce within a country, let alone across countries.

The major resource of the poor is their own labor. Trade liberalization affects a poor family in two ways. First, it affects the wages they earn and (if there are labor-market imperfections) whether they remain employed. If they are farmers, it affects the income they earn from the sales of products. Second, it affects the prices of the goods and services they consume. If trade liberalization raises staple food prices, producers (often poor farmers) will gain, while subsistence farmers will be unaffected and consumers (often the urban poor) will suffer. For example, in Peru, poor farmers produce little sorghum but much coffee. As a first pass, then, the liberalization of coffee trade will raise coffee prices (and relieve poverty) while action on sorghum prices will not. A converse case is maize farmers in Mexico, who will probably be harmed as the North American Free Trade Agreement drives down prices (Levy and Wijnbergen 1992).

Trade liberalization affects prices directly by reducing taxes and subsidies but also has indirect effects—that is, via the demand and supply of particular goods and factors. Thus, for example, the prices of nontradable services (for example, health services) or unskilled labor may change significantly and ultimately have a greater effect on poverty. Such indirect effects, however, are less predictable and often receive less weight in decisionmaking. These indirect effects can be mitigated to the extent the poor can change their behavior, for example by switching to a crop whose price has gone up.

Trade liberalization is likely to be associated with reduced poverty in the long run. In the short run, given the diverse nature of the poor, there is no presumption that trade liberalization has any predictable or immediate impact on poverty. The effects depend on the individual's precise circumstances and forecasting the effects requires detailed information and analysis.

Source: Bruno, Ravallion, and Squire 1996; World Bank 1990, 1996.

ment, though resources used in such programs are themselves a social cost and there is no conclusive evidence on their effectiveness. Nonetheless, there may be reasons for a government to take a more active role. Households may not be able to finance the cost of private sector retraining if capital markets are not well developed. In addition, the private return to retraining may be low for certain groups of disadvantaged workers, whereas the social benefits may be higher when improved social cohesion is taken into consideration. The effectiveness of retraining programs tends to be higher if they are demand driven, so that, for example, apprenticeships in the private sector subsidized by governments may work better than government-sponsored training programs.

Retrained Hungarian workers had slightly improved chances of re-employment at slightly higher wages compared to nonparticipants who were re-employed. The most significant difference was that participants obtained longer-term employment, indicating the potential for retraining to have a positive effect on the lifetime income of participants. It is not clear, however, if the benefits of the program were sufficient to justify the costs. The government-sponsored PROBECAT training program in Mexico provides short-term skills training to unemployed workers. A recent study found that it was effective in reducing the length of unemployment for participants with prior work experience and in raising the earnings of men. It had no effect on the fate of trainees without prior work experience or on women re-entering the work force. More generally, the costs and benefits of retraining need to be evaluated on a case by case basis.[31]

Conclusion

Given sound complementary policies, adjustment costs associated with trade liberalization are unlikely to present an adequate reason for delays in opening up to the outside world. But there is much that policymakers can do to minimize such costs. Perhaps the most important complementary policies are ensuring macroeconomic stability and the credibility of policies so as to foster a quick, sustained, private investment response in newly competitive sectors of the economy. Structural policy reforms to improve labor market flexibility and reform of the state enterprise sector may provide important complementary support. Of course, each of these policies is likely to be of great economic value on its own. The mutually supportive relations between trade, macroeconomic, labor market, and other policies may then serve to increase the credibility and payoffs to each.

In general, trade liberalization is expected to yield important net social gains. It is likely to play a significant role in poverty reduction both by raising returns to unskilled labor, where (as in many developing countries) it is the relatively abundant factor of production and, more significantly in the longer term, by contributing to faster overall economic growth. However, the private costs of adjustment for specific groups of entrepreneurs and workers in protected industries may sometimes still be significant. Apart from suggesting a need for policymakers to develop an adequate political strategy in support of reforms, this consideration also suggests the desirability for reasons of equity of carefully designing social safety nets to assist especially vulnerable individuals or groups who may be adversely affected by reforms.

Notes

1. See Matusz (1997) and Neary (1982) for more complete descriptions of this measure of adjustment costs.

2. Estimates of the efficiency gains from trade reform associated with reallocation of resources to more productive uses range from 1–2 percent of GDP per year up to as much as 10 percent of GDP per year if production is characterized by increasing returns to scale. In addition, elimination of incentives to smuggle, lobby, evade tariffs, and so on can generate an additional indirect benefit that has been estimated at over 6 percent of GDP in countries such as India and Turkey. Some of this evidence is cited in Thomas, Nash, and others (1991). Recent research also provides evidence that trade liberalization may improve medium-term growth by improving incentives to invest and long-run growth by boosting productivity growth.

3. In this study by Papageorgiou, Choksi, and Michaely (1990), as well as in most of the studies summarized later in this chapter, it is not possible to disentangle the myriad forces that might influence employment levels. Although trade liberalization occurred during the time frame examined, there may have also been changes in macroeconomic policy, the rate of technological innovation, the growth of the labor force, and so on. In addition, the focus on manufacturing employment may mask changes in employment (either positive or negative) that may have occurred elsewhere in the economy.

4. See Parker, Riopelle, and Steel (1995) on five African countries. The reforms undertaken by these countries went beyond trade liberalization to regulatory and financial reforms and reforms in public enterprises and the tax structure. The study considered reforms to have been the most extensive and thorough in Ghana, followed by Mali and Malawi, with Senegal and Tanzania having the least exten-

sive reforms. See Dabee and Milner (1996) on Mauritius; Foroutan and Nash (1996) on Senegal.

5. See Revenga (1995) on Mexico and Rama (1994b) on Uruguay. The burden of adjustment was, however, distributed quite unevenly in Mexico. Between 1984 and 1990 employment in tobacco, plastics, and footwear fell by 12, 20, and 22 percent, respectively. By contrast, employment in electrical machinery, metal products, ceramics, and printing and publishing rose by 13, 17, 26, and 38 percent, respectively. Using industry-level data for Uruguay, Rama finds that a 10 percent reduction in the implicit rate of protection was associated with a 5 percent reduction in employment.

6. See Currie and Harrison (forthcoming). Even among firms that were most affected by liberalization (around 25 percent of the sample) Currie and Harrison find that a 10 percent reduction in the tariff rate was associated with only a 1.6 percent reduction in employment. The authors suggest that the slightness of the employment impact at the firm level was due to firms adjusting profit margins and increasing productivity.

7. In fact, it is possible that plants were able to attain lower employment levels through natural attrition. Revenga (1995) also found that such liberalization was associated with an increase in the average wage. She conjectures that the average wage reflected a change in the skill mix of employment (see box 3-2).

8. See Devarajan, Ganem, and Thierfelder (1997). These are projected changes in labor demand, not changes in employment. Part of the shift in labor demand may be reflected in a changed wage structure rather than a change in employment patterns (see box 3-2). The authors of this study project wage changes, but do not report projected employment changes.

9. Because artificially protected sectors can be expected to continue to grow at the same rate as the overall economy, the magnitude of the distortion grows in absolute terms. The benefits of liberalization are therefore not only permanent, but they also grow in absolute magnitude as the economy grows.

10. Conceptually, liberalization could result in unemployed capital and land in addition to unemployed labor. However, because of limitations on available data, unemployed labor is often the sole focus of formal studies of adjustment costs.

11. Theoretical explorations of the impact of trade reforms under different labor market structures include Edwards and Edwards (1990) and Agenor and Aizenmann (1995).

12. See Alderman, Canagarajah, and Younger (1995) for Ghana; Haltiwanger and Singh (1996) for Hungary. The figure for unemployment duration in Hungary was derived by extrapolating from the rate at which unemployed workers were finding jobs in November 1992.

13. Berry and Sabot (1978) survey evidence on labor markets. Squire and Suthiwart-Narueput (1997) discuss the role of noncompliance in blunting the impact of regulations. See Currie and Harrison (forthcoming) for Morocco.

14. This view of the association between labor market distortions and trade protection is also made in Krueger (1988) and Rama and Tabellini (1995).

15. The study (Nogues 1991) suggests a second hypothesis, namely that entrepreneurs did not believe the reforms would be lasting and therefore found it more profitable in the long run to resist reforms than to adjust their workforce. Feliciano (1994) attributes the lack of impact of trade reform on employment in Mexico to restrictions on dismissals.

16. See Fallon and Lucas (1993) for India and Zimbabwe; Rama (1994b) for Sri Lanka; Thomas, Nash, and others (1991) for Madagascar.

17. The design of the tax system can also affect the flexibility of factor markets. Mussa (1982) notes that entrepreneurs move their capital from one activity to another only if the increase in the present discounted value of the stream of returns from the alternative use exceeds the costs of retooling. A proportional income tax will distort this decision and slow the rate at which capital adjusts to changes in the economic environment by reducing the marginal benefits of redeploying capital. One way to circumvent this problem is to provide an investment tax credit whereby entrepreneurs can deduct adjustment costs from taxable income.

18. Pindyck and Solimano (1993) and Leahy and Whited (1995) discuss the impact of uncertainty on investment. Roberts and Tybout (1996) discuss the anatomy of export booms.

19. Edwards and Edwards (1990) and Edwards (1994) survey discussions of the sequencing of reforms and describe the Southern Cone experience. See World Bank (1997b) on the role of exchange rate and fiscal policies in recent experience.

20. Based on fifty-three countries with data available for both 1980 and 1994 (World Bank 1997c).

21 See Blejer and Cheasty (1990) on the fiscal effects of trade reform; Bevan (1995) on Kenya.

22. Assaad (1996), Robbins (1996), and Basu, Fields, and Debgupta (1996) study the efficacy of various financial incentives in inducing voluntary separations from the public sector. Thomas, Nash and others (1991) note that losses by heavily indebted import-competing firms may also contribute to accumulation of bad debts in the banking system, which if left unchecked, may ultimately force the government to undertake a costly bailout. They note that adequate prudential supervision and regulation of the financial sector, including prompt action to write off bad debts, can greatly contribute to minimizing such effects.

23. The study also reports that the failure rate for micro- and small enterprises is also very high, with the rate of closures in the Dominican Republic being in excess of 20 percent in the early 1990s. In such dynamic labor markets, net employment changes may understate the gross numbers suffering some period of job loss but, given the fast pace of change, the average duration of unemployment should be relatively short.

24. Rodrik (1994) argues that reform becomes politically more difficult as the ratio of private costs to net social benefits increases. In principle, this ratio can range from a value of zero (where there are no losers and only winners) to infinity (where a policy is purely redistributive, having no net social benefits).

25. Of course, the same argument can be applied to suggest that, in the absence of other considerations, reforms that are implemented should receive strong support since they then become the status quo.

26. See Kaufman, Bazdresch, and Heredia (1994) for Mexico; Foroutan and Nash (1996) for Senegal.

27. See Rodrik (1989) on speed and credibility; Dewatripont and Roland (1992) on gradualism.

28. See Edwards (1997) and Panagariya and Rodrik (1993) on uniform tariffs.

29. See Jacobson, LaLonde, and Sullivan (1993a, b) on U.S. workers. A displaced worker is defined as one whose job loss results from the plant closings and mass layoffs associated with economic restructuring. See Rama and MacIsaac (1996) on Ecuador; Tansel (1996) on Turkey. The economic rents collected by these workers tend to overstate the expected private costs of adjustment that might accrue to a worker earning market wages.

30. Issues in design of social welfare nets are discussed in Subbarao (1997) and IMF (1995a and b).

31. O'Leary (1995) discusses the measurement of the effectiveness of labor market programs in Hungary and Poland. See also World Bank (1995b, box 17.1).

References

Agenor, Pierre-Richard, and Joshua Aizenman. 1995. "Trade Liberalization and Unemployment." IMF Working Paper WP/95/20. International Monetary Fund, Fiscal Affairs Department, Washington, D.C.

Alderman, Harold, Sudharshan Canagarajah, and Stephen Younger. 1995. "A Comparison of Ghanian Civil Servants' Earnings before and after Retrenchment." *Journal of African Economies* 4(2): 259–88.

Assaad, Ragui. 1996. "An Analysis of Compensation Programs for Redundant Workers in Egyptian Public Enterprise." Paper presented at a World Bank conference on Public Sector Retrenchment and Efficient Compensation Schemes. World Bank, Policy Research Department, Washington, D.C.

Baldwin, Richard E., and Elena Seghezza. 1996. "Growth and Trade." World Bank, International Economics Department, Washington, D.C.

Baldwin, Robert E., John H. Mutti, and J. David Richardson. 1980. "Welfare Effects on the United States of a Significant Multilateral Tariff Reduction." *Journal of International Economics* 10(3): 405–23.

Banerji, Arup, and Hafez Ghanem. 1997. "Does the Type of Political Regime Matter for Trade and Labor Market Policies?" *The World Bank Economic Review* 11(1): 171–94.

Basu, Kaushik, Gary Fields, and Shub Debgupta. 1996. "Retrenchment, Labor Laws and Government Policy: An Analysis with Special Reference to India." Paper presented at a World Bank conference on Public Sector Retrenchment and Efficient Compensation Schemes. World Bank, Policy Research Department, Washington, D.C.

Berry, Albert, and R. H. Sabot. 1978. "Labor Market Performance in Developing Countries: A Survey." *World Development* 6.

Bevan, David. 1995. "Fiscal Implications of Trade Liberalization." IMF Working Paper WP/95/50. International Monetary Fund, Fiscal Affairs Department, Washington, D.C.

Bleany, Michael, Merle Holden, and Carolyn Jenkins. 1996. "South Africa." Africa Economic Research Consortium, Nairobi.

Blejer, Mario I., and Adrienne Cheasty. 1990. "Fiscal Implications of Trade Liberalization." In Vito Tanzi, ed., *Fiscal Policy in Open Developing Economies*. Washington, D.C.: International Monetary Fund.

Bruno, Michael, Martin Ravallion, and Lyn Squire. 1996. "Equity and Growth in Developing Countries: Old and New Perspectives on the Policy Issues." Policy Research Working Paper 1563. World Bank, Policy Research Department, Washington, D.C.

Currie, Janet, and Ann Harrison. Forthcoming. "Sharing the Costs: The Impact of Trade Reform on Capital and Labor in Morocco." *Journal of Labor Economics*.

Dabee, Beealsingh, and Chris Milner. 1996. "Evaluating Trade Liberalization in Mauritius." African Economic Research Consortium, Nairobi.

de Melo, Jaime, and David Roland-Holst. 1994. "Economywide Costs of Protection and Labor Market Rigidities." In Michael Connolly and Jaime de Melo, eds. *The Effects of Protectionism on a Small Country: The Case of Uruguay*. A Regional and Sectoral Study. Washington, D.C.: World Bank.

de Melo, Jaime, and David Tarr. 1990. "Welfare Costs of U.S. Quotas in Textiles, Steel and Autos." *Review of Economics and Statistics* 72(1): 489–97.

Demery, Lionel, and Lyn Squire. 1996. "Macroeconomic Adjustment and Poverty in Africa: An Emerging Picture." *World Bank Research Observer* 11:39–59.

Dewatripont, Mathias, and Gerard Roland. 1992. "The Virtues of Gradualism and Legitimacy in the Transition to a Market Economy." *Economic Journal* 102(411): 291–300.

Devarajan, Shantayanan, Hafez Ghanem, and Karen Thierfelder. 1997. "Economic Reform and Labor Unions: A General-Equilibrium Analysis Applied to Bangladesh and Indonesia." *The World Bank Economic Review* 11(1): 145–70.

Dixon, Peter B., B. R. Parmenter, and Alan A. Powell. 1984. "Trade Liberalization and Labor Market Disruption." *Journal of Policy Modeling* 6(4): 431–54.

Edwards, Sebastian. 1990. "The Sequencing of Economic Reform: Analytical Issues and Lessons from Latin American Experiences." *The World Economy* 13(3): 1–14.

———. 1994. "Macroeconomic Stabilization in Latin America: Recent Experience and Sequencing Issues." IPR Working Paper Series 79. Institute for Policy Reform, Washington, D.C.

———. 1997. "Trade Reforms, Uniform Tariffs and the Budget." In Mario I. Blejer and Teressa Ter-Minassian, eds., *Macroeconomic Dimensions of Public Finance: Essays in Honour of Vito Tanzi*. New York: Rutledge.

Edwards, Sebastian, and Alejandra Cox Edwards. 1990. "Labor Market Distortions and Structural Adjustments in Developing Countries." NBER Working Paper 3346. National Bureau of Economic Research, Cambridge, Mass.

Fallon, Peter R., and Robert E. B. Lucas. 1993. "Job Security Regulations and the Dynamic Demand for Industrial Labor in India and Zimbabwe." *Journal of Development Economics* 40(4): 241–75.

Feliciano, Zadia M. 1994. "Workers and Trade Liberalization: The Impact of Trade Reforms in Mexico on Wages and Employment." Harvard University, Cambridge, Mass.

Fernandez, Raquel, and Dani Rodrik. 1991. "Resistance to Reform: Status Quo Bias in the Presence of Individual-Specific Uncertainty." *American Economic Review* 81(5): 1146–55.

Finger, J. Michael. 1991. "Trade Policy in the United States." In D.A. Salvataore, ed., *A Handbook of Trade Policies*. Westport, Conn.: Greenwood Publishing Group.

———. 1996. "Legalized Backsliding: Safeguard Provisions in GATT." In Will Martin and L. Alan Winters, eds., *The Uruguay Round and the Developing Countries*. Cambridge: Cambridge University Press.

Foroutan, Faezah, and John Nash. 1996. "Senegal." World Bank, International Economics Department, Washington, D.C.

Haggard, Stephen, and Steven Webb, eds. 1994. *Voting for Reform*. Washington, D.C.: World Bank

Haltiwanger, John, and Manisha Singh. 1996. "Cross-Country Evidence on Public Sector Retrenchment." Paper presented at a World Bank conference on Public Sector Retrenchment and Efficient Compensation Schemes. World Bank, Policy Research Department, Washington, D.C.

Harrison, Ann, and Ana Revenga. 1995. "Factor Markets and Trade Policy Reform." World Bank, International Economics Department, Washington, D.C.

Hoddinott, John. 1996. "Wages and Unemployment in an Urban African Labour Market." *Economic Journal*. 106(439): 1610–26.

International Monetary Fund. 1995a. *Social Dimensions of the IMF's Policy Dialogue*. Pamphlet Series 47. Washington, D.C.

———. 1995b. "Social Safety Nets for Economic Transition: Options and Recent Experience." IMF Paper PPAA/95/3. Washington, D.C.

Jacobson, Louis S., Robert J. LaLonde, and Daniel G. Sullivan. 1993a. "Earnings Losses of Displaced Workers." *American Economic Review* 83(4): 685–709.

———. 1993b. "Long-term Earnings Losses of High-Seniority Displaced Workers." *Economic Perspectives* 17(6): 2–20.

Kaufman, Robert, Carlos Bazdresch, and Blanca Heredia. 1994. "Mexico: Radical Reform in a Dominant Party System." In Stephen Haggard and Steven Webb, eds. *Voting for Reform.* Washington, D.C.: World Bank

Krueger, Anne. 1978. *Foreign Trade Regimes and Economic Development: Liberalization Attempts and Consequences.* Cambridge, Mass.: National Bureau of Economic Research and Ballinger Publishing Co.

———. 1988. "The Relationships between Trade, Employment and Development." In Gustav Ranis and T. Paul Schultz, eds. *The State of Development Economics—Progress and Perspectives.* Oxford: Basil Blackwell.

Leahy, John V., and Toni M. Whited. 1995. "Effect of Uncertainty on Investment: Some Stylized Facts." NBER Working Paper 4986. National Bureau of Economic Research, Cambridge, Mass.

Levine, R., and D. Renelt. 1992. "A Sensitivity Analysis of Cross-Country Growth Regressions." *American Economic Review* 82(4): 942–63.

Levy, Victor, and John L. Newman. 1989. "Wage Rigidity: Micro and Macro Evidence on Labor Market Adjustment in the Modern Sector." *The World Bank Economic Review* 3(1): 97–117.

Levy, Santiago, and Sweder van Wijnbergen. 1992. "Mexican Agriculture in the Free Trade Agreement: Transition Problems in Economic Reform." OECD Development Centre Technical Paper 63 1–92. Paris.

Liedholm, Carl, and Donald C. Mead. 1995. "The Dynamic Role of Micro and Small Enterprises in the Development Process." GEMINI Action Research Program I, Final Report.

Magee, Stephen P. 1972. "The Welfare Effects of Restrictions on U.S. Trade." *Brookings Papers on Economic Activity 3.* Washington, D.C.: Brookings Institution.

Matusz, Steven. 1997. "Adjusting to Trade Liberalization." Background paper for *Global Economic Prospects and the Developing Countries 1997.* Department of Economics, Michigan State University.

Michalopoulos, Constantine, and David Tarr, eds. 1994. *Trade in the New Independent States.* Studies of Economies in Transformation 13. Washington, D.C.: World Bank.

Michalopoulos, Constantine, and David Tarr. 1996. *Trade Performance and Policy in the New Independent States.* Directions in Development Series. Washington, D.C.: World Bank.

Mills, Bradford F., and David E. Sahn. 1995. "Reducing the Size of the Public Sector Workforce: Institutional Constraints and Human Consequences in Guinea." *Journal of Development Studies* 31(4): 505–28.

Mussa, Michael. 1982. "Government Policy and the Adjustment Process." In Jagdish N. Bhagwati, ed. *Import Competition and Response.* Chicago: University of Chicago Press.

Mutti, John. 1978. "Aspects of Unilateral Trade Policy and Factor Adjustment Costs." *Review of Economics and Statistics.* 6(1): 102–10.

Nabli, Mustapha. 1990. "The Political Economy of Trade Liberalization in Developing Countries." *Open Economies Review* 1(2): 111–45.

Neary, J. Peter. 1982. "Intersectoral Capital Mobility, Wage Stickiness, and the Case for Adjustment Assistance." In Jagdish N. Bhagwati, ed., *Import Competition and Response.* Chicago: University of Chicago Press.

Nogues, Julio. 1991. "Trade, Employment, and Growth in Peru Since WWII." In Demetris Papageorgiou, Michael Michaely, and Armeane Choski, eds. *Liberalizing Foreign Trade.* Oxford: Basil Blackwell.

O'Leary, Christopher J. 1995. "Performance Indicators: A Management Tool for Active Labour Programmes in Hungary and Poland." *International Labour Review* 134: 729–51.

Orazem, Peter, Milan Vodopivec, and Ruth Wu. 1995. "Worker Displacement during the Transition: Experience from Slovenia." Policy Research Working Paper 1449. World Bank, Policy Research Department, Transition Economics Division, Washington, D.C.

OECD (Organization for Economic Cooperation and Development). 1996. "Trade and Competition: Frictions after the Uruguay Round." Paris: OECD.

Palmeter, N. D. 1988. "The Antidumping Emperor." *Journal of World Trade Law* 22: 5–7.

Pangariya, Arvind, and Dani Rodrik. 1993. "Political Economy Arguments for a Uniform Tariff." *International Economic Review.* 34(3): 687–703.

Papageorgiou, Demetrios, Armeane M. Choksi, and Michael Michaely. 1990. *Liberalizing Foreign Trade in Developing Countries: The Lessons of Experience.* Washington, D.C.: World Bank.

Parker, Ronald L., Randall Riopelle, and William F. Steel. 1995. *Small Enterprises Adjusting to Liberalization in Five African Countries.* World Bank Discussion Paper 271. Washington, D.C.: World Bank.

Pindyck, Robert, and Andres Solimano. 1993. "Economic Instability and Aggregate Investment." NBER Working Paper 4380. National Bureau of Economic Research, Cambridge, Mass.

Pritchett, Lant, and Geeta Sethi. 1994. "Tariff Rates, Tariff Revenue, and Tariff Reform: Some New Facts." *The World Bank Economic Review.* 8(1): 1–16.

Rama, Martin. 1994a. "Flexibility in Sri Lanka's Labor Market." Policy Research Working Paper 1262. World Bank, Policy Research Department, Trade Policy Division, Washington, D.C.

———. 1994b. "The Labor Market and Trade Reform in Manufacturing." In Michael Connolly and Jaime de Melo, eds., *The Effects of Protectionism on a Small Country: The Case of Uruguay.* Washington, D.C.: World Bank.

Rama, Martin, and Donna MacIsaac. 1996. "Activity, Earnings and Welfare after Retrenchment: Central Bank

Employees in Ecuador." Paper presented at a World Bank conference on Public Sector Retrenchment and Efficient Compensation Schemes. World Bank, Policy Research Department, Washington, D.C.

Rama, Martin, and Guido Tabellini. 1995. *Endogeneous Distortions in Product and Labor Markets.* CEPR Discussion Paper 1143. London: Center for Economic Policy Research.

Revenga, Ana. 1995. "Employment and Wage Effects of Trade Liberalization: The Case of Mexican Manufacturing." Policy Research Working Paper 1524. World Bank, Latin American and the Caribbean Country Department II, Washington, D.C.

Robbins, Donald. 1996a. "Evidence on Trade and Wages in the Developing World." HIID Development Discussion Paper 557. Harvard Institute of International Development, Cambridge, Mass.

———. 1996b. "Public Sector Retrenchment: A Case Study of Argentina." Paper presented at a World Bank conference on Public Sector Retrenchment and Efficient Compensation Schemes. World Bank, Policy Research Department, Washington, D.C.

Roberts, Mark J., and James R. Tybout. 1996. *The Micro Anatomy of Export Booms.* Directions in Development Series. Washington, D.C.: World Bank.

Rodrik, Dani. 1989. "Credibility of Trade Reform: A Policymaker's Guide." *World Economy* (March).

———. 1994. "The Rush to Free Trade in the Developing World: Why So Late? Why Now? Will it Last?" In Stephan Haggard and Steven B. Webb, eds., *Voting for Reform: Democracy, Political Liberalization, and Economic Adjustment.* Washington, D.C.: World Bank.

Schaffner, Julie Anderson. 1993. "Rural Labor Legislation and Permanent Agricultural Employment in Northeastern Brazil." *World Development* 21(5): 705–19.

Squire, Lyn, and Sethaput Suthiwart-Narueput. 1997. "The Impact of Labor Market Regulations." *The World Bank Economic Review* 11(1): 119–43.

Steel, William F., and Leila M. Webster. 1992. "How Small Enterprises in Ghana Have Responded to Adjustment." *The World Bank Economic Review* 6(3): 423–38.

Subbarao, K. 1997. *Safety Net Programs and Poverty Reduction: Lessons from Cross-Country Experience.* Directions in Development Series, Washington, D.C.: World Bank.

Tansel, Aysit. 1996. "Workers Displaced Due to Privatization in Turkey: Before Versus after Displacement." Paper pre-sented at a World Bank conference on Public Sector Retrenchment and Efficient Compensation Schemes. World Bank, Policy Research Department, Washington, D.C.

Thomas, Vinod, John Nash, and others. 1991. *Best Practices in Trade Policy Reform.* Oxford: Oxford University Press.

Wacziarg, Romain. 1997. "Measuring the Dynamic Gains from Trade." Background paper for *Global Economic Prospects and the Developing Countries 1997.* World Bank, International Economics Department, Washington, D.C.

Williamson, John. 1994. *The Political Economy of Policy Reform.* Washington, D.C.: Institute for International Economics.

Williamson, John, and Stephen Haggard. 1994. "The Political Conditions for Economic Reform." In John Williamson, ed., *The Political Economy of Policy Reform.* Washington, D.C.: Institute for International Economies.

Winters, L. Alan, and Wendy E. Takacs. 1991. "Labour Adjustment Costs and British Footwear Protection." *Oxford Economic Papers* 43(3): 479–501.

Wood, Adrian. 1997. "Openness and Wage Inequality in Developing Countries: The Latin American Challenge to the East Asian Conventional Wisdom." *World Bank Economic Review* 11(1): 33–57.

World Bank. 1988. *World Development Report 1988: Public Finance in Development.* New York: Oxford University Press.

———. 1990. *World Development Report 1990: Poverty.* New York: Oxford University Press.

———. 1992. "Trade Policy Reforms under Adjustment Programs." World Bank, Operations Evaluation Department, Washington, D.C.

———. 1995a. *Bureaucrats in Business.* World Bank Policy Research Series. New York: Oxford University Press.

———. 1995b. *World Development Report 1995: Workers in an Integrating World.* New York: Oxford University Press.

———. 1996. *Global Economic Prospects and the Developing Countries 1996.* Washington, D.C.

———. 1997a. "Poverty and Income Distribution in a High Growth Economy: Chile 1987–1995." World Bank, Latin America and the Caribbean Region, Country Department II, Washington, D.C.

———. 1997b. *The Road to Financial Integration: Private Capital Flows to Developing Countries.* World Bank Policy Research Series. New York: Oxford University Press.

———. 1997c. *World Development Indicators 1997.* New York: Oxford University Press.

Appendix 1

Regional economic prospects

East Asia and Pacific

Growth in developing East Asia and Pacific slipped to about 8.5 percent in 1996 from near 10 percent the year before and an average of over 10 percent in the first half of the 1990s. In many countries tighter macroeconomic policies were adopted to reduce inflationary pressures and growing current account deficits. Tighter credit in the wake of the giant construction boom in the region in the first half of the 1990s contributed to a downturn in property prices and the emergence of bad debt problems in the banking sector in some Southeast Asian countries. A slump in regional export growth to 4 percent from 22 percent in 1995 also contributed to slower output growth. The export slowdown was largely the result of cyclical and special factors (see box 1-1 in chapter 1). Preliminary data for 1997 confirm a strong export recovery in China and Malaysia, although Thailand's performance remains weak (figure A1-1). Market pressure led to more or less severe adjustment of several currencies.

In China tight money and firmer controls over new investment by state-owned enterprises slowed output growth to 9.7 percent in 1996 from near 13 percent in 1991–95. Inflation fell to 8 percent from a 24 percent high in 1994. Tighter monetary policies and fiscal restraint also contributed to slowing 1996 output growth in Indonesia (by half a percentage point), Malaysia (1 percentage point), and Thailand (2 percentage points). With slower export growth, all three Southeast Asian countries ran larger current account deficits: 4 percent of GDP in Indonesia and 8 percent in Malaysia and Thailand. In Thailand a more severe export slowdown, the accumulation of bad debt problems in the financial sector, and a downgrading of sovereign debt ratings led to capital outflows and forced a sharp devaluation of the currency and a switch to a floating rate regime in 1997. Currencies in Indonesia, Malaysia, the Philippines, and even Singapore also came under pressure. While it is clear that growth in the more severely affected countries will slow in the next one to two years, the outbreak of a Mexico-style crisis appears unlikely. In most Southeast Asian countries domestic savings ratios are significantly higher than they were in Mexico before the crisis, while overall debt and debt service relative to exports are lower.

Elsewhere in the region, Vietnam continued to register exceptional export- and foreign-investment-led growth of about 9.5 percent. Growth among the small Pacific island economies of the region averaged only a little over 2 percent a year in 1987–95, but picked up to an estimated average 4–5 percent in 1995 and 1996. Significant output growth was achieved in Western

There is a strong export recovery for some

Figure A1-1 East Asia's export growth, 1993–97
(*Current U.S. dollars, year-on-year, three-month moving average*)

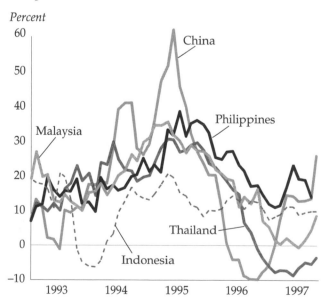

Source: IMF *International Financial Statistics*; Bloomberg; and World Bank staff estimates.

Samoa, which is pursuing economic reforms including privatization of state-owned enterprises and trade and financial sector reforms. In Fiji and the Solomon islands expansionary fiscal policies and continued high gold and timber production are underpinning economic growth but are unlikely to be sustainable in the medium term. Given the traditionally large role of the public sector and relatively high levels of trade protection, outward- and private-sector-oriented reforms will be important for the future in many of the island economies.

The external environment for East Asian and Pacific countries in 1997–2006 should remain broadly favorable. Solid world trade growth in the 6–7 percent range is expected to provide ample opportunity for export growth of 9–10 percent. Most countries are also expected to experience terms of trade gains because of lower primary commodity prices. While the U.S. dollar six-month LIBOR is projected to run about one percentage point higher than the average for 1991–96, the impact on regional interest payments would be relatively minor, about 0.5 percent of export revenues. Private capital flows to the region should continue to grow strongly in the coming decade, attracted by rapid growth and relatively open economies, although, as recent events indicate, avoidance of overheating and proper management of inflows will be important. Given a broadly favorable external environment and the demonstrated ability of regional policymakers to adapt quickly to changing circumstances, the long-term outlook remains good, although the risks have increased. Growth is expected

Growth is slowing to a more sustainable long-run pace

Table A1-1 East Asia forecast summary
(Annual percentage change or ratio)

Indicator	1987–96	Baseline 1997–2006
Real GDP	9.2	7.6
Consumption per capita	6.6	6.3
GDP per capita	7.7	6.6
Population 16–65 years	1.4	1.3
Median inflation[a]	7.0	6.4
Gross domestic investment/GDP	34.3	38.2
Budget deficit/GDP	–1.1	–1.2
Export volume[b]	12.4	9.6
Current account/GDP	–1.2	–1.6
Debt/exports[c]	98.0	66.0

a. GDP deflator.
b. Goods and nonfactor services.
c. Ratio of long-term debt outstanding and disbursed to exports of goods and nonfactor services plus net worker remittances.
Source: World Bank baseline forecast, June 1997.

to average a little more than 7.5 percent in the next decade, only slightly lower than last year's forecast (table A1-1). The principal risks to the projections come less from the external scenario and more from domestic policy weaknesses. The risks are greater in countries more exposed to external shocks by larger current account deficits, greater external debt, more fragile banking sectors, or a loss of competitiveness in recent years. Here a sharp, unanticipated rise in international interest rates or a slump in investor confidence and capital inflows could have more adverse impacts than currently expected.

The region's aggregate current account deficit is expected to remain quite modest over the next ten years, at less than 2 percent of GDP. Deficits in individual Southeast Asian countries have reached as high as 8–10 percent of GDP in recent years, though. Reducing these imbalances will require higher domestic savings or lower investment—or both. But with savings rates already high (36 percent with China and 30 percent without) and public finances in rough balance, more of the burden of adjustment may need to fall on private investment, especially to raise its efficiency. Apart from tighter macroeconomic policies, reducing high rates of effective protection that foster inefficient investments in some manufacturing sectors will be essential. Improvements in financial sector performance will also be critical in ensuring better discipline in investment selection and performance, for example to avoid excessive property lending. This will require improvements in prudential regulation and supervision, as well as better legal frameworks (such as bankruptcy procedures to deal with bad debts). More flexible exchange rate policies, adequate investment in physical infrastructure and labor quality, and liberalization of service sectors may be essential in ensuring the continued transition to higher value added and technologically more demanding production.

South Asia

The South Asia region is projected to average 5.9 percent growth over the next decade (table A1-2), a 0.5 percentage point increase on last year's projection. The revision is made chiefly on the basis of accumulating evidence that economic reforms have taken root and will grow despite governmental changes stemming from the region's vigorous but volatile democratic politics. Commitment to further reforms is being strengthened by the robust supply response to earlier ones, especially in India. Although political and economic instability are having more adverse effects in other countries of the region, there are signs that improving relations between countries may open the door to a reduction of military-political tensions, more concentration on reforms, and greater appreciation of the benefits of regional economic cooperation. India, Bangladesh, and Nepal signed agreements resolving long-standing disputes on the sharing of river waters. Moves to infuse reality into hitherto merely formal arrangements for freer regional trade appear to have gained ground.

The Indian economy grew 6–7 percent in 1994–96. Exports have boomed, growing at an unprecedented 15 percent real rate in 1992–95 and remaining close to the rate of world trade growth in 1996. Stabilization and reforms since 1991 have removed entry barriers, increased domestic competition, and liberalized the trade and foreign investment regime to some extent. Reforms have moved ahead despite changes of government in both 1996 and 1997. Changes over the past year include further liberalization of the investment regime and opening up critical infrastructure sectors to the private sector. Private investment increased by 4 percentage points to 18 percent of GDP between 1994 and 1996, pushing up the overall investment rate from 22 to 26 percent. The 1997–98 budget cut the average import-weighted tariff to 20 percent, with further reductions to come. Other policy changes over the past year included more incremental reforms aimed at improving financial system performance and deregulating agriculture (one of the fastest growing export sectors in recent years). Reductions in corporate and personal tax rates in the budget were unexpectedly large.

Big challenges remain though. Central among them is reducing a fiscal deficit running around 9 percent of GDP in the past few years, which, among other diverse and pervasive ill effects, hampers investment from being raised to the 30 percent-plus rates prevalent in East Asia. Inadequate private sector provision, lack of competition, and poor regulation contribute to severe shortages of infrastructure and low service sector productivity in many areas, seriously constraining potential growth. Such reductions in the budget deficit as there have been over the past five years have largely been achieved at the expense of infrastructure and other investment spending. Overregulation of agriculture and agro-industry continue to constrain opportunities in rural areas, where most people—and most of the poor—live.

In Pakistan growth declined to 3.1 percent in 1996–97, the result of weak performance in agriculture and large-scale manufacturing. Fiscal deficits substantially exceeded targets, and the current account deficit remained at 6–7 percent of GDP. A new and well-supported government was elected in early 1997. Faced with a looming balance-of-payments crisis, the new government presented proposals for sweeping structural and fiscal reforms. In Sri Lanka and Bangladesh political instability and persistent institutional weaknesses remain problems. Poor weather cramped Sri Lankan growth in 1996. Tourism revenues fell 30 percent due to the civil war, while a 40 percent increase in military spending contributed to a worsening of the fiscal situation. Even so, a strengthening of the government in local council elections may provide a better basis for bringing the fourteen-year civil war to an end. In Bangladesh elections in 1996 ended months of political turmoil, allowing the new government to launch further reforms, including measures to regulate the banking sector. Since growth is constrained by low savings and investment rates, the government aims to improve the environment for private investments. Measures include rationalization and restructuring of state-owned enterprises as a prelude to privatization.

Despite often tough political and institutional conditions, countries in the region are persevering with major economic reforms. The external environment for the region should prove favorable, with lower oil prices contributing to improved terms of trade and the phasing out of the Multifibre Arrangement under the Uruguay Round expanding market access for the region's apparel industries. On balance, the risks to current forecasts for growth may prove to be more on the upside than the down.

Latin America and the Caribbean

The year 1996 saw a better than expected upturn in the region's growth—real output grew about 3.5 percent, up from 0.8 percent in 1995—boosted by a strong

---

Reforms take root, growth is expected to strengthen

Table A1-2 South Asia forecast summary
(Annual percentage change or ratio)

Indicator	1987–96	Baseline 1997–2006
Real GDP	5.4	5.9
Consumption per capita	2.6	2.6
GDP per capita	3.3	4.1
Population 16–65 years	2.4	2.4
Median inflation[a]	9.5	6.6
Gross domestic investment/GDP	22.4	29.5
Budget deficit/GDP	–8.2	–5.0
Export volume[b]	9.8	10.4
Current account/GDP	–2.8	–2.1
Debt/exports[c]	253.0	168.0

a. GDP deflator.
b. Goods and nonfactor services.
c. Ratio of long-term debt outstanding and disbursed to exports of goods and nonfactor services plus net worker remittances.
Source: World Bank baseline forecast, June 1997.

surge in exports and in gross domestic investment. Net private capital flows to the region surged to $74 billion from $54 billion in 1995, while prices for external debt instruments of countries in the region soared.

Much of this turnaround came from Argentina and Mexico, where output had fallen sharply in 1995 in the aftermath of the Mexican peso crisis. Prompt adjustment measures in both countries allowed a quick 4–5 percent recovery in output accompanied by a resurgence of private capital inflows. In Mexico stabilization of the exchange rate at a competitive level contributed to a 15–20 percent surge in both exports and investment. Mexico was able to obtain $22.4 billion in gross bonds, loans, and equity issues from the international financial markets, compared with $10 billion in 1995, with short-term debt constituting only about 5 percent of total foreign indebtedness. In Argentina buoyant exports and investment could result in 1997 output growth markedly outpacing earlier official projections of 5 percent.

Most other countries in the region, however, saw growth slow. The median pace of growth in the region slipped to 3.2 percent from 3.7 percent in 1995. In Brazil GDP growth slowed to 3.1 percent from 4.2 percent in 1995, in part as a result of high real interest rates of 10–20 percent. Brazil has made several fundamental economic improvements in the 1990s, including trade liberalization and macroeconomic stabilization under the Real Plan of 1994. Inflation fell from 2,000 percent in 1994 to 11 percent by the end of 1996. Privatization of the large state enterprise sector, which began in the early 1990s, appears set to accelerate. Nevertheless, some key vulnerabilities remain. The tight monetary policy implicit in the Real Plan and enormous foreign capital inflows contributed to an appreciation of the real exchange rate and an increase in the current account deficit to more than 3 percent of GDP in 1996 from near balance in 1994. Further large increases in external deficits over the next couple of years could increase vulnerability to external shocks, such as a significant increase in U.S. interest rates. Progress on fiscal consolidation, the most important way in which to increase national savings and relax upward pressure on interest and exchange rates, has been less than desired, with the public sector deficit falling to 3.9 percent of GDP in 1996 from 5 percent in 1995, against a target of 2.5 percent.

Boosted by economic reforms and higher coffee prices, growth in the Central American countries picked up to around 4 percent in the first half of the 1990s from less than 1 percent in the 1980s. Fiscal tightening in a number of countries, a slowing in workers' remittances, and a downturn in coffee prices contributed to slowing the subregion's growth to 2.4 percent in 1996. In the aggregate the Caribbean island economies have experienced virtually no growth so far in the 1990s (0.2 percent a year). Strong growth in the Dominican Republic was offset by sluggishness in Jamaica (due in part to a financial sector crisis) and contraction in Haiti. The outlook for countries in Central America and the Caribbean is for modest growth averaging 3.5–4 percent a year in 1997–2006. Appreciation of real exchange rates in a number of countries has eroded competitiveness in the U.S. market relative to Mexico. The expected decline in the real price of key commodities for the region (bananas, coffee, bauxite, oil, sugar) will continue to exert pressure on current accounts.

Raising domestic savings rates to allow higher investment and faster growth without undue reliance on foreign borrowing is an important objective for many countries in the region. Between 1990 and 1994, in the lead-up to the Mexico crisis, the region's domestic saving to GDP ratio fell by 3 percentage points while foreign saving rose by the same amount. Much of these inflows went to finance higher consumption rather than investment. The position was reversed in 1995–96, when savings rates rose by 3 percent of GDP for the region excluding Brazil. Increases amounted to more than 5 percentage points in Mexico and Venezuela; 1–2 percentage points in Colombia, Peru, and many Central American countries; and less than 1 percentage point in Argentina (figure A1-2). Apart from fiscal consolidation, many countries are undertaking longer-term structural reforms to improve domestic savings rates, for example, moving to fully funded pension systems and introducing financial and banking sector reforms that should improve the confidence of savers. The main exception to the trend toward higher domestic saving has been Brazil, where the savings rate fell by 4 percentage points between 1994 and 1996, while foreign saving (the current account deficit) rose by 3 percentage points.

Given the enormous gains in macroeconomic stabilization and structural reforms achieved by the region over the past decade, and with most countries in the region continuing to move ahead with reforms, regional growth is expected to improve from 2.3 percent in 1987–96 to a little over 4 percent in 1997–2006, or 2.7 percent in per capita terms (table A1-3). Growth is expected to be somewhat higher in the second part of the forecast period, in part because policies to increase domestic savings, particularly microeconomic measures aimed at private savers, may take time to design, implement, and take effect. Higher unemployment and approaching elections in many countries may prove a test of how far governments have truly moved away from populist traditions.

Regional output growth in the early part of the projection period is also assumed to be subdued by orderly macroeconomic adjustment in Brazil over the next few years. However, if Brazil's current account

Figure A1-2 Domestic saving and current account balance
Percentage of GDP

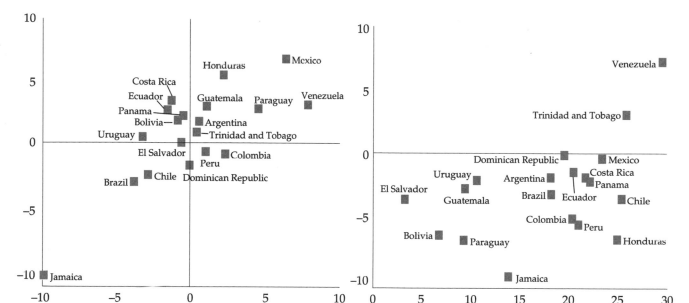

Change in domestic saving and current account balance between 1994 and 1996

Change in current account balance

Domestic saving and current account balance, 1996

Current account balance

Source: World Bank data.

deficit continued to rise at the same rate as in 1995–96, the risk of a capital flow reversal and a quicker adjustment would increase, especially if foreign interest rates were to rise substantially. In this eventuality the knock-on effects on other countries in the region could be larger than those in the Mexican peso crisis because Brazil is an important export market for many of these countries. The increased reliance on volatile portfolio flows for external financing over the past year in a range of countries might also add to vulnerability if there were a surge in U.S. interest rates, in particular where macroeconomic imbalances and banking sector vulnerabilities are high.

The region's export volumes grew 10 percent a year in the 1990s, with 60 percent of the growth from members of Mercosur and NAFTA. Half the export growth enjoyed by Mercosur member countries was due to trade within the group, reflecting both one-off increases in the level of trade due to tariff and quota reductions and large capital inflows. Regional trading arrangements are becoming increasingly important to the region's development strategy and have contributed to consolidating its outward orientation. For

A marked rise in per capita income growth is expected

Table A1-3 Latin America and the Caribbean forecast summary
(Annual percentage change or ratio)

Indicator	1987–96	Baseline 1997–2006
Real GDP	2.3	4.2
Consumption per capita	1.0	2.4
GDP per capita	0.5	2.7
Population 16–65 years	2.4	2.1
Median inflation[a]	20.4	9.1
Gross domestic investment/GDP	20.9	24.4
Budget deficit/GDP	−3.6	−0.2
Export volume[b]	6.7	6.5
Current account/GDP	−1.8	−2.7
Debt/exports[c]	210.0	150.0

a. GDP deflator.
b. Goods and nonfactor services.
c. Ratio of long-term debt outstanding and disbursed to exports of goods and nonfactor services plus net worker remittances.
Source: World Bank baseline forecast, June 1997.

the future, it remains important that these arrangements continue to serve as building blocks for greater integration with the world economy.

Europe and Central Asia

Growth among transition economies in the Europe and Central Asia region in 1996 generally turned out lower than expected, a result of continued decline in Russian and Ukrainian output, slower export growth in the Central and Eastern European countries, and the initial effects of austerity measures in several countries. Nonetheless, fundamentals supporting growth remain favorable for the near and medium term. Improving conditions in EU export markets and continued strength in investment should support a rebound in the Central and Eastern European countries' growth toward 4–4.5 percent. Increasingly stable macroeconomic conditions in Russia, Ukraine, and several other countries of the former Soviet Union are likely to boost real incomes and consumption, setting the stage for a pick-up in investment spending. Although there are risks of policy slippage in some countries of the former Soviet Union, a favorable scenario would see stabilization of output in 1997, with growth accelerating to 5–6 percent by the turn of the century (figure A1-3).

Recent developments have underscored the difficult macroeconomic issues being addressed by all the Central and Eastern European countries. Strong capital inflows to the Czech Republic, Hungary, and Poland have complicated management of the money supply and exchange and interest rates at a time when export growth has weakened and the risk of domestic "overheating" in some countries has increased. Reducing inflation to EU levels will also present significant challenges. After some years marked by lack of effective policy implementation, tighter macroeconomic policies were introduced in Romania following elections. But financial crises in Bulgaria and Albania and concerns regarding banking systems in the Baltic countries highlight the underlying fragility of financial systems in the region and the continuing diversity of performance.

One of the more promising developments in the first half of the 1990s was the strong export performance of the Baltic states, the Czech Republic, Hungary, Poland, Russia, and the Slovak Republic. Export growth in leading countries of Central and Eastern Europe reached 20 percent by 1995 (in ECU terms), reflecting strong import demand in the EU and gains in market share in several sectors, supported by substantial inflows of FDI. But with the recent downturn in EU activity, export growth in Central and Eastern Europe decelerated sharply to 5 percent in 1996–97. At the same time, continued strength in

domestic demand and imports led to widening trade and current account deficits—in the Czech Republic to 8–9 percent of GDP. In the early months of 1997 measures to slow the pace of credit expansion and consumption and import growth were introduced in some countries.

In Russia crude oil and gas export volumes rose about 4 percent in 1996. Overall export revenues were further boosted by higher oil and metals prices. Prospects for longer-term export performance are somewhat less encouraging, as oil output has dropped to its lowest level in thirty years, sapped by delays in development and infrastructure maintenance projects. With expected declines in world crude oil prices over the longer term, total export revenues are anticipated to grow modestly unless new investment and efficiency improvements are achieved.

Private capital flows to the region were flat at around $30 billion in 1996, though this masked wide variations. Countries such as the Czech Republic, Hungary, and Poland continued to receive significant inflows of FDI and rising portfolio equity investment in stock markets. A $1.2 billion seven-year Russian Eurobond was well received, following a five-year $1 billion issue in November 1996. Earlier Paris and London Club reschedulings, covering some 60 percent of outstanding claims on Russia, set the stage for improved perceptions of creditworthiness. And foreign flows into equities and T-bills have risen in recent months.

Growth will revive in all parts of the region

Figure A1-3 GDP growth in transition economies, 1991–96 and 1997–2006

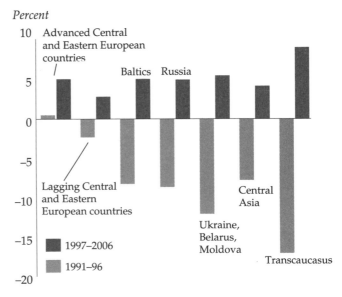

Source: World Bank data and projections.

If all goes according to plan, the year 2002 will see both the full implementation of the European Monetary Union (EMU) and the admission of the first new members from Central and Eastern Europe into the EU. The transition phase leading up to the EMU could have some adverse short-run implications for these countries, however, including slower EU growth, a decline in discretionary official development assistance because of EMU fiscal criteria, and the possibility of heightened anti-immigration sentiment given the necessary labor market adjustments in the EU. The EMU also implies significant additional challenges for harmonization of policy. Even though the aspiring entrants have made great progress in developing market institutions, harmonizing rules to EU standards, and upgrading financial sector technologies, there is still much to be done. But the long-run benefits of integration with the EMU bloc could be significant in principle, including slightly higher long-run growth and lower inflation and interest rates.

Growth in Central and Eastern European countries is expected to recover modestly to 3.5 percent in 1997 from 3 percent in 1996, restrained by cooling con-

*A return to positive growth
gradually spreads through the region*

Table A1-4 Europe and Central Asia forecast summary
(Annual percentage change or ratio)

Indicator	1987–96	Baseline 1997–2006
Real GDP	–2.6	4.5
Consumption per capita	–0.8	3.5
GDP per capita	–3.1	4.0
Population 16–65 years	0.6	0.8
Median inflation[a]	29.5	12.4
Gross domestic investment/GDP	32.4	29.6
Budget deficit/GDP	–7.8	–3.0
Export volume[b]	3.3	5.5
Current account/GDP	1.1	–0.2
Debt/exports[c]	132	100
Memorandum items		
GDP of middle-income		
Western Europe	3.3	4.0
GDP of Central and		
Eastern Europe	–1.2	4.5
GDP of former Soviet Union	–5.3	4.8

a. GDP deflator.
b. Goods and nonfactor services.
c. Ratio of long-term debt outstanding and disbursed to exports of goods and nonfactor services plus net worker remittances.
Source: World Bank baseline forecast, June 1997.

sumer demand, the delayed effects of the export slowdown on investment, and the start of adjustment in Romania. Gradual recovery in EU markets, Hungary's emergence from earlier adjustment efforts, and catch-up by the later reformers should support growth of 4–5 percent through 2000 (table A1-4). Closer integration with the EU should allow a longer-run growth path of about 5 percent.

Signs of recovery should become more prominent in Russia and Ukraine later this year and in 1998, based on continuing progress in stabilization, rising real incomes, and consumer spending. Although supportive policy elements will need to be in place (particularly with respect to budgetary arrears), improving business confidence and increasing FDI should underpin a sharper upturn in private investment later in the decade, leading to growth of 3–4 percent by 1998 and to longer-term advances of 5–6 percent.

Measures to foster private sector activity are central to achieving medium-term growth of 5 percent across the region. In the Baltic states these include continuing fiscal adjustment, improvements in banking supervision, and export promotion. In Central Asia crucial issues encompass a consolidation of gains in fiscal reform and stabilization, and development of the productive and export potential of the agriculture, energy, and extractive sectors. Among the Transcaucasus republics improvements in the political climate and in investor confidence are expected to support growth, particularly in the service sector, while exploitation of Caspian Sea oil should underpin longer-term prospects.

Middle East and North Africa

Economic growth in the Middle East and North Africa region over the past decade of a little over 2 percent a year was close to the lowest among all developing regions (table A1-5). Excluding war-affected Iraq, growth in 1987–96 is estimated to have averaged 3 percent—or only 0.2 percent in per capita terms. Combined with fast labor force growth, the sluggish performance of output growth contributed to the highest unemployment rates among all developing regions, around 15 percent (figure A1-4). However, projections for the next decade have been raised by around 0.5 percentage point from *Global Economic Prospects 1996* to 3.6 percent on the basis of more evidence that reforms are moving ahead and becoming consolidated in some countries, though not to an extent sufficient to generate the desirable major improvements in growth. Growth will also be restrained by the erosion of regional oil exporters' incomes as a result of expected long-run declines in real oil prices. High sociopolitical tensions in some countries will also continue to check the enthusiasm of domestic and foreign investors.

Over the past year economic reform moved ahead in nearly all the Middle East and North African countries bordering the Mediterranean. In Egypt (the largest of these countries by population), macroeconomic stabilization has reduced the fiscal deficit from 17 percent of GDP in 1991 to about 1 percent in 1996. Inflation came down from over 22 percent to below 7 percent. External creditworthiness has been restored with a negligible current account deficit and foreign exchange reserves worth around seventeen months of imports. Progress on structural reform, though more modest, has continued, with significant trade liberalization to be implemented under the country's 1996 agreement with the IMF and an Association Agreement being negotiated under the EU's Mediterranean Initiative. Privatization also accelerated, though it remains small in relation to the size of the state-owned enterprise sector as a whole. The importance of further structural reforms is underlined by the still sluggish pace of export growth, which is estimated to have averaged around 4 percent in volume terms in 1991–96.

Jordan, the other main reforming country in the Mashreq, signed an Association Agreement with the EU in April 1997. Tariffs on almost 500 manufactured goods imported from the EU will be removed beginning in 1999, and on most others later. Reforms also continued to move ahead in the Maghreb countries with the 1996 signing of EU Association Agreements by Morocco and Tunisia. However, in some cases the most significant trade liberalization is scheduled to take place later, with increases in effective protection rates occurring earlier. Care needs to be taken that the momentum of reform does not slacken. Despite difficult domestic political conditions, Algeria has also moved ahead with trade liberalization and privatization. Although private capital flows to the Middle East and North Africa region are the lowest (relative to GDP) of all developing regions, they are rising in response to recent reforms, with most FDI flows going to Egypt, Morocco, and Tunisia, as well as some portfolio flows to Egypt and Morocco.

In Iran higher than expected oil prices in the past two years have led to recovery in growth to 4–5 percent, as well as improvements in trade and fiscal balances and ability to service external debt. Structural reforms have made less progress, however. Privatization or restructuring of the large and generally inefficient state enterprise sector has run out of steam. Extensive, variable, and less than transparent bureaucratic regulation acts as a check on private investment. Nevertheless, the outcome of recent presidential elections may open the way to more structural reforms.

The urgency of reforms is heightened by high unemployment throughout the Middle East and North Africa. In Algeria, Iraq, and the West Bank

Per capita incomes are expected to recover after a decade of declines

Table A1-5 Middle East and North Africa forecast summary

(Annual percentage change or ratio)

Indicator	1987–96	Baseline 1997–2006
Real GDP	2.2	3.6
Consumption per capita	–0.8	1.3
GDP per capita	–0.6	1.1
Population 16–65 years	3.1	2.8
Median inflation[a]	7.8	6.5
Gross domestic investment/GDP	22.5	23.9
Budget deficit/GDP	–5.0	–3.0
Export volume[b]	5.2	5.1
Current account/GDP	–3.0	–1.5
Debt/exports[c]	230.0	165.0

a. GDP deflator.
b. Goods and nonfactor services.
c. Ratio of long-term debt outstanding and disbursed to exports of goods and nonfactor services plus net worker remittances.
Source: World Bank baseline forecast, June 1997.

Unemployment is highest in the Middle East and North Africa

Figure A1-4 Regional unemployment rates in the early 1990s

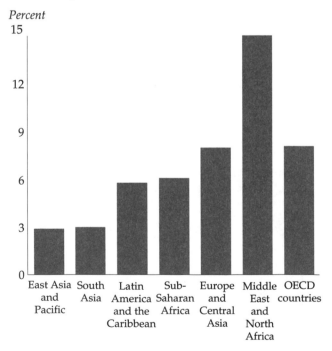

Percent

Source: Filmer 1995; ILO, various years; World Bank 1995 and staff estimates.

and Gaza, unemployment is more than 20 percent. For Egypt, Jordan, Lebanon, Morocco, and Tunisia it is close to 15 percent. Real wages are back to their levels of the 1970s and poverty levels have increased in some countries. The region's population growth and age structure is such that the labor force will be expanding at almost 3 percent a year in the next decade. In the absence of progress in creating more and better jobs and improving labor productivity and wages, social tensions are likely to rise. So, intensification of structural reform is necessary to ensure that the recovery currently under way in some countries is more employment intensive than in the past.

Sub-Saharan Africa

Growth in Sub-Saharan Africa is projected to average a little more than 4 percent a year in the coming decade, more than double the pace of the preceding ten years (table A1-6). Yet regional per capita income, rising at a little over 1 percent a year, would be no higher in 2006 than in 1982 (in constant 1987 U.S. dollars) and 5 percent lower than in 1974. So the coming decade would only represent the recovery of ground lost over twenty years.

Given the poor performance of the past, how realistic is even this modest projection? The discussion of the regional outlook in chapter 1 notes that one reason for expecting an improvement in growth is the gradual and painfully achieved (though still

---

Moderate improvement is expected in most economic indexes

Table A1-6 Sub-Saharan Africa forecast summary
(*Annual percentage change or ratio*)

Indicator	1987–96	Baseline 1997–2006
Real GDP	2.0	4.1
Consumption per capita	−1.0	1.0
GDP per capita	−0.8	1.2
Population 16–65 years	3.1	3.1
Median inflation[a]	10.2	8.3
Gross domestic investment/GDP	18.2	21.1
Budget deficit/GDP	−6.7	−4.5
Export volume[b]	2.8	5.6
Current account/GDP	−2.1	−2.4
Debt/exports[c]	330.0	270.0

a. GDP deflator.
b. Goods and nonfactor services.
c. Ratio of long-term debt outstanding and disbursed to exports of goods and nonfactor services plus net worker remittances.
Source: World Bank baseline forecast, June 1997.

---

modest) spread and firming of commitment to economic reform over the past decade. Countries that have gone furthest with adjustment and structural reforms are already among the better performers in the region. Countries in the CFA franc zone launched a major revitalization of reforms in 1994 and achieved around 5 percent growth in 1995–96. Outside the CFA zone, Ethiopia, Kenya, Tanzania, and Uganda in East Africa and Ghana in West Africa achieved median growth of 4.1 percent in 1987–96, outperforming the 3 percent median for the region as a whole.

A second factor is political stabilization in southern and, perhaps, central Africa. South Africa and Angola, accounting for 45 percent and 2.5 percent of regional GDP, were gripped by civil strife and grew by only about 1 percent a year in 1981–94. With peace, South Africa grew around 3.5 percent a year in 1995–96. If it sustains even this modest growth over the next decade, regional GDP growth will be boosted by more than 0.5 percentage point. Output in the Democratic Republic of Congo (formerly Zaire) may have fallen by about 4 percent a year over the past decade. A return to more stable conditions following the recent political transition would also provide a fillip to regional growth. A third factor is that Sub-Saharan Africa's terms of trade fell by 3 percent a year on average in 1981–94, reducing income in terms of purchasing power for imports by perhaps 0.75 percent of GDP a year. Given a somewhat less severe projected decline in primary commodity prices over the next decade, income losses from this source might amount to only 0.1–0.2 percent of GDP.

There are of course significant risks attached to growth forecasts for Sub-Saharan Africa. Most obvious, there are uncertainties attached to any long-run forecast for commodity prices. Some of the largest economies in the region also continue to face significant policy challenges. In 1996 South Africa saw a downturn in net foreign capital inflows, a widening current account deficit, a sharp fall in the rand exchange rate, and higher inflation and interest rates. The fiscal deficit remained at a high 4 percent of GDP, and 1997 growth is widely expected to slip back below 3 percent. The government's plan to pursue fiscal consolidation, privatization, trade liberalization, and reforms of labor markets are opposed by many in the ruling alliance. In Nigeria high oil prices over the past two years allowed a swing from budget deficits averaging 12 percent of GDP in 1990–94 to likely surpluses in 1996–97, but there are few signs of significant improvements in fundamental policies. Government controls over interest rates and a dual exchange rate system (which subsidizes dollars for government use at one-fourth the price for the private market) remain in place, while progress on privatization or public sector reform has slowed significantly.

References

Filmer, Deon. 1995. "Estimating the World at Work." Policy Research Working Paper 1488. Background paper for *World Development Report 1995*. World Bank, World Development Report Office, Washington, D.C.

ILO (International Labor Organization). Various years. *World Labor Report.* Geneva: International Labor Office.

———. Various years. *Yearbook of Labor Statistics.* Geneva: International Labor Office.

World Bank. 1995. *Will Arab Workers Prosper or Be Left Out in the Twenty-first Century?* Regional Perspectives on *World Development Report 1995.* Washington, D.C.

Appendix 2

Studies of adjustment costs of trade liberalization

Table A2-1 Studies of adjustment costs of trade liberalization

Author	Summary	Findings
Economywide studies Baldwin, Mutti, and Richardson (1980)	The authors construct a model of 367 sectors of the U.S. economy to investigate the potential effects of a 50 percent multilateral tariff reduction. They account for idled capital.	Benefit-cost ratio of 2.4 after one year, 24 over the infinite horizon.
Dixon, Parmenter, and Powell (1984)	The authors construct a model of the Australian economy to investigate the effects of a 25 percent liberalization.	Depending on the scenario, 2–14 percent of the workforce would have to switch occupations over two years. This compares with natural turnover of 32–142 percent.
de Melo and Roland-Holst (1990)	The authors model trade liberalization for Uruguay, taking into account administered protection and rent seeking behavior.	Liberalization would entail the relocation of 5 percent of the labor force. The authors do not provide a benchmark with which this figure can be compared.
Industry studies de Melo and Tarr (1990)	This general equilibrium study focuses on U.S. textiles, steel, and automobiles. The authors incorporate earlier findings on long-term earnings losses for displaced workers.	Considering only efficiency gains from reform, they find a benefit-cost ratio of 17.
Mutti (1978)	The author studies the U.S. iron and steel, machine tools, industrial chemicals, motor vehicles, and electrical machinery industries.	The benefit-cost ratios calculated by the author range from 1.3 to 24.4. These numbers are generally smaller than findings of other studies because the assumed durations of unemployment were long.

Note: Excludes studies discussed in the text. See references to chapter 3.

Global economic indicators

Table 1 Growth of real GDP, 1966–2006
(current 1995 dollars and 1987 prices and exchange rates—average annual percentage growth)

	1995 GDP (US$ billions)	1966–73	1974–90	1991–95	1995	1996 estimate	1997–2006 forecast
World	**28,340**	**5.2**	**3.0**	**2.0**	**2.5**	**2.9**	**3.4**
High-income	**23,220**	**4.9**	**2.9**	**2.0**	**2.2**	**2.5**	**2.8**
Industrial countries	22,110	4.8	2.8	1.8	2.0	2.3	2.7
G-7 countries	19,080	4.7	2.9	1.8	1.9	2.3	2.6
United States	7,255	3.0	2.6	2.6	2.0	2.4	—
Japan	5,110	10.0	3.8	1.1	0.9	3.6	—
G-4 Europe	6,150	4.4	2.3	1.3	2.4	1.4	2.5
Germany[a]	2,415	4.3	2.0	1.8	2.1	1.4	—
Other industrial	3,030	4.9	2.3	1.5	2.7	2.3	2.9
Other high-income	1,110	9.2	6.5	7.0	7.2	5.8	5.6
Low- and middle-income	**5,120**	**6.7**	**3.3**	**2.3**	**3.8**	**4.5**	**5.4**
Excluding Eastern Europe and former Soviet Union	4,100	6.3	3.4	5.0	4.8	5.6	5.5
Asia	1,685	5.5	6.2	8.2	8.5	7.9	7.1
East Asia and Pacific	1,250	7.5	7.3	10.5	9.7	8.6	7.6
China	700	8.5	8.7	12.8	10.7	9.7	—
Indonesia	200	6.4	6.7	7.7	8.2	7.8	—
South Asia	435	3.7	4.9	4.6	5.8	6.5	5.9
India	325	3.7	4.8	4.6	6.1	6.8	—
Latin America and the Caribbean	1,625	6.9	2.6	3.2	0.2	3.4	4.2
Brazil	690	9.8	3.6	2.7	3.0	2.9	—
Argentina	280	4.3	0.4	5.7	–4.6	4.3	—
Mexico	250	6.8	3.4	1.1	–7.2	5.1	—
Europe and Central Asia	1,050	6.6	3.1	–6.4	–0.8	–0.3	4.5
Russian Federation[b]	360	6.6	3.6	–9.8	–4.3	–6.0	—
Turkey	165	4.9	4.2	3.2	7.0	6.4	—
Poland	120	7.3	0.3	2.4	6.6	6.1	—
Middle East and North Africa	460	8.7	1.4	2.6	3.1	4.1	3.6
Iran	105	10.2	–0.3	4.2	2.7	3.6	—
Egypt	60	3.7	7.1	3.4	4.6	4.3	—
Algeria	42	6.3	4.3	0.1	4.4	4.2	—
Sub-Saharan Africa	300	4.7	2.2	1.5	3.9	3.8	4.1
South Africa	135	4.9	2.1	0.7	3.1	3.5	—
Nigeria	25	6.5	1.0	2.6	2.3	2.1	—

Note: Growth rates over intervals are computed using least squares method.
a. Data prior to 1991 cover Federal Republic of Germany.
b. Data prior to 1992 cover former Soviet Union.
Source: World Bank data and staff estimates.

Real GDP growth, 1987–2006

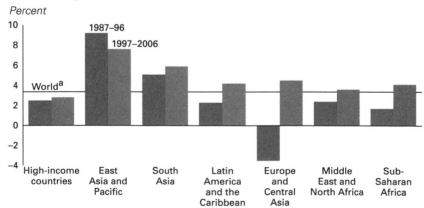

a. World data for 1997–2006.

Table 2 Growth of real GDP per capita, 1966–2006

(current 1995 dollars and 1987 prices and exchange rates—average annual percentage growth)

	1995 GDP per capita (US$)	1966–73	1974–90	1991–95	1995	1996 estimate	1997–2006 forecast
World	**5,050**	**2.9**	**1.2**	**0.5**	**1.1**	**1.4**	**2.0**
High-income	**25,845**	**3.8**	**2.1**	**1.3**	**1.6**	**1.9**	**2.3**
Industrial countries	27,200	3.8	2.1	1.1	1.4	1.8	2.2
G-7 countries	28,330	3.8	2.1	1.1	1.3	1.8	2.2
United States	27,000	1.9	1.5	1.6	1.1	1.4	—
Japan	40,800	8.7	3.0	0.8	0.7	3.3	—
G-4 Europe	24,065	3.8	2.1	0.9	2.1	1.2	2.5
Germany[a]	27,500	3.7	2.1	1.2	1.7	1.3	—
Other industrial	21,745	4.0	1.7	1.0	2.2	1.9	2.6
Other high-income	12,980	6.7	4.7	5.8	6.0	4.7	4.8
Low- and middle-income	**1,195**	**3.8**	**1.4**	**0.5**	**2.1**	**2.7**	**3.8**
Excluding Eastern Europe and former Soviet Union	1,085	3.6	1.3	3.3	3.1	3.8	3.8
Asia	600	2.8	4.3	6.8	7.0	6.4	5.7
East Asia and Pacific	790	4.7	5.6	9.1	8.6	7.4	6.6
China	580	5.7	7.1	11.5	9.9	8.6	—
Indonesia	1,040	3.9	4.6	5.9	6.6	6.2	—
South Asia	360	1.2	2.6	2.6	3.9	4.6	4.1
India	350	1.4	2.6	2.7	4.3	4.9	—
Latin America and the Caribbean	3,520	4.2	0.4	1.4	−1.5	1.7	2.7
Brazil	4,325	7.1	1.4	1.2	1.6	1.6	—
Argentina	8,100	2.7	−1.1	4.4	−5.9	3.4	—
Mexico	2,725	3.4	1.0	−0.8	−8.8	3.2	—
Europe and Central Asia	2,220	5.5	2.2	−6.7	−1.0	−0.8	4.0
Russian Federation[b]	2,400	5.6	2.9	−9.8	−4.2	−5.9	—
Turkey	2,700	2.3	1.8	1.5	5.4	4.7	—
Poland	3,050	6.5	−0.5	2.2	6.4	5.9	—
Middle East and North Africa	2,000	5.8	−1.7	−0.1	0.8	1.4	1.1
Iran	1,650	7.0	−3.6	1.4	0.2	0.6	—
Egypt	1,045	1.5	4.5	1.4	2.8	2.5	—
Algeria	1,485	3.3	1.2	−2.1	2.4	1.9	—
Sub-Saharan Africa	520	2.0	−0.7	−1.1	1.1	0.8	1.2
South Africa	3,230	2.3	−0.4	−1.5	0.8	1.2	—
Nigeria	215	3.6	−2.0	−0.3	−0.7	−0.8	—

Note: Growth rates over intervals are computed using least squares method.
a. Data prior to 1991 cover Federal Republic of Germany.
b. Data prior to 1992 cover former Soviet Union.
Source: World Bank data and staff estimates.

Real per capita GDP growth, 1987–2006

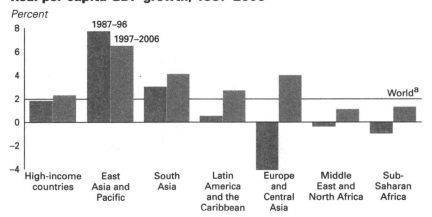

a. World data for 1997–2006.

Table 3 Inflation: GDP deflators, 1966–2006

(1987=100; percentage change)

	1966–73	1974–90	1991–95	1995	1996 estimate	1997–2006 forecast
World	**5.0**	**7.6**	**5.0**	**4.3**	**3.2**	**3.3**
High-income[a]	**5.4**	**6.6**	**3.1**	**2.5**	**1.8**	**2.0**
Industrial countries	5.4	6.4	3.0	2.4	1.7	1.9
G-7 countries	5.3	6.1	3.0	2.3	1.6	1.7
United States	4.9	6.0	3.2	2.5	2.0	—
Japan	5.8	3.3	1.2	1.5	0.0	—
G-4 Europe	5.4	8.1	4.1	2.8	2.3	1.8
Germany[b]	4.9	3.5	5.2	2.0	1.0	—
Other industrial	5.8	7.8	3.1	3.1	2.2	2.6
Other high-income	5.1	12.5	5.7	4.6	5.2	4.4
Low- and middle-income[a]	**4.5**	**10.7**	**12.6**	**11.5**	**9.2**	**7.8**
Excluding Eastern Europe and former Soviet Union	4.5	10.9	12.0	10.9	8.8	7.5
Asia	5.6	8.4	9.0	8.5	7.2	6.4
East Asia and Pacific	5.4	7.4	6.7	8.4	7.0	6.4
China	–1.7	3.8	11.9	12.8	10.7	—
Indonesia	65.6	13.3	8.1	9.4	9.0	—
South Asia	5.8	8.5	10.1	8.5	7.5	6.6
India	6.2	8.1	10.3	8.0	7.5	—
Latin America and the Caribbean	5.1	18.0	17.8	13.1	11.4	9.1
Brazil	22.8	145.0	765.0	77.8	16.9	—
Argentina	24.0	255.0	26.0	4.5	4.3	—
Mexico	5.9	47.5	17.5	35.6	27.3	—
Europe and Central Asia	2.4	5.1	44.2	25.7	25.0	12.4
Russian Federation[c]	0.5	2.0	427.0	180.0	50.0	—
Turkey	10.8	46.2	75.0	82.5	92.5	—
Poland	1.2	31.4	35.8	27.4	25.8	—
Middle East and North Africa	4.2	9.6	6.7	8.2	6.5	6.5
Iran	5.6	16.9	32.1	39.7	43.6	—
Egypt	2.2	11.3	12.6	12.0	8.4	—
Algeria	4.5	10.5	28.5	28.2	22.2	—
Sub-Saharan Africa	4.1	10.1	11.3	11.3	8.1	8.3
South Africa	6.4	14.5	11.6	10.2	11.5	—
Nigeria	10.7	14.5	38.0	57.4	48.2	—

Note: Deflators are in local currency units. Growth rates over intervals are computed using least squares method.

a. High-income group inflation rates are GDP-weighted averages of local currency inflation; low- and middle-income group rates are medians.

b. Data prior to 1991 cover Federal Republic of Germany.

c. Data prior to 1992 cover former Soviet Union.

Source: World Bank data and staff estimates.

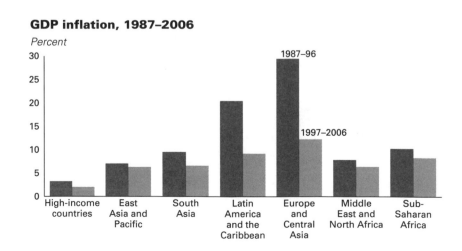

GDP inflation, 1987–2006

Table 4 Current account balance, 1970–2006
(percentage of GDP)

	1995 current account balance (US$ billions)	1970–80	1981–90	1991–95	1995	1996 estimate	1997–2006 forecast
World	**–50.0**	**0.0**	**–0.5**	**–0.3**	**–0.2**	**–0.2**	**–0.2**
High-income	**36.5**	**0.1**	**–0.3**	**0.1**	**0.2**	**0.1**	**0.2**
Industrial countries	20.0	–0.1	–0.5	–0.1	0.1	–0.1	0.1
G-7 countries	–31.0	0.1	–0.5	–0.2	–0.2	–0.3	–0.3
United States	–148.0	0.0	–2.1	–1.4	–2.0	–2.2	—
Japan	110.0	0.7	2.3	2.6	2.1	1.4	—
G-4 Europe	16.0	0.2	0.4	–0.5	0.3	0.6	0.5
Germany[a]	–21.5	0.5	2.6	–0.9	–0.9	–0.6	—
Other industrial	51.0	–0.9	–0.7	0.7	1.7	1.9	1.7
Other high-income	16.5	3.7	6.9	1.3	1.5	2.2	1.7
Low- and middle-income	**–86.5**	**–0.1**	**–1.1**	**–1.6**	**–1.6**	**–1.4**	**–1.6**
Excluding Eastern Europe and former Soviet Union	–90.0	–0.7	–2.5	–2.3	–2.0	–1.7	–2.0
Asia	–40.0	–1.2	–2.3	–1.7	–2.3	–1.9	–1.7
East Asia and Pacific	–28.7	–1.1	–1.7	–1.4	–2.1	–1.7	–1.6
China	1.6	–0.4	0.1	0.8	0.2	0.1	—
Indonesia	–7.0	–1.4	–3.1	–2.3	–3.5	–1.7	—
South Asia	–11.3	–1.5	–3.5	–2.3	–2.6	–2.5	–2.1
India	–5.5	–0.1	–2.2	–1.1	–1.7	–1.5	—
Latin America and the Caribbean	–30.0	–2.8	–1.8	–2.5	–1.8	–2.0	–2.7
Brazil	–17.8	–4.1	–1.5	–0.3	–2.5	–3.1	—
Argentina	–2.4	–0.3	–2.1	–1.9	–0.8	–1.8	—
Mexico	–0.7	–3.5	–0.8	–5.4	–0.3	–0.6	—
Europe and Central Asia	–3.5	0.4	2.0	0.6	–0.3	–0.4	–0.2
Russian Federation[b]	14.0	2.0	2.9	2.7	2.2	2.0	—
Turkey	–2.3	–2.0	–1.3	–0.7	–1.4	–1.9	—
Poland	–4.2	–0.9	–1.4	–3.9	3.7	–5.0	—
Middle East and North Africa	–1.5	6.5	–3.6	–3.7	–0.3	1.4	–1.5
Iran	4.0	2.4	0.4	–1.4	2.3	4.4	—
Egypt	0.0	–8.2	–4.6	3.3	0.0	0.1	—
Algeria	–2.3	6.8	–0.5	0.2	–5.5	–2.6	—
Sub-Saharan Africa	–11.5	–2.0	–2.8	–2.5	–3.8	–3.2	–2.4
South Africa	–3.5	–1.7	0.6	0.3	–2.6	–2.4	—
Nigeria	–3.5	0.7	–0.1	–1.3	–8.7	–3.3	—

Note: Current account balance includes net official transfers. The world balance is a statistical discrepancy item. Shares over intervals are period averages.
a. Data prior to 1991 cover Federal Republic of Germany.
b. Data prior to 1992 cover former Soviet Union.
Source: World Bank data and staff estimates.

Ratio of current account balance to GDP, 1987–2006

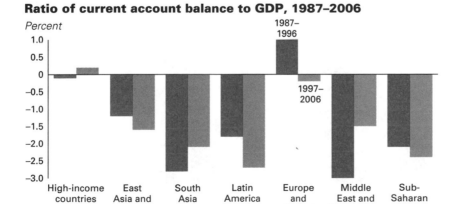

Table 5 Exports of goods, 1995
(percent)

Region/country	Merchandise exports (US$ millions)	Average annual growth 1981–94	Effective market growth 1981–94
World	**5,074,031**	**5.5**	**5.5**
All developing	**1,051,011**	**4.9**	**5.2**
Asia	**400,159**	**11.3**	**6.9**
East Asia and Pacific	353,822	11.8	7.3
China	148,797	11.9	8.1
Fiji	607	3.2	5.9
Indonesia	45,417	9.5	6.5
Malaysia	74,045	13.9	11.5
Myanmar	846	2.0	4.2
Papua New Guinea	2,654	7.3	5.8
Philippines	17,502	5.2	6.7
Thailand	56,440	16.8	6.3
Vietnam	5,300	—	—
South Asia	**46,337**	**8.1**	**4.9**
Bangladesh	3,173	9.4	5.3
India	30,764	7.6	6.2
Nepal	348	9.6	4.7
Pakistan	7,992	8.9	5.6
Sri Lanka	3,798	8.5	4.0
Latin America and the Caribbean	**220,395**	**4.3**	**5.9**
Argentina	20,967	3.1	5.1
Bolivia	1,101	3.7	6.1
Brazil	46,506	5.0	5.6
Chile	16,039	7.3	5.7
Colombia	9,764	12.5	5.5
Costa Rica	2,611	6.9	5.7
Dominican Republic	765	–5.5	6.7
Ecuador	4,307	4.0	2.5
El Salvador	998	0.3	5.0
Guatemala	2,050	1.0	6.0
Jamaica	1,414	2.8	4.4
Mexico	79,800	10.8	10.4
Panama	605	5.5	4.4
Paraguay	895	9.7	4.9
Peru	5,575	1.0	5.8
Trinidad and Tobago	2,456	–0.7	5.3
Uruguay	2,117	1.9	4.8
Venezuela	18,324	3.3	6.5
Europe and Central Asia	**245,323**	**1.0**	**2.6**
Armenia	248	—	—
Azerbaijan	550	—	—
Belarus	4,156	—	—
Europe and Central Asia (continued)			
Bulgaria	5,110	–12.3	–5.2
Czech Republic	21,647	—	—
Estonia	1,967	—	—
Georgia	140	—	—
Greece	11,180	6.6	3.9
Hungary	12,540	0.7	1.1
Kazakstan	4,584	—	—
Kyrgyz Republic	380	—	—
Latvia	1,283	—	—
Lithuania	2,707	—	—
Moldova	720	—	—
Poland	22,892	4.8	1.9
Romania	7,548	–10.5	2.2
Russian Federation	81,137	—	—
Slovak Republic	8,552	—	—
Slovenia	8,286	—	—
Tajikistan	707	—	—
TFYR Macedonia	1,130	—	—
Turkmenistan	1,939	—	—
Turkey	21,600	6.7	4.0
Ukraine	11,567	—	—
Uzbekistan	3,371	—	—
Middle East and North Africa	**115,700**	**1.2**	**5.6**
Algeria	9,810	2.2	4.9
Bahrain	4,044	4.0	6.5
Egypt, Arab Rep.	3,770	0.5	4.1
Iran, Islamic Rep.	16,000	7.1	10.5
Iraq	373	–21.0	5.0
Jordan	1,769	5.0	2.6
Morocco	4,824	3.9	4.4
Oman	6,260	11.6	4.5
Saudi Arabia	48,150	–0.1	6.4
Syrian Arab Rep.	3,970	8.6	3.1
Tunisia	5,475	8.2	3.5
Yemen, Rep.	973	2.0	9.8
Sub-Saharan Africa	**69,433**	**2.3**	**4.9**
Angola	3,880	9.5	5.2
Botswana	1,910	5.5	3.0
Côte d'Ivoire	3,400	1.7	4.2
Cameroon	1,410	7.0	4.3
Ethiopia	423	–3.7	3.7
Gabon	2,670	2.7	4.8
Ghana	1,440	6.5	4.6
Kenya	1,856	5.5	1.5
Sub-Saharan Africa (continued)			
Madagascar	364	0.4	5.2
Nigeria	9,950	1.9	6.1
Senegal	720	0.1	3.6
South Africa	27,860	1.4	4.7
Sudan	475	–3.3	6.5
Zambia	1,140	–0.9	5.6
Zimbabwe	1,980	1.9	4.2
High-income	**4,023,020**	**5.6**	**5.4**
Industrial	3,428,088	5.0	5.0
G-7	2,491,647	4.7	5.3
Canada	192,197	5.5	6.5
France	286,694	4.3	4.4
Germany	511,771	4.1	4.1
Italy	231,336	4.6	4.4
Japan	443,116	3.7	5.6
United Kingdom	241,790	4.2	4.6
United States	584,743	6.1	6.1
Other industrial	936,441	5.7	4.4
Australia	53,085	6.9	6.4
Austria	58,100	6.9	3.7
Belgium and Luxembourg	168,307	4.6	4.1
Denmark	49,036	4.8	4.1
Finland	39,573	2.8	3.8
Iceland	1,804	2.2	3.8
Ireland	43,681	9.7	4.4
Netherlands	195,516	5.1	4.2
New Zealand	13,736	4.1	6.1
Norway	41,746	7.2	3.0
Portugal	22,584	10.1	4.3
Spain	91,716	7.6	4.3
Sweden	79,908	3.9	4.4
Switzerland	77,649	6.4	4.5
Other high-income	594,932	10.5	6.9
Brunei	2,440	–0.4	—
Hong Kong (China)	173,871	16.1	7.1
Israel	19,028	6.3	5.5
Korea, Rep.	125,058	10.8	6.5
Kuwait	13,036	–1.2	6.2
Qatar	3,365	1.0	6.0
Singapore	118,265	13.8	7.4
Taiwan (China)	111,680	9.3	9.9
United Arab Emirates	21,700	7.6	6.4

Note: Merchandise exports are f.o.b. in current U.S. dollars. Growth rates are for export volumes. Effective market growth is a weighted average of import volume growth in the country's export markets. Growth rates over intervals are computed using least squares method.
Source: See technical notes.

Merchandise exports as share of GDP, 1995
Percent

Average annual growth of export volumes, 1981–94
Percent

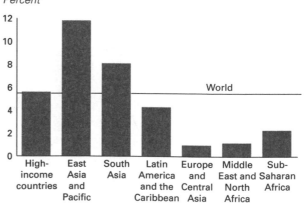

Table 6 Imports of goods, 1995

(percent)

Region/country	Merchandise imports (US$ millions)	Average annual growth 1981–94	Merchandise imports/ GDP
World	**5,124,036**	**5.5**	**18.2**
All developing	**1,126,429**	**2.8**	**21.6**
Asia	**424,664**	**8.6**	**24.9**
East Asia and Pacific	364,913	9.9	28.8
China	129,113	10.3	18.5
Fiji	864	0.8	41.8
Indonesia	40,918	4.7	20.3
Malaysia	77,751	11.3	91.1
Myanmar	1,335	4.2	13.4
Papua New Guinea	1,451	–0.1	29.6
Philippines	28,337	7.6	38.2
Thailand	73,654	15.7	44.1
Vietnam	7,500	—	37.1
South Asia	59,751	4.0	13.7
Bangladesh	6,496	2.8	22.3
India	34,522	4.1	10.5
Nepal	1,374	5.2	31.2
Pakistan	11,461	3.6	18.9
Sri Lanka	5,185	5.8	40.1
Latin America and the Caribbean	**238,214**	**2.6**	**14.6**
Argentina	20,123	6.0	7.2
Bolivia	1,424	1.6	23.2
Brazil	53,783	3.1	7.8
Chile	15,914	6.7	23.6
Colombia	13,853	1.7	17.1
Costa Rica	3,274	6.7	35.5
Dominican Republic	2,976	3.0	24.7
Ecuador	4,193	0.3	23.4
El Salvador	2,853	4.8	29.4
Guatemala	3,135	4.8	21.2
Jamaica	2,757	3.1	56.1
Mexico	72,500	12.7	29.0
Panama	2,565	1.8	34.6
Paraguay	2,235	10.1	24.9
Peru	9,224	2.3	15.7
Trinidad and Tobago	1,713	–7.0	33.2
Uruguay	2,867	5.8	16.1
Venezuela	11,978	–1.9	16.0
Europe and Central Asia	**278,476**	**4.5**	**24.8**
Armenia	661	—	23.3
Azerbaijan	681	—	18.1
Belarus	5,257	—	24.5
Europe and Central Asia (continued)			
Bulgaria	5,800	–11.3	44.9
Czech Republic	26,444	—	59.1
Estonia	2,354	—	53.2
Georgia	436	—	10.1
Greece	25,480	7.8	28.1
Hungary	15,073	1.4	34.5
Kazakstan	4,108	—	18.0
Kyrgyz Republic	439	—	13.9
Latvia	1,810	—	29.0
Lithuania	3,083	—	37.3
Moldova	822	—	48.4
Poland	29,050	6.6	24.7
Romania	9,424	–1.4	28.5
Russian Federation	60,916	—	17.0
Slovak Republic	8,500	—	49.0
Slovenia	9,452	—	51.0
Tajikistan	690	—	37.7
TFYR Macedonia	1,260	—	64.0
Turkmenistan	994	—	25.4
Turkey	35,710	9.8	21.7
Ukraine	11,379	—	14.3
Uzbekistan	2,951	—	12.8
Middle East and North Africa	**108,929**	**–3.8**	**23.4**
Algeria	10,350	–4.9	25.0
Bahrain	3,626	0.3	71.7
Egypt, Arab Rep.	11,700	–2.8	19.3
Iran, Islamic Rep.	11,100	–0.8	10.6
Iraq	783	–27.5	—
Jordan	3,697	–2.3	55.6
Morocco	8,563	5.1	26.4
Oman	4,248	1.0	35.1
Saudi Arabia	27,458	–5.4	21.9
Syrian Arab Rep.	4,616	–2.7	27.6
Tunisia	7,903	4.2	43.8
Yemen, Rep.	3,200	–4.8	69.2
Sub-Saharan Africa	**76,146**	**–1.0**	**26.0**
Angola	1,700	2.8	27.5
Botswana	1,800	7.5	41.7
Côte d'Ivoire	2,300	–2.6	22.8
Cameroon	1,100	–4.6	13.8
Ethiopia	960	–1.9	16.2
Gabon	870	–2.6	18.5
Ghana	1,960	5.7	31.7
Kenya	2,948	0.3	32.4
Sub-Saharan Africa (continued)			
Madagascar	532	–1.7	16.6
Nigeria	6,990	–8.6	29.2
Senegal	970	–0.3	19.9
South Africa	30,555	0.8	22.8
Sudan	870	–3.2	13.4
Zambia	970	–1.7	23.6
Zimbabwe	2,690	0.5	40.8
High-income	**3,997,607**	**6.2**	**17.5**
Industrial	3,365,736	5.7	15.4
G-7	2,466,192	5.9	13.1
Canada	168,426	6.0	29.6
France	274,972	5.0	17.9
Germany	448,132	6.1	18.6
Italy	204,062	5.1	18.8
Japan	335,882	6.8	6.6
United Kingdom	263,760	5.1	23.9
United States	770,958	6.3	11.1
Other industrial	899,544	5.2	29.8
Australia	61,286	4.5	17.6
Austria	67,300	6.3	28.8
Belgium and Luxembourg	154,206	4.2	57.3
Denmark	43,223	3.7	25.1
Finland	28,114	2.3	22.4
Iceland	1,756	0.6	24.9
Ireland	32,300	5.5	53.1
Netherlands	176,123	5.0	44.5
New Zealand	13,958	4.7	24.5
Norway	32,702	3.2	22.4
Portugal	32,322	10.0	31.6
Spain	114,831	11.1	20.6
Sweden	64,438	4.3	28.2
Switzerland	76,985	2.6	25.6
Other high-income	631,871	10.2	57.0
Brunei	1,940	3.9	38.9
Hong Kong (China)	192,774	12.6	134.2
Israel	29,632	6.1	32.2
Korea, Rep.	135,119	11.5	29.6
Kuwait	7,139	–5.0	26.8
Qatar	2,165	–0.1	28.4
Singapore	124,507	10.4	148.8
Taiwan (China)	103,571	13.7	39.7
United Arab Emirates	22,800	4.8	58.3

Note: Merchandise imports are c.i.f. in current U.S. dollars. Growth rates are for import volumes. Growth rates over intervals are computed using least squares method.

Source: See technical notes.

Merchandise imports as share of GDP, 1995
Percent

Average annual growth of import volumes, 1981–94
Percent

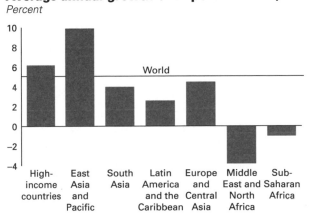

Table 7 Direction of merchandise trade, 1995
(percentage of world trade)

Source of exports	High-income importers							Developing importers						World
	United States	European Union	Japan	Other indus-trial	All indus-trial	Other high-income	All high-income	Sub-Saharan Africa	Asia	Europe and Central Asia	Middle East and North Africa	Latin America and the Caribbean	All low- and middle-income	
High-income	10.8	32.0	3.9	6.4	53.2	8.3	61.4	1.1	7.4	3.5	1.7	3.8	17.4	78.8
Industrial	8.5	30.4	2.7	6.0	47.6	6.3	53.9	0.9	4.3	3.3	1.5	3.4	13.5	67.4
United States	..	2.4	1.3	2.9	6.6	1.7	8.3	0.1	0.8	0.2	0.3	1.9	3.3	11.6
European Union (15)	2.7	24.1	0.9	2.4	30.1	1.8	31.9	0.7	1.4	2.9	1.1	1.0	7.1	39.0
Japan	2.4	1.4	..	0.4	4.2	2.3	6.5	0.1	1.6	0.1	0.1	0.4	2.3	8.8
Other industrial	3.3	2.4	0.5	0.3	6.6	0.5	7.1	..	0.4	0.1	0.1	0.1	0.8	7.9
Other high-income[a]	2.3	1.6	1.3	0.4	5.6	2.0	7.6	0.1	3.1	0.2	0.2	0.3	3.9	11.4
Low- and middle-income	4.2	5.5	2.0	0.6	12.3	2.9	15.2	0.4	2.0	1.9	0.6	1.2	6.0	21.2
Sub-Saharan Africa	0.2	0.5	0.1	0.1	0.9	0.1	1.0	0.2	0.1	..	..	..	0.3	1.3
Developing Asia	1.5	1.3	1.4	0.3	4.4	2.2	6.6	0.1	0.8	0.2	0.2	0.1	1.4	8.0
Europe and Central Asia	0.2	2.1	0.1	0.1	2.4	0.1	2.5	..	0.2	1.6	0.1	0.1	2.1	4.6
Middle East and North Africa	0.2	0.8	0.3	0.1	1.4	0.4	1.8	0.1	0.7	0.1	0.2	..	1.1	2.9
Latin America and the Caribbean	2.1	0.8	0.2	0.1	3.2	0.1	3.3	..	0.1	0.1	0.1	0.9	1.2	4.5
World	**15.0**	**37.4**	**6.0**	**7.0**	**65.4**	**11.2**	**76.6**	**1.5**	**9.3**	**5.4**	**2.3**	**4.9**	**23.4**	**100.0**

.. Is not meaningful or is less than 0.1 percentage point.
Note: Expressed as a share (percent) of total world exports. World exports in 1995 amounted to some $5,000 billion.
a. *Other high-income* includes the Asian newly industrialized economies, several oil exporters of the Gulf region, and Israel.
Source: IMF Direction of Trade Statistics; UN Comtrade database.

Share of merchandise imports from developing countries, 1995

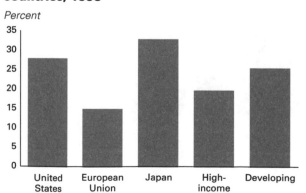

Percent

Direction of merchandise exports, 1995

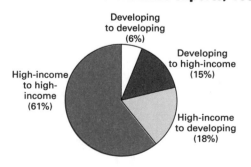

Table 8 Growth of merchandise trade in nominal dollars, 1985–95

(average annual percentage growth)

Source of exports	High-income importers							Developing importers						World
	United States	European Union	Japan	Other industrial	All industrial	Other high-income	All high-income	Sub-Saharan Africa	Asia	Europe and Central Asia	Middle East and North Africa	Latin America and the Caribbean	All low- and middle-income	World
High-income	**7.8**	**11.2**	**12.2**	**9.1**	**10.2**	**17.0**	**10.9**	**6.0**	**16.0**	**12.1**	**1.9**	**12.0**	**11.2**	**11.0**
Industrial	7.2	11.0	11.8	9.1	10.0	15.8	10.5	5.3	13.5	11.9	1.8	11.7	9.9	10.4
United States	..	9.1	11.0	10.0	9.8	15.0	10.7	3.6	13.4	6.9	3.0	11.9	10.4	10.6
European Union (15)	6.7	11.3	17.2	8.9	10.7	16.6	11.0	5.3	14.5	13.9	2.5	13.1	10.2	10.8
Japan	6.2	11.9	..	3.9	7.5	16.2	9.8	9.3	13.1	−1.3	−4.0	9.6	9.3	9.7
Other industrial	8.3	9.4	8.1	11.7	8.8	14.8	9.1	2.2	12.1	1.0	2.2	7.2	7.1	8.9
Other high-income	10.7	14.8	13.1	9.7	12.2	21.8	13.9	11.1	21.1	18.9	3.3	16.7	18.3	15.2
Low- and middle-income	**11.3**	**7.4**	**8.0**	**10.4**	**8.8**	**17.0**	**10.0**	**9.3**	**13.1**	**4.9**	**2.0**	**11.0**	**7.9**	**9.3**
Sub-Saharan Africa	5.0	1.8	5.5	5.3	3.0	15.1	3.6	12.1	14.1	2.7	8.8	−2.6	8.6	4.6
Developing Asia	17.7	18.5	11.3	17.4	15.4	18.2	16.2	16.4	19.4	4.7	6.5	19.5	13.9	15.8
Europe and Central Asia	12.9	10.2	9.4	2.6	10.1	22.7	10.5	−0.6	9.1	6.7	−3.2	16.2	5.8	8.1
Middle East and North Africa	3.8	0.9	0.7	7.9	1.5	11.3	2.8	8.8	10.8	−4.1	4.6	−5.1	5.3	3.7
Latin America and the Caribbean	10.0	5.2	6.3	9.0	8.4	15.3	8.6	−0.5	7.8	−1.1	2.1	13.5	9.6	8.8
World	**8.7**	**10.5**	**10.6**	**9.2**	**9.9**	**17.0**	**10.7**	**6.8**	**15.3**	**8.9**	**2.0**	**11.8**	**10.3**	**10.6**

.. Is not meaningful or is less than 0.1 percentage point.

Note: Growth rates are compound averages.

Source: IMF Direction of Trade Statistics; UN Comtrade database.

Table 9 Structure of long-term public and publicly guaranteed (PPG) debt, 1995

(percentage of long-term PPG debt)

	Con-cessional	Nonconcessional			Con-cessional	Nonconcessional	
		Variable	Fixed			Variable	Fixed
All developing	**30.0**	**33.8**	**36.2**	Dominican Republic	55.5	25.2	19.4
				Ecuador	15.8	47.5	36.7
Asia	**48.3**	**21.4**	**30.3**	El Salvador	54.9	19.5	25.6
East Asia and Pacific	39.0	25.0	36.0	Guatemala	50.1	21.1	28.8
China	18.4	28.7	53.0	Jamaica	41.0	25.2	33.9
Indonesia	44.8	31.2	24.0				
Malaysia	19.8	27.0	53.2	Mexico	1.7	48.6	49.8
Myanmar	90.9	0.0	9.1	Panama	11.0	66.9	22.1
				Paraguay	59.3	7.4	33.3
Papua New Guinea	55.9	22.3	21.8	Peru	24.3	38.8	36.9
Philippines	38.0	30.1	31.9	Trinidad and Tobago	3.9	54.2	42.0
Thailand	41.9	15.8	42.4	Uruguay	6.4	48.8	44.8
Vietnam	92.9	—	—	Venezuela	0.4	55.4	44.2
South Asia	**66.7**	**14.3**	**19.0**	**Europe and Central Asia**	**15.5**	**45.1**	**39.4**
Bangladesh	98.2	0.3	1.5	Armenia	47.5	51.2	1.3
India	54.7	18.1	27.3	Azerbaijan	14.7	85.3	0.0
Nepal	97.7	0.0	2.3	Belarus	38.0	52.1	9.9
Pakistan	68.6	18.6	12.8	Bulgaria	2.9	73.8	23.3
Sri Lanka	91.0	3.0	5.9	Czech Republic	1.4	35.9	62.7
Latin America and				Estonia	30.1	60.0	9.8
the Caribbean	**14.5**	**45.4**	**40.2**	Georgia	8.5	40.2	51.2
Argentina	4.4	43.7	51.9	Hungary	2.3	27.5	70.1
Bolivia	61.7	12.1	26.2	Kazakstan	5.3	84.6	10.2
Brazil	3.0	60.1	36.9	Kyrgyz Republic	79.0	17.3	3.7
Chile	4.9	70.1	25.0				
Colombia	7.7	47.0	45.4	Latvia	44.9	31.6	23.5
Costa Rica	29.0	24.5	46.4	Lithuania	21.0	34.9	44.1

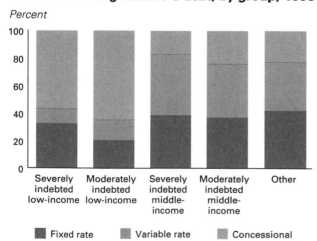

Structure of long-term PPG debt, by group, 1995

Percent

Severely indebted low-income · Moderately indebted low-income · Severely indebted middle-income · Moderately indebted middle-income · Other

■ Fixed rate ▨ Variable rate ▧ Concessional

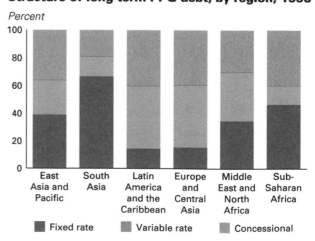

Structure of long-term PPG debt, by region, 1995

Percent

East Asia and Pacific · South Asia · Latin America and the Caribbean · Europe and Central Asia · Middle East and North Africa · Sub-Saharan Africa

■ Fixed rate ▨ Variable rate ▧ Concessional

Table 9 (continued)

	Con-cessional	Nonconcessional Variable	Fixed		Con-cessional	Nonconcessional Variable	Fixed
Europe and Central Asia (continued)				Syrian Arab Rep.	90.1	0.0	9.9
Moldova	36.6	61.4	1.9	Tunisia	38.0	21.9	40.0
Poland	27.0	59.3	13.7	Yemen, Rep.	63.8	1.4	34.8
Romania	11.1	33.5	55.4				
				Sub-Saharan Africa	**46.7**	**13.7**	**39.7**
Russian Federation	22.1	44.7	33.2	Angola	15.7	8.4	76.0
Slovak Republic	25.0	22.3	52.7	Botswana	51.4	15.0	33.6
Slovenia	2.8	76.0	21.3	Côte d'Ivoire	39.4	42.9	17.7
Tajikistan	4.0	94.2	1.8	Cameroon	52.2	10.2	37.6
Turkmenistan	5.3	76.3	18.4	Ethiopia	83.2	1.3	15.4
Turkey	15.8	24.0	60.2	Gabon	24.0	15.0	61.0
Ukraine	1.0	76.0	23.0	Ghana	83.4	0.6	15.9
Uzbekistan	14.0	67.7	18.3	Kenya	67.0	5.6	27.4
				Madagascar	62.8	8.0	29.2
Middle East and North Africa	**34.7**	**35.3**	**30.0**	Nigeria	5.0	18.6	76.4
Algeria	10.1	51.4	38.5				
Egypt, Arab Rep.	65.6	3.9	30.5	Senegal	75.8	8.1	16.0
Jordan	48.5	25.1	26.4	Sudan	49.5	16.4	34.0
Morocco	24.7	40.9	34.4	Zambia	68.4	6.7	24.9
Oman	20.5	51.8	27.8	Zimbabwe	47.2	17.1	35.7

Source: World Bank data.

Ten highest ratios of non-concessional debt to GDP, 1995

(percent)

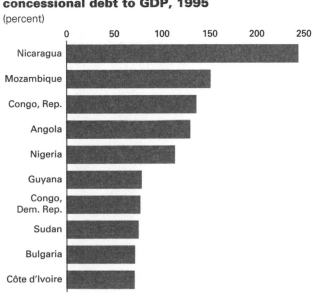

101

Table 10 Long-term net resource flows to developing countries, 1995
(US$ millions)

	Total	Percentage of GDP	Private				Official		
			Total	Net debt flows	FDI	Portfolio equity flows	Total	Official development assistance	Other
All developing countries	**237,197**	**4.55**	**184,189**	**56,613**	**95,489**	**32,087**	**53,008**	**45,199**	**7,808**
Asia	**104,169**	**6.11**	**89,328**	**18,706**	**53,567**	**17,055**	**14,841**	**9,803**	**5,038**
East Asia and Pacific	95,764	7.55	84,137	17,646	51,776	14,715	11,628	6,470	5,158
China	51,870	7.43	44,339	5,683	35,849	2,807	7,531	1,734	5,797
Indonesia	12,999	6.46	11,649	2,428	4,348	4,873	1,350	1,074	276
Malaysia	11,856	13.90	11,924	3,825	5,800	2,299	−69	−38	−31
Myanmar	95	0.95	61	36	10	16	34	35	−1
Papua New Guinea	931	18.99	578	−325	453	450	353	329	23
Philippines	4,234	5.71	4,605	1,166	1,478	1,961	−371	343	−714
Thailand	9,753	5.84	9,143	4,921	2,068	2,154	610	716	−107
Vietnam	881	4.35	237	−67	150	155	643	705	−62
South Asia	**8,405**	**1.93**	**5,191**	**1,060**	**1,791**	**2,340**	**3,214**	**3,334**	**−120**
Bangladesh	906	3.11	10	−25	2	33	896	912	−16
India	3,282	1.00	3,592	775	1,300	1,517	−311	−237	−74
Nepal	287	6.52	−2	−10	8	0	289	289	0
Pakistan	2,511	4.14	1,443	305	409	729	1,068	1,092	−24
Sri Lanka	631	4.89	140	15	63	61	491	496	−5
Latin America and the Caribbean	**66,884**	**4.10**	**54,261**	**24,174**	**22,897**	**7,190**	**12,624**	**5,032**	**7,592**
Argentina	8,650	3.08	7,204	5,674	1,319	211	1,447	602	845
Bolivia	748	12.20	191	41	150	0	557	465	92
Brazil	17,783	2.58	19,097	9,827	4,859	4,411	−1,314	444	−1,757
Chile	2,481	3.69	4,230	2,261	1,695	274	−1,749	63	−1,812
Colombia	3,342	4.13	3,741	1,109	2,501	131	−399	89	−487
Costa Rica	275	2.98	384	−13	396	1	−109	−10	−99
Dominican Republic	281	2.34	237	−34	271	0	44	12	32
Ecuador	867	4.83	561	90	470	1	306	240	66
El Salvador	170	1.75	8	−30	38	0	161	121	40
Guatemala	169	1.14	85	10	75	0	83	132	−49
Jamaica	188	3.82	188	21	167	0	0	82	−83
Mexico	23,443	9.38	13,068	5,586	6,963	520	10,374	−65	10,440
Panama	221	2.98	228	−12	220	20	−7	0	−7
Paraguay	343	3.82	174	−26	200	0	169	159	11
Peru	4,119	7.00	3,532	26	1,895	1,611	587	255	332
Trinidad and Tobago	330	6.39	271	−28	299	0	59	20	39
Uruguay	241	1.35	217	88	124	4	24	51	−28
Venezuela	634	0.85	470	−438	900	7	165	25	140
Europe and Central Asia	**40,570**	**3.61**	**30,059**	**10,072**	**17,215**	**2,772**	**10,511**	**10,125**	**387**
Armenia	200	7.05	8	0	8	0	192	190	3
Azerbaijan	270	7.18	110	0	110	0	160	88	72
Belarus	287	1.33	103	83	20	0	183	156	27
Bulgaria	454	3.52	489	−46	135	400	−34	55	−89
Czech Republic	5,675	12.67	5,596	2,946	2,568	82	79	83	−4
Estonia	291	6.58	207	−1	201	7	84	22	63
Georgia	169	3.93	0	0	0	0	169	169	0
Hungary	7,628	17.45	7,841	2,839	4,519	483	−213	243	−456
Kazakstan	1,000	4.39	500	216	284	0	500	158	342
Kyrgyz Republic	187	5.90	15	0	15	0	172	194	−23
Latvia	269	4.30	224	44	180	0	44	27	18
Lithuania	307	3.71	194	116	73	4	113	42	71
Moldova	197	11.58	79	15	64	0	118	102	16
Poland	8,375	7.12	5,058	478	3,659	921	3,318	3,364	−47
Romania	1,415	4.28	687	267	419	1	728	316	412

Table 10 (continued)

	Total	Percentage of GDP	Private				Official		
			Total	Net debt flows	FDI	Portfolio equity flows	Total	Official development assistance	Other
Russian Federation	2,121	0.59	1,115	–1,043	2,017	141	1,006	868	138
Slovak Republic	855	4.93	653	410	183	60	202	136	66
Slovenia	778	4.20	838	662	176	0	–59	2	–62
Tajikistan	106	5.80	15	0	15	0	91	55	37
Turkmenistan	28	0.72	19	19	0	0	9	1	8
Turkey	1,249	0.76	2,000	485	885	630	–751	9	–760
Ukraine	710	0.89	247	–20	267	0	463	88	375
Uzbekistan	488	2.11	235	120	115	0	254	46	207
Middle East and North Africa	**2,420**	**0.52**	**1,414**	**1,559**	**–347**	**203**	**1,006**	**5,149**	**–4,143**
Algeria	1,005	2.43	129	123	5	1	876	489	387
Egypt, Arab Rep.	1,210	2.00	294	–306	598	2	916	1,218	–302
Iran, Islamic Rep.	58	0.06	17	0	17	0	41	41	0
Jordan	546	8.22	–143	–197	43	11	690	567	123
Morocco	388	1.20	572	132	290	150	–184	303	–487
Oman	136	1.12	126	–28	150	5	10	24	–15
Syrian Arab Rep.	285	2.12	43	–22	65	0	242	268	–26
Tunisia	907	5.03	751	487	264	0	157	150	7
Yemen, Rep.	145	3.14	–2	–2	0	0	147	131	16
Sub-Saharan Africa	**23,154**	**7.91**	**9,128**	**2,102**	**2,157**	**4,868**	**14,026**	**15,091**	**–1,065**
Angola	891	14.40	523	123	400	0	368	385	–17
Botswana	100	2.31	64	–6	70	0	36	76	–40
Côte d'Ivoire	680	6.75	36	14	19	3	644	969	–325
Cameroon	206	2.59	49	–53	102	0	157	278	–121
Ethiopia	627	10.57	–42	–49	7	0	669	652	17
Gabon	170	3.62	–125	–75	–50	0	295	221	74
Ghana	1,078	17.44	525	29	230	267	553	579	–27
Kenya	500	5.50	–42	–74	32	0	542	703	–161
Madagascar	230	7.18	4	–6	10	0	226	233	–8
Nigeria	312	1.30	453	–203	650	6	–141	–15	–126
Senegal	394	8.10	–24	–25	1	0	419	460	–41
Sudan	184	2.82	0	0	0	0	184	165	18
Zambia	482	11.74	30	–36	66	0	452	548	–96
Zimbabwe	450	6.82	99	41	40	18	351	367	–16

Source: World Bank data.

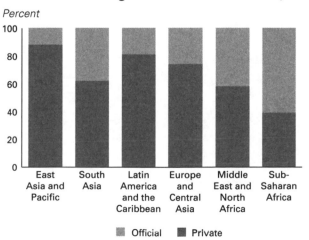

Distribution of long-term net resource flows, 1995

Percent

Official   Private

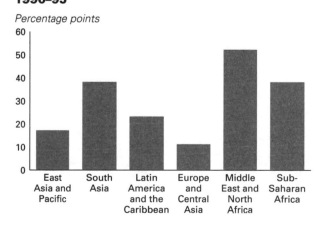

Change in share of private long-term flows, 1990–95

Percentage points

103

Table 11 Manufactures unit value, LIBOR, and commodity prices, selected years, 1965–96

		1965	1970	1973	1974	1975	1976	1977	1978	1979	1980	1981
G-5 unit value index of manufactures[a]		22	25	33	41	45	46	50	58	66	72	72
LIBOR[b]		5.0	8.9	9.4	10.8	7.7	6.1	6.4	9.2	12.2	14.0	16.7
Commodity price indexes[c]	*Weights (percent)*											
Petroleum		6	5	12	48	46	51	55	57	135	161	155
Nonfuel commodities		40	44	68	91	75	87	109	101	116	125	108
Agriculture	69.1	42	45	75	98	80	98	127	116	130	138	118
Food	29.4	42	46	91	132	100	86	90	99	113	137	123
Beverages	16.9	47	57	73	87	82	156	268	199	208	182	146
Raw materials	22.8	37	36	57	63	54	71	71	76	93	104	90
Metals and minerals	28.1	37	41	50	61	53	61	66	68	85	95	83
Fertilizers	2.7	39	30	60	195	158	76	75	73	100	129	122
Commodity prices	*Units*											
Agriculture												
Cocoa	cents/kg	37	67	113	156	125	204	379	340	329	260	208
Coffee	cents/kg	100	115	137	145	144	315	517	359	382	347	287
Tea[d]	cents/kg	107	90	86	117	120	128	214	160	167	180	161
Sugar	cents/kg	5	8	21	66	45	26	18	17	21	63	37
Bananas	$/mt	159	165	165	184	247	257	275	287	326	379	401
Wheat	$/mt	59	55	140	180	149	133	103	128	160	173	175
Rice	$/mt	119	126	293	517	341	235	252	346	313	411	459
Maize	$/mt	55	58	98	132	120	112	95	101	116	125	131
Coconut oil	$/mt	348	397	513	998	394	418	578	683	985	674	570
Palm oil	$/mt	273	260	378	669	434	407	530	600	654	584	571
Soybean oil	$/mt	270	286	436	832	563	438	580	607	662	598	507
Soybeans	$/mt	117	117	290	277	220	231	280	268	298	296	288
Cotton	cents/kg	63	63	136	142	116	169	155	157	169	205	185
Rubber	cents/kg	50	41	68	75	56	77	81	99	126	142	112
Other												
Logs	$/cm	35	43	68	82	68	92	93	97	170	196	155
Sawnwood	$/cm	157	175	224	247	223	264	265	272	366	396	349
Urea	$/mt	—	48	95	316	198	112	127	145	173	222	216
Metals and minerals												
Copper	$/mt	1,290	1,413	1,786	2,059	1,237	1,401	1,310	1,367	1,985	2,182	1,742
Aluminum	$/mt	474	556	589	674	797	896	1,050	1,088	1,230	1,456	1,263
Nickel	$/mt	1,735	2,846	3,373	3,825	4,570	4,974	5,203	4,610	5,986	6,519	5,953
Gold	($/toz)	35	36	97	159	161	125	148	193	307	608	460
Phosphate rock	$/mt	13	11	14	55	67	36	31	29	33	47	50
Steel products index (1990 =100)		25	31	46	66	52	54	53	68	76	79	82
Energy												
Crude petroleum	$/bbl	1.4	1.2	2.8	11.0	10.4	11.6	12.6	12.9	31.0	36.9	35.5
Coal	$/mt	—	—	—	—	—	—	33.4	39.6	35.4	43.1	56.5

a. Unit value index in U.S. dollar terms (1990=100) of manufactures exported from the G-5 countries (France, Germany, Japan, United Kingdom, and United States), weighted by the country's exports to developing countries.
b. London interbank offer rate on six-month U.S. dollar deposits.

Price indexes relative to manufactures unit value index, 1985–96

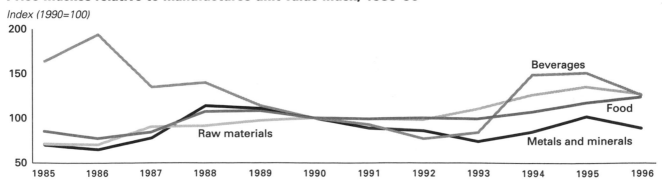

Index (1990=100)

	1982	1983	1984	1985	1986	1987	1988	1989	1990	1991	1992	1993	1994	1995	1996
	71	70	68	69	81	89	95	95	100	102	107	106	110	119	114
	13.6	9.9	11.3	8.6	6.8	7.3	8.1	9.3	8.4	6.1	3.9	3.4	5.1	6.1	5.6

	1982	1983	1984	1985	1986	1987	1988	1989	1990	1991	1992	1993	1994	1995	1996
	143	130	125	119	63	79	64	78	100	85	83	74	69	75	89
	95	103	104	91	92	93	111	107	100	95	92	91	112	122	115
	103	112	117	100	103	99	110	106	100	98	94	99	123	131	125
	96	104	106	85	77	84	107	108	100	99	100	99	107	117	124
	148	156	176	164	194	135	140	114	100	93	77	84	149	151	126
	80	88	87	71	70	90	91	97	100	99	98	110	126	135	127
	75	82	74	70	65	78	114	111	100	89	86	74	85	102	89
	105	98	98	89	89	94	109	106	100	102	96	84	93	104	120

	1982	1983	1984	1985	1986	1987	1988	1989	1990	1991	1992	1993	1994	1995	1996
	174	212	240	225	207	199	158	124	127	120	110	112	140	143	146
	309	291	319	323	429	251	303	239	197	187	141	156	331	333	269
	164	216	292	181	173	167	163	187	205	172	170	168	158	153	169
	19	19	11	9	13	15	22	28	28	20	20	22	27	29	26
	374	429	370	380	382	393	478	547	541	560	473	443	439	445	470
	160	157	152	136	115	113	145	169	136	129	151	140	150	177	208
	272	257	232	197	186	215	277	299	271	293	268	235	268	321	338
	109	136	136	112	88	76	107	112	109	107	104	102	108	123	166
	464	730	1,155	590	297	442	565	517	337	433	578	450	608	670	752
	445	501	729	501	257	343	437	350	290	339	394	378	528	628	531
	447	527	724	572	342	334	463	432	447	454	429	480	616	625	552
	245	282	282	224	208	216	304	275	247	240	236	255	252	259	305
	160	185	179	132	106	165	140	167	182	168	128	128	176	213	177
	86	106	96	76	81	98	118	97	86	83	86	83	113	158	139
	146	138	157	122	139	202	201	191	177	191	210	390	308	256	253
	339	328	352	307	329	401	402	485	533	553	607	758	821	740	741
	159	135	171	136	107	117	155	132	157	172	140	107	148	212	205
	1,480	1,592	1,377	1,417	1,374	1,783	2,602	2,848	2,662	2,339	2,281	1,913	2,307	2,936	2,295
	992	1,439	1,251	1,041	1,150	1,565	2,551	1,951	1,639	1,302	1,254	1,139	1,477	1,806	1,506
	4,838	4,673	4,752	4,899	3,881	4,872	13,778	13,308	8,864	8,156	7,001	5,293	6,340	8,228	7,501
	376	423	360	318	368	446	437	381	383	362	344	360	384	384	388
	42	37	38	34	34	31	36	41	41	43	42	33	33	35	39
	71	67	70	61	62	72	94	106	100	99	88	91	93	107	96
	32.7	29.7	28.6	27.2	14.4	18.2	14.7	17.8	22.9	19.4	19.0	16.8	15.9	17.2	20.4
	52.2	44.5	48.6	46.6	43.9	36.2	37.1	40.5	41.7	41.5	40.6	38.0	36.5	39.2	37.2

c. Indexes are in current U.S. dollar terms (1990=100).
d. Tea prices are average for auctions at Calcutta, Colombo, London, and Nairobi/Mombasa; previous editions reported London auction prices only.
Source: World Bank data.

Price indexes relative to manufactures unit value index, 1985–96

Index (1990=100)

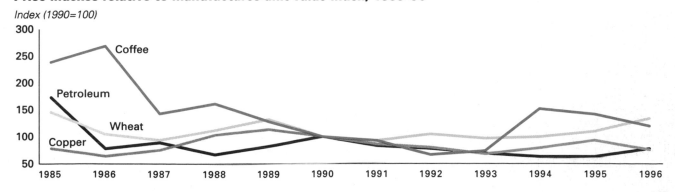

105

Technical notes

The principal sources for the data in this statistical annex are the World Bank's central databases.

Regional aggregates are based on the classification of economies by income group and region, following the Bank's standard definitions (see country classification tables that follow). Debt and finance data refer to the 136 countries that report to the Bank's Debtor Reporting System (see the World Bank's *Global Development Finance 1997*). Small economies have generally been omitted from the tables but are included in the regional totals.

Current price data are reported in U.S. dollars.

Notes on tables

Tables 1 through 4. Projections are consistent with those highlighted in chapter 1 and appendix 1.

Tables 5 and 6. Merchandise exports and imports exclude trade in services. Imports are reported on a c.i.f. basis. Growth rates are based on constant price data, which are derived from current values deflated by relevant price indexes. Effective market growth is the export-weighted import growth rate of the country's trading partners. The UNCTAD trade database is the principal source for data through 1995; in some cases these data have been supplemented by IMF and UN Comtrade databases or by World Bank staff estimates. Trade figures for countries of the former Soviet Union now reflect the total of non-CIS and intra-CIS exports and imports.

Tables 7 and 8. Growth rates are compound averages and are computed for current dollar measures of trade.

Table 9. Long-term debt covers public and publicly guaranteed external debt but excludes IMF credits. Concessional debt is debt with an original grant element of 25 percent or more. Nonconcessional variable interest rate debt includes all public and publicly guaranteed long-term debt with an original grant element of less than 25 percent whose terms depend on movements of a key market rate. This item conveys information about the borrower's exposure to changes in international interest rates. For complete definitions, see *Global Development Finance 1997*.

Table 10. Long-term net resource flows are the sum of net resource flows on long-term debt (excluding IMF) plus non–debt-creating flows. Foreign direct investment refers to the net inflows of investment from abroad. Portfolio equity flows are the sum of country funds, depository receipts, and direct purchases of shares by foreign investors. For complete definitions, see *Global Development Finance 1997*.

Table 11. Commodity price data are collected by the International Economics Department of the World Bank. World Bank commodity price series for wheat, rice, rubber, sawnwood, and crude petroleum were revised in April 1995. As a result, commodity price indexes are not strictly comparable to previous editions of *Global Economic Prospects*.

Classification of economies

Table 1 Classification of economies by income and region, 1997–98

Income group	Subgroup	Sub-Saharan Africa — East and Southern Africa	Sub-Saharan Africa — West Africa	Asia — East Asia and Pacific	Asia — South Asia	Europe and Central Asia — Eastern Europe and Central Asia	Europe and Central Asia — Rest of Europe	Middle East and North Africa — Middle East	Middle East and North Africa — North Africa	Americas
Low-income		Angola Burundi Comoros Congo, Dem. Rep." Eritrea Ethiopia Kenya Lesotho Madagascar Malawi Mozambique Rwanda Somalia Sudan Tanzania Uganda Zambia Zimbabwe	Benin Burkina Faso Cameroon Central African Republic Chad Congo, Rep. Côte d'Ivoire Equatorial Guinea Gambia, The Ghana Guinea Guinea-Bissau Liberia Mali Mauritania Niger Nigeria São Tomé and Principe Senegal Sierra Leone Togo	Cambodia China Lao PDR Mongolia Myanmar Vietnam	Afghanistan Bangladesh Bhutan India Nepal Pakistan Sri Lanka	Armenia Azerbaijan Bosnia and Herzegovina Kyrgyz Republic Moldova Tajikistan		Yemen, Rep.		Guyana Haiti Honduras Nicaragua
Middle-income	Lower	Botswana Djibouti Namibia Swaziland	Cape Verde	Fiji Indonesia Kiribati Korea, Dem. Rep. Marshall Islands Micronesia, Fed. Sts. Papua New Guinea Philippines Solomon Islands Thailand Tonga Vanuatu Western Samoa	Maldives	Albania Belarus Bulgaria Estonia Georgia Kazakstan Latvia Lithuania Macedonia, FYR[b] Romania Russian Federation Turkmenistan Ukraine Uzbekistan Yugoslavia, Fed. Rep.[c]	Turkey	Iran, Islamic Rep. Iraq Jordan Lebanon Syrian Arab Republic West Bank and Gaza	Algeria Egypt, Arab Rep. Morocco Tunisia	Belize Bolivia Colombia Costa Rica Cuba Dominica Dominican Republic Ecuador El Salvador Guatemala Jamaica Panama Paraguay Peru St. Vincent and the Grenadines Suriname Venezuela
	Upper	Mauritius Mayotte Seychelles South Africa	Gabon	American Samoa Malaysia		Croatia Czech Republic Hungary Poland Slovak Republic Slovenia	Isle of Man Malta	Bahrain Oman Saudi Arabia	Libya	Antigua and Barbuda Argentina Barbados Brazil Chile Grenada Guadeloupe Mexico Puerto Rico St. Kitts and Nevis St. Lucia Trinidad and Tobago Uruguay
Subtotal:	157	26	23	21	8	27	3	10	5	34

Table 1 *(continued)*

| Income group | Subgroup | Sub-Saharan Africa | | Asia | | Europe and Central Asia | | Middle East and North Africa | | |
		East and Southern Africa	West Africa	East Asia and Pacific	South Asia	Eastern Europe and Central Asia	Rest of Europe	Middle East	North Africa	Americas
High-income	*OECD countries*			Australia Japan Korea, Rep. New Zealand			Austria Belgium Denmark Finland France Germany Greece Iceland Ireland Italy Luxembourg Netherlands Norway Portugal Spain Sweden Switzerland United Kingdom			Canada United States
	Non-OECD countries	Réunion		Brunei French Polynesia Guam Hong Kong (China)[d] Macao New Caledonia N. Mariana Islands Singapore OAE[e]			Andorra Channel Cyprus Faeroe Islands Greenland Liechtenstein Monaco	Israel Kuwait Qatar United Arab Emirates		Aruba Bahamas, The Bermuda Cayman Islands French Guiana Martinique Netherlands Antilles Virgin Islands (U.S.)
Total:	210	27	23	34	8	27	28	14	5	44

a. Formerly Zaire.
b. Former Yugoslav Republic of Macedonia.
c. Federal Republic of Yugoslavia (Serbia/Montenegro).
d. As of July 1, 1997, Hong Kong is a part of China.
e. Other Asian economies—Taiwan (China).

Definitions of groups

For operational and analytical purposes, the World Bank's main criterion for classifying economies is gross national product (GNP) per capita. Every economy is classified as low-income, middle-income (subdivided into lower-middle and upper-middle), or high-income. Other analytical groups, based on geographic regions and levels of external debt, are also used.

Low-income and middle-income economies are sometimes referred to as developing economies. The use of the term is convenient; it is not intended to imply that all economies in the group are experiencing similar development or that other economies have reached a preferred or final stage of development. Classification by income does not necessarily reflect development status.

These tables classify all World Bank member countries as well as all other economies with populations of more than 30,000.

Income group: Economies are divided according to 1996 GNP per capita, calculated using the *World Bank Atlas* method. The groups are low-income, $785 or less; lower-middle-income, $786–$3,115; upper-middle-income, $3,116–$9,635; and high-income, $9,636 or more.

Indebtedness: Standard World Bank definitions of severe and moderate indebtedness, averaged over three years (1993–95) are used to classify economies in this table. *Severely indebted* means either of the two key ratios is above a critical level: present value of debt service to GNP (80 percent) and present value of debt service to exports (220 percent). *Moderately indebted* means either of the two key ratios exceeds 60 percent of, but does not reach, the critical level. For economies that do not report detailed debt statistics to the World Bank Debtor Reporting System (DRS), present value calculation is not possible. Instead, the following methodology is used to classify the non-DRS economies. *Severely indebted* means three of four key ratios (averaged over 1993–95) are above a critical level: debt to GNP (50 percent), debt to exports (275 percent), debt service to exports (30 percent), and interest to exports (20 percent). *Moderately indebted* means three of the four key ratios exceed 60 percent of, but do not reach, the critical level. All other classified low- and middle-income economies are listed as *less-indebted.*

Table 2 Classification of economies by income and indebtedness, 1997–98

Income group	Subgroup	Severely indebted		Moderately indebted	Less indebted		Not classified by indebtedness

Low-income		Afghanistan
		Angola
		Burundi
		Cambodia
		Cameroon
		Central African
		  Republic
		Congo, Dem.
		  Rep.[a]
		Congo, Rep.
		Côte d'Ivoire
		Equatorial
		  Guinea
		Ethiopia
		Ghana
		Guinea
		Guinea-Bissau
		Guyana
		Honduras
		Kenya
		Liberia
		Madagascar
		Malawi
		Mali
			Mauritania
			Mozambique
			Myanmar
			Nicaragua
			Niger
			Nigeria
			Rwanda
			São Tomé
			  and Principe
			Sierra Leone
			Somalia
			Sudan
			Tanzania
			Togo
			Uganda
			Vietnam
			Yemen, Rep.
			Zambia
				Bangladesh
				Benin
				Burkina Faso
				Chad
				Comoros
				Gambia, The
				Haiti
				India
				Lao PDR
				Pakistan
				Senegal
				Zimbabwe
					Armenia
					Azerbaijan
					Bhutan
					China
					Kyrgyz Republic
					Lesotho
					Moldova
					Mongolia
					Nepal
					Sri Lanka
					Tajikistan
							Bosnia and Herzegovina
							Eritrea

Middle-income	*Lower*	Bolivia
		Bulgaria
		Cuba
		Ecuador
		Iraq
		Jamaica
		Jordan
		Panama
		Peru
		Syrian Arab Republic
				Algeria
				Colombia
				Egypt, Arab Rep.
				Indonesia
				Macedonia, FYR[b]
				Morocco
				Papua New Guinea
				Philippines
				Russian Federation
				St. Vincent and the Grenadines
				Tunisia
				Turkey
				Venezuela
				Western Samoa
					Albania
					Belarus
					Belize
					Botswana
					Cape Verde
					Costa Rica
					Djibouti
					Dominica
					Dominican
					  Republic
					El Salvador
					Estonia
					Fiji
					Georgia
					Guatemala
					Iran, Islamic
					  Rep.
					Kazakstan
					Kiribati
						Korea, Dem.
						  Rep.
						Latvia
						Lebanon
						Lithuania
						Maldives
						Namibia
						Paraguay
						Romania
						Solomon Islands
						Suriname
						Swaziland
						Thailand
						Tonga
						Turkmenistan
						Ukraine
						Uzbekistan
						Vanuatu
							Marshall Islands
							Micronesia, Fed. Sts.
							West Bank and Gaza
							Yugoslavia, Fed. Rep.[c]

	Upper	Argentina
		Brazil
		Gabon
		Mexico
				Chile
				Hungary
				Poland
				Trinidad and Tobago
				Uruguay
					Antigua and
					  Barbuda
					Bahrain
					Barbados
					Croatia
					Czech Republic
					Grenada
					Libya
					Malaysia
					Malta
					Mauritius
					Oman
					Saudi Arabia
					Seychelles
					Slovak Republic
					Slovenia
						South Africa
						St. Kitts and
						  Nevis
						St. Lucia
							American Samoa
							Guadeloupe
							Isle of Man
							Mayotte
							Puerto Rico

Table 2 *(continued)*

Income group	Subgroup	Severely indebted	Moderately indebted	Less indebted	Not classified by indebtedness	
High-income	*OECD countries*				Australia Austria Belgium Canada Denmark Finland France Germany Greece Iceland Ireland Italy Japan	Korea, Rep. Luxembourg Netherlands New Zealand Norway Portugal Spain Sweden Switzerland United Kingdom United States
	Non-OECD countries				Andorra Aruba Bahamas, The Bermuda Brunei Cayman Islands Channel Islands Cyprus Faeroe Islands French Guiana French Polynesia Guam Greenland Hong Kong (China)[d] Israel Kuwait Liechtenstein	Macao Martinique Monaco Netherlands Antilles New Caledonia N. Mariana Islands Qatar Réunion Singapore United Arab Emirates Virgin Islands (U.S.) OAE[e]
Total:	210	52	31	63	64	

Note: For definitions of country groups and indebtedness indicators, see Definition of Groups at the end of table 1.

a. Formerly Zaire.

b. Former Yugoslav Republic of Macedonia.

c. Federal Republic of Yugoslavia (Serbia/Montenegro).

d. As of July 1, 1997, Hong Kong is a part of China.

e. Other Asian economies—Taiwan (China.)

Distributors of World Bank Publications

Prices and credit terms vary from country to country. Consult your local distributor before placing an order.

ARGENTINA
Oficina del Libro Internacional
Av. Cordoba 1877
1120 Buenos Aires
Tel: (54 1) 815-8354
Fax: (54 1) 815-8156

AUSTRALIA, FIJI, PAPUA NEW GUINEA, SOLOMON ISLANDS, VANUATU, AND WESTERN SAMOA
D.A. Information Services
648 Whitehorse Road
Mitcham 3132
Victoria
Tel: (61) 3 9210 7777
Fax: (61) 3 9210 7788
E-mail: service@dadirect.com.au
URL: http://www.dadirect.com.au

AUSTRIA
Gerold and Co.
Weihburggasse 26
A-1011 Wien
Tel: (43 1) 512-47-31-0
Fax: (43 1) 512-47-31-29
URL: http://www.gerold.co/at.online

BANGLADESH
Micro Industries Development
Assistance Society (MIDAS)
House 5, Road 16
Dhanmondi R/Area
Dhaka 1209
Tel: (880 2) 326427
Fax: (880 2) 811188

BELGIUM
Jean De Lannoy
Av. du Roi 202
1060 Brussels
Tel: (32 2) 538-5169
Fax: (32 2) 538-0841

BRAZIL
Publicações Tecnicas Internacionais Ltda.
Rua Peixoto Gomide, 209
01409 Sao Paulo, SP.
Tel: (55 11) 259-6644
Fax: (55 11) 258-6990
E-mail: postmaster@pti.uol.br
URL: http://www.uol.br

CANADA
Renouf Publishing Co. Ltd.
5369 Canotek Road
Ottawa, Ontario K1J 9J3
Tel: (613) 745-2665
Fax: (613) 745-7660
E-mail: order.dept@renoufbooks.com
URL: http://www.renoufbooks.com

CHINA
China Financial & Economic
Publishing House
8, Da Fo Si Dong Jie
Beijing
Tel: (86 10) 6333-8257
Fax: (86 10) 6401-7365

COLOMBIA
Infoenlace Ltda.
Carrera 6 No. 51-21
Apartado Aereo 34270
Santafé de Bogotá, D.C.
Tel: (57 1) 285-2798
Fax: (57 1) 285-2798

COTE D'IVOIRE
Center d'Edition et de Diffusion Africaines
(CEDA)
04 B.P. 541
Abidjan 04
Tel: (225) 24 6510;24 6511
Fax: (225) 25 0567

CYPRUS
Center for Applied Research
Cyprus College
6, Diogenes Street, Engomi
P.O. Box 2006
Nicosia
Tel: (357 2) 44-1730
Fax: (357 2) 46-2051

CZECH REPUBLIC
National Information Center
prodejna, Konviktska 5
CS – 113 57 Prague 1
Tel: (42 2) 2422-9433
Fax: (42 2) 2422-1484
URL: http://www.nis.cz/

DENMARK
SamfundsLitteratur
Rosenoerns Allé 11
DK-1970 Frederiksberg C
Tel: (45 31) 351942
Fax: (45 31) 357822

ECUADOR
Libri Mundi
Libreria Internacional
P.O. Box 17-01-3029
Juan Leon Mera 851
Quito
Tel: (593 2) 521-606; (593 2) 544-185
Fax: (593 2) 504-209
E-mail: librimu1@librimund.com.ec
E-mail: librimu2@librimund.com.ec

EGYPT, ARAB REPUBLIC OF
Al Ahram Distribution Agency
Al Galaa Street
Cairo
Tel: (20 2) 578-6083
Fax: (20 2) 578-6833

The Middle East Observer
41, Sherif Street
Cairo
Tel: (20 2) 393-9732
Fax: (20 2) 393-9732

FINLAND
Akateeminen Kirjakauppa
P.O. Box 128
FIN-00101 Helsinki
Tel: (358 0) 121 4418
Fax: (358 0) 121-4435
E-mail: akatilaus@stockmann.fi
URL: http://www.akateeminen.com/

FRANCE
World Bank Publications
66, avenue d'Iéna
75116 Paris
Tel: (33 1) 40-69-30-56/67
Fax: (33 1) 40-69-30-68

GERMANY
UNO-Verlag
Poppelsdorfer Allee 55
53115 Bonn
Tel: (49 228) 212940
Fax: (49 228) 217492

GREECE
Papasotiriou S.A.
35, Stournara Str.
106 82 Athens
Tel: (30 1) 364-1826
Fax: (30 1) 364-8254

HAITI
Culture Diffusion
5, Rue Capois
C.P. 257
Port-au-Prince
Tel: (509) 23 9260
Fax: (509) 23 4858

HONG KONG, MACAO
Asia 2000 Ltd.
Sales & Circulation Department
Seabird House, unit 1101-02
22-28 Wyndham Street, Central
Hong Kong
Tel: (852) 2530-1409
Fax: (852) 2526-1107
E-mail: sales@asia2000.com.hk
URL: http://www.asia2000.com.hk

HUNGARY
Euro Info Service
Margitszigeti Europa Haz
H-1138 Budapest
Tel: (36 1) 111 6061
Fax: (36 1) 302 5035
E-mail: euroinfo@mail.matav.hu

INDIA
Allied Publishers Ltd.
751 Mount Road
Madras – 600 002
Tel: (91 44) 852-3938
Fax: (91 44) 852-0649

INDONESIA
Pt. Indira Limited
Jalan Borobudur 20
P.O. Box 181
Jakarta 10320
Tel: (62 21) 390-4290
Fax: (62 21) 390-4289

IRAN
Ketab Sara Co. Publishers
Khaled Eslamboli Ave., 6th Street
Delafrooz Alley No. 8
P.O. Box 15745-733
Tehran 15117
Tel: (98 21) 8717819; 8716104
Fax: (98 21) 8712479
E-mail: ketab-sara@neda.net.ir

Kowkab Publishers
P.O. Box 19575-511
Tehran
Tel: (98 21) 258-3723
Fax: (98 21) 258-3723

IRELAND
Government Supplies Agency
Oifig an tSoláthair
4-5 Harcourt Road
Dublin 2
Tel: (353 1) 661-3111
Fax: (353 1) 475-2670

ISRAEL
Yozmot Literature Ltd.
P.C. Box 56055
3 Yohanan Hasandlar Street
Tel Aviv 61560
Tel: (972 3) 5285-397
Fax: (972 3) 5285-397

R.O.Y. International
PO Box 13056
Tel Aviv 61130
Tel: (972 3) 5461423
Fax: (972 3) 5461442
E-mail: royil@netvision.net.il

Palestinian Authority/Middle East
Index Information Services
P.O.B. 19502 Jerusalem
Tel: (972 2) 6271219
Fax: (972 2) 6271634

ITALY
Licosa Commissionaria Sansoni SPA
Via Duca Di Calabria, 1/1
Casella Postale 552
50125 Firenze
Tel: (55) 645-415
Fax: (55) 641-257
E-mail: licosa@ftbcc.it
URL: http://www.ftbcc.it/licosa

JAMAICA
Ian Randle Publishers Ltd.
206 Old Hope Road, Kingston 6
Tel: 809-927-2085
Fax: 809-977-0243
E-mail: irpl@colis.com

JAPAN
Eastern Book Service
3-13 Hongo 3-chome, Bunkyo-ku
Tokyo 113
Tel: (81 3) 3818-0861
Fax: (81 3) 3818-0864
E-mail: orders@svt-ebs.co.jp
URL: http://www.bekkoame.or.jp/~svt-ebs

KENYA
Africa Book Service (E.A.) Ltd.
Quaran House, Mfangano Street
P.O. Box 45245
Nairobi
Tel: (254 2) 223 641
Fax: (254 2) 330 272

KOREA, REPUBLIC OF
Daejon Trading Co. Ltd.
P.O. Box 34, Youida, 706 Seoun Bldg
44-6 Youido-Dong, Yeongchengpo-Ku
Seoul
Tel: (82 2) 785-1631/4
Fax: (82 2) 784-0315

MALAYSIA
University of Malaya Cooperative
Bookshop, Limited
P.O. Box 1127
Jalan Pantai Baru
59700 Kuala Lumpur
Tel: (60 3) 756-5000
Fax: (60 3) 755-4424

MEXICO
INFOTEC
Av. San Fernando No. 37
Col. Toriello Guerra
14050 Mexico, D.F.
Tel: (52 5) 624-2800
Fax: (52 5) 624-2822
E-mail: infotec@rtn.net.mx
URL: http://rtn.net.mx

NEPAL
Everest Media International Services (P) Ltd.
GPO Box 5443
Kathmandu
Tel: (977 1) 472 152
Fax: (977 1) 224 431

NETHERLANDS
De Lindeboom/InOr-Publikaties
P.O. Box 202, 7480 AE Haaksbergen
Tel: (31 53) 574-0004
Fax: (31 53) 572-9296
E-mail: lindeboo@worldonline.nl
URL: http://www.worldonline.nl/~lindeboo

NEW ZEALAND
EBSCO NZ Ltd.
Private Mail Bag 99914
New Market
Auckland
Tel: (64 9) 524-8119
Fax: (64 9) 524-8067

NIGERIA
University Press Limited
Three Crowns Building Jericho
Private Mail Bag 5095
Ibadan
Tel: (234 22) 41-1356
Fax: (234 22) 41-2056

NORWAY
NIC Info A/S
Book Department, Postboks 6512 Etterstad
N-0606 Oslo
Tel: (47 22) 97-4500
Fax: (47 22) 97-4545

PAKISTAN
Mirza Book Agency
65, Shahrah-e-Quaid-e-Azam
Lahore 54000
Tel: (92 42) 735 3601
Fax: (92 42) 576 3714

Oxford University Press
5 Bangalore Town
Sharae Faisal
PO Box 13033
Karachi-75350
Tel: (92 21) 446307
Fax: (92 21) 454/7640
E-mail: oup@oup.khi.erum.com.pk

Pak Book Corporation
Aziz Chambers 21, Queen's Road
Lahore
Tel: (92 42) 636 3222; 636 0885
Fax: (92 42) 636 2328
E-mail: pbc@brain.net.pk

PERU
Editorial Desarrollo SA
Apartado 3824, Lima 1
Tel: (51 14) 285380
Fax: (51 14) 286628

PHILIPPINES
International Booksource Center Inc.
1127-A Antipolo St, Barangay, Venezuela
Makati City
Tel: (63 2) 896 6501; 6505; 6507
Fax: (63 2) 896 1741

POLAND
International Publishing Service
Ul. Piekna 31/37
00-677 Warzawa
Tel: (48 2) 628-6089
Fax: (48 2) 621-7255
E-mail: books%ips@ikp.atm.com.pl
URL: http://www.ipscg.waw.pl/ips/export/

PORTUGAL
Livraria Portugal
Apartado 2681, Rua Do Carmo 70-74
1200 Lisbon
Tel: (1) 347-4982
Fax: (1) 347-0264

ROMANIA
Compani De Librarii Bucuresti S.A.
Str. Lipscani no. 26, sector 3
Bucharest
Tel: (40 1) 613 9645
Fax: (40 1) 312 4000

RUSSIAN FEDERATION
Isdatelstvo <Ves Mir>
9a, Lolpachniy Pereulok
Moscow 101831
Tel: (7 095) 917 87 49
Fax: (7 095) 917 92 59

SINGAPORE, TAIWAN, MYANMAR, BRUNEI
Asahgate Publishing Asia Pacific Pte. Ltd.
41 Kallang Pudding Road #04-03
Golden Wheel Building
Singapore 349316
Tel: (65) 741-5166
Fax: (65) 742-9356
E-mail: ashgate@asianconnect.com

SLOVENIA
Gospodarski Vestnik Publishing Group
Dunajska cesta 5
1000 Ljubljana
Tel: (386 61) 133 83 47; 132 12 30
Fax: (386 61) 133 80 30
E-mail: repansekj@gvestnik.si

SOUTH AFRICA, BOTSWANA
International Subscription Service
P.O. Box 41095
Craighall
Johannesburg 2024
Tel: (27 11) 880-1448
Fax: (27 11) 880-6248
E-mail: iss@is.co.za

Oxford University Press
5 Bangalore Town
Sharae Faisal
PO Box 13033
Karachi-75350
Tel: (92 21) 446307
Fax: (92 21) 454/7640
E-mail: oup@oup.khi.erum.com.pk

SPAIN
Mundi-Prensa Libros, S.A.
Castello 37
28001 Madrid
Tel: (34 1) 431-3399
Fax: (34 1) 575-3998
E-mail: libreria@mundiprensa.es
URL: http://www.mundiprensa.es/

Mundi-Prensa Barcelona
Consell de Cent, 391
08009 Barcelona
Tel: (34 3) 488-3492
Fax: (34 3) 487-7659
E-mail: barcelona@mundiprensa.es

SRI LANKA, THE MALDIVES
Lake House Bookshop
100, Sir Chittampalam Gardiner Mawatha
Colombo 2
Tel: (94 1) 32105
Fax: (94 1) 432104
E-mail: LHL@sri.lanka.net

SWEDEN
Wennergren-Williams AB
P. O. Box 1305
S-171 25 Solna
Tel: (46 8) 705-97-50
Fax: (46 8) 27-00-71
E-mail: mail@wwi.se

SWITZERLAND
Librairie Payot Service Institutionnel
Côtes-de-Montbenon 30
1002 Lausanne
Tel: (41 21) 341-3229
Fax: (41 21) 341-3235

ADECO Van Diemen EditionsTechniques
Ch. de Lacuez 41
CH1807 Blonay
Tel: (41 21) 943 2673
Fax: (41 21) 943 3605

TANZANIA
Oxford University Press
Maktaba Street, PO Box 5299
Dar es Salaam
Tel: (255 51) 29209
Fax: (255 51) 46822

THAILAND
Central Books Distribution
306 Silom Road
Bangkok 10500
Tel: (66 2) 235-5400
Fax: (66 2) 237-8321

TRINIDAD & TOBAGO, AND THE CARRIBBEAN
Systematics Studies Unit
9 Watts Street
Curepe
Trinidad, West Indies
Tel: (809) 662-5654
Fax: (809) 662-5654
E-mail: tobe@trinidad.net

UGANDA
Gustro Ltd.
PO Box 9997, Madhvani Building
Plot 16/4 Jinja Rd.
Kampala
Tel: (256 41) 254 763
Fax: (256 41) 251 468

UNITED KINGDOM
Microinfo Ltd.
P.O. Box 3, Alton, Hampshire GU34 2PG
England
Tel: (44 1420) 86848
Fax: (44 1420) 89889
E-mail: wbank@ukminfo.demon.co.uk
URL: http://www.microinfo.co.uk

VENEZUELA
Tecni-Ciencia Libros, S.A.
Centro Cuidad Comercial Tamanco
Nivel C2, Caracas
Tel: (58 2) 959 5547; 5035; 0016
Fax: (58 2) 959 5636

ZAMBIA
University Bookshop, University of Zambia
Great East Road Campus
P.O. Box 32379
Lusaka
Tel: (260 1) 252 576
Fax: (260 1) 253 952

ZIMBABWE
Longman Zimbabwe (Pvt.)Ltd.
Tourle Road, Ardbennie
P.O. Box ST125
Southerton
Harare
Tel: (263 4) 6216617
Fax: (263 4) 621670

06/1997

0240